WITHDRAWN
Library
College of St. Scholastica
Duluth, Minn.

ACTON'S POLITICAL PHILOSOPHY

ACTON'S POLITICAL PHILOSOPHY

An Analysis

By
G. E. FASNACHT
Sometime Lecturer, University College, Oxford

With a Foreword by
SIR HAROLD BUTLER, K.C.M.G., C.B.

NEW YORK
THE VIKING PRESS
1953

Copyright 1952 by The Viking Press, Inc.

JC
223
.A35
F3
1953

Made and printed in Great Britain

TO THE MEMORY OF
KENNETH LEYS
Fellow of University College

FOREWORD

By Sir Harold Butler, K.C.M.G., C.B.

At a time of much confusion in political thought Mr. Fasnacht has rendered a great service by bringing together all the varied aspects of Lord Acton's political philosophy. With his vast erudition and universal outlook Acton was better equipped than any modern English thinker to expound the true nature of the problems which now beset us. Because he never drew the strands of his thought together into a systematic pattern, its range and depth have been too little appreciated. Though his mind was encyclopaedic, his published writings were fragmentary. By supplementing them with a mass of new material derived from his unpublished manuscripts Mr. Fasnacht has sought to bring his whole philosophy of politics into focus.

Though unfamiliar with the setting in which the history of the last fifty years has placed them, Acton's profound insight enabled him to grasp the essence of our present dilemmas. From the trends already evident in his own time he deduced the conflict of ideas to which they must lead. On the one side was freedom, the ethical, almost the religious, purpose of human society, the mainspring of its conscience. On the other was power, constantly seeking to curb or destroy liberty by generating new forms of autocracy. The rise of socialism was a revolt against the economic autocracy of feudalism and industrialism. In Acton's view, "as much socialism as is economically sound and which is not totalitarian or despotic is part of the remedy for the ills of society." But socialism might become "the worst enemy freedom has ever had to encounter," if it attempted to place the whole of economic life under the control of the State.

So, too, democracy was a revolt against the political autocracy of absolute monarchs or dictators, but democracy itself might breed a new kind of despotism. "Popular power may be tainted with the same poison as personal power." The authority of the people must be restrained by constitutional checks and balances to safeguard freedom and the protection of minorities. "The will of a whole people cannot make just that which is unjust." Acton had an ingrained fear of popular dictatorship. He believed that the British constitution as developed in the eighteenth and nineteenth centuries was one of the supreme achievements in the art of self-government, yet it is significant that he regarded the federal principle embodied in the American constitution as offering greater security against democratic tyranny.

From these few examples it may be seen how relevant Acton's philosophy appears to our present political perplexities. Indeed, its study is perhaps even more important to us than it was to his contemporaries. For that reason this book is a timely and valuable contribution to the thinking of all lovers of liberty in this time of doubt and transition.

It is with very deep regret that I have to record the death of Sir Harold Butler while these pages are in the Press. This Foreword must be one of the last things he wrote. I am greatly privileged to print it, and even more by his great interest and kindness. G. E. F.

CONTENTS

	PAGE
PREFACE	xi
ACKNOWLEDGEMENTS	xiii
ABBREVIATIONS	xiv
INTRODUCTION	1

CHAPTER
I.	THE THEORY OF CONSCIENCE	33
II.	THE IDEA OF DEVELOPMENT	48
III.	THE ENGLISH AND AMERICAN POLITICAL TRADITIONS	64
IV.	THE STATE, GOVERNMENT, AND DEMOCRACY	81
V.	SOCIALISM	117
VI.	NATIONALITY AND POWER	126
VII.	THE IMPORTANCE OF IDEAS	140
	Note on Hume	148
VIII.	THE ADVANCEMENT OF LEARNING	150
IX.	THE HISTORY OF FREEDOM	165
X.	ACTON'S RELATION TO OTHER THINKERS	185

APPENDICES:
I.	THE ECONOMIC FACTOR	207
II.	ACTON'S CRITICS	222
III.	MORAL JUDGMENTS	224
IV.	ENGLISH HISTORIANS	226
V.	PROBLEMS OF ACTON INTERPRETATION	228
VI.	NATURAL SCIENCE	228
VII.	ANALYSIS OF ACTON MS. Add. 4955	229
VIII.	ADAM SMITH	241
IX.	GROTIUS	241
X.	ROTHE AND VINET	242
XI.	FURTHER EXTRACTS FROM THE ACTON MSS.	243

BIBLIOGRAPHY	245
THE ACTON MANUSCRIPTS	247
INDEX	248

The rights of man on earth are the consequence of the rights of God in Heaven.

> Acton to Mary Gladstone,
> 8 Oct. 1887
> (*Letters to Mary Gladstone*,
> 2nd ed., p. 179)

Conscience cannot prevail in politics without science.

> Acton MSS., Add. 5434

Political Science is in its infancy.

> Acton MSS., Add. 5504

PREFACE

ACTON's thought is simple in logical structure, but complex in form, and concentrated in expression. His political theory turns on the sovereignty of the developed conscience, the conscience guided by experience and knowledge. The action of conscience in history comes under the law of development, that is, continuity and progress. Freedom, in its simplest sense, is free agency, which distinguishes history from any necessary process whether natural or logical. In its ethical sense it means, primarily, freedom to do one's moral duty, which, politically as well as morally, entails self-government. The two elements, freedom of conscience and development, Acton believed were shown in combination in the English and American political traditions. For Acton, natural rights and history are not opposed, because the marrow of history itself, in his view, is ethical.

The extreme logical simplicity of Acton's thought is hidden by the fragmentary, complex, and concentrated form of its expression. The fragmentary form was dictated by his desire not to appear doctrinaire. The complexity results from his attempt to focus light simultaneously from every available source, as, for example, when he writes of Whiggism: Locke displayed the metaphysical, Somers and Holt the legal, Burnet the ecclesiastical, Leibniz its universal basis. It would not have occurred to most thinkers to relate Locke's empiricism and Leibniz's *lex continui* simultaneously to the study of the revolution of 1688. At the same time he tried to follow many different counsels of perfection, for example, to state a stronger case for the view he rejected than its supporters could provide, and to avoid emphasis on his own view. Finally, he speaks in three different characters, as a historian, as a political scientist, and as a philosopher. It must also be remembered that Acton's views were always developing. His philosophy of history is an attempt to raise Hegel to a higher level and a wider view. The higher level is the sovereignty of conscience, the wider view is, in his own words, "all that goes to weave the web of social life." His philosophy of history is a vision of the development of freedom, or, as he himself put it, an illumination of the soul.

As far as practicable I have given Acton's views in his own words, as it is not possible in any other way to avoid misrepresenting him.[1]

The material used in this book falls into three broad categories: (1) work Acton himself published; (2) letters, which were written with no expectation of publication; (3) manuscript notes, intended for no eyes but his own. It is the material in the first category which has the greatest authority.

G. E. FASNACHT

[1] It is Acton's mature philosophy, after he had reached the age of forty (1874), on which the present analysis is concentrated. Earlier views have been retained where later evidence was lacking, or where there seemed no good reason to doubt that he continued to hold substantially similar views later. In some instances it has been necessary to quote a passage more than once when it throws light on different aspects of Acton's thought. Acton himself writes: "The source of our ideas is not in us. They pour in from all sides and springs. It takes time to assimilate them. The principle of selection, the point of contact, the link, is what a man finds in himself—and he must be mature before it has done its work, and given unity to the whole." (Add. 4940.)

The key to Acton's mind is the value he placed on (1) French thought, (2) German learning, (3) English and American experience.

In "French thought" is included the Swiss school, from de Staël to Vinet, which Acton termed the natural complement of the French mind.

ACKNOWLEDGEMENTS

My warmest thanks are due to the Warden and Fellows of Nuffield College for the grant which made possible the research on which this book is based, and in particular to Sir Henry Clay, then Warden, to Lord Lindsay, at that time Master of Balliol and Sub-Warden of Nuffield, for their encouragement and advice, to Dr. G. P. Gooch for unbounded kindness, and to the Reverend K. K. M. Leys, to whom my debt can never be repaid. To Sir Harold Butler, Mr. R. C. K. Ensor, the Provost of Oriel, Professor G. D. H. Cole, Mr. Carritt, Mr. Douglas Woodruff, and Professor Ulrich Noack of the University of Würzburg I am also under the deepest obligation of gratitude. Finally, I must thank the Editors and Proprietors of the *Contemporary Review* and the *Hibbert Journal* for permission to reprint material that appeared in those periodicals, and the Delegates of the Oxford University Press for allowing me to use parts of Chapters V and VI, which were separately published in pamphlet form under the title *Lord Acton on Nationality and Socialism*.

G. E. F.

ABBREVIATIONS

Add.	*Additional Manuscripts*, Cambridge University Library
C.M.H.	*Cambridge Modern History*
Corr.	*Lord Acton's Correspondence*, Vol. I
E.H.R.	*English Historical Review*
E.S.S.	*Encyclopaedia of the Social Sciences*
F.R.	*Lectures on the French Revolution*
Gasquet	Gasquet: *Lord Acton and his Circle*
Hawarden Letters	*Some Hawarden Letters*
H.E.	*Historical Essays and Studies*
H.F.	*History of Freedom and other Essays*
H.F.R.	*Home and Foreign Review*
J.M.H.	*Journal of Modern History*
L.M.G.	*Letters of Lord Acton to Mary Gladstone*
L.M.H.	*Lectures on Modern History*
N.B.R.	*North British Review*

INTRODUCTION

ACTON defined the central point in his philosophy of politics in his inaugural lecture as Regius Professor at Cambridge in 1895 (*aetat.* 61):

What do people mean who proclaim that liberty is the palm, and the prize, and the crown, seeing that it is an idea of which there are two hundred definitions, and that this wealth of interpretation has caused more bloodshed than anything, except theology? Is it Democracy as in France, or Federalism as in America, or the national independence which bounds the Italian view, or the reign of the fittest, which is the ideal of Germans? I know not whether it will ever fall within my sphere of duty to trace the slow progress of that idea through the chequered scenes of our history, and to describe how subtle speculations touching the nature of conscience promoted a nobler and more spiritual conception of the liberty that protects it, until the guardian of rights developed into the guardian of duties which are the cause of rights, and that which had been prized as the material safeguard for treasures of earth became sacred as security for things that are divine. All that we require is a work-day key to history, and our present need can be supplied without pausing to satisfy philosophers. Without inquiring how far Sarasa or Butler, Kant or Vinet, is right as to the infallible voice of God in man, we may easily agree in this, that where absolutism reigned, by irresistible arms, concentrated possessions, auxiliary churches, and inhuman laws, it reigns no more; that commerce having risen against land, labour against wealth, the State against the forces dominant in society, the division of power against the State, the thought of individuals against the practice of ages, neither authorities nor minorities, nor majorities can command implicit obedience; and, where there has been long and arduous experience, a rampart of tried conviction and accumulated knowledge, where there is a fair level of general morality, education, courage and self-restraint, there, if there only, a society may be found that exhibits the condition of life towards which, by elimination of failures, the world has been moving through the allotted space. You will know it by outward signs: Representation, the extinction of slavery, the reign of opinion, and the like; better still by less apparent evidences: the security of the weaker groups and the liberty of conscience, which, effectually secured, secures the rest.[1]

Acton was discussing the new period constituted by the last four centuries, in which, he believed, real if slow progress could be discerned. Progress, in Acton's use of the term, means progress towards liberty.

Acton's conception of freedom was not negative. He attempted to safeguard himself against this misconception by adding a quotation from Brisson: Freedom is the name that the sovereign conscience takes when it emerges to model society in accordance with the dictates of reason.[2] Acton's philosophy is ethical and historical. While it can be described as the historical philosophy of politics, it must be added that for Acton the marrow of history itself is ethical. The historical aspect must, however, be stressed, for Acton was not only the most learned English historian of his day, but he regarded the scientific study of history, which began in the second quarter of the nineteenth century, as a movement in the human mind deeper and more serious than the Renaissance itself.[3] It is a view to which all the social sciences are now committed by the historical method.

Acton's view of continuity and progress, evolution and development will be more fully considered in a later chapter. Here it may be noted that he adopts the argument of Leibniz, that history is the demonstration of religion. Similarly, what Acton meant by conscience—what is highest and best in man—will need fuller discussion. Acton does not regard conscience as infallible, in spite of the arguments of Butler and Kant and Vinet. But he obviously sympathizes with the seventeenth-century doctrine that it is better to follow even an erring conscience, as also does, for example, Mr. Carritt.[4] He who is prepared to commit the least sin against conscience is in principle prepared to commit the greatest.

Writing to Lady Blennerhassett in 1879, at the age of forty-five, Acton said that his standpoint was that of a man who rejected everything in Catholicism that was inconsistent with

[1] *L.M.H.*, pp. 12-13.
[2] *Ibid.*, p. 327.
[3] *Ibid.*, p. 14.
[4] *Ethical and Political Thinking*, Chap. 2.

liberty, and everything in politics that was inconsistent with Catholicism:

> Let me try as briefly as possible and without argument to tell you what is in fact a very simple, obvious, and not interesting story. It is the story of a man who started in life believing himself a sincere Catholic and a sincere Liberal; who therefore renounced everything in Catholicism which was not compatible with liberty, and everything in Politics which was not compatible with Catholicity. As an English Liberal, I judged that of the two parties—of the two doctrines—which have governed England for 200 years, that one was most fitted to the divine purpose which upheld civil and religious liberty. Therefore I was among those who think less of what is than what ought to be, who sacrifice the real to the ideal, interest to duty, authority to morality.
>
> To speak quite plainly, as this is a confession, not an apology, I carried farther than others the Doctrinaire belief in mere Liberalism, identifying it altogether with morality, and holding the ethical standard and purpose to be supreme and sovereign.
>
> I carried this principle into the study of history when I had the means of getting beyond the common limit of printed books. . . .
>
> That is my entire Capital. . . . It is nothing but the mere adjustment of religious history to the ethics of Whiggism.[1]

Five years later Acton wrote to Mary Gladstone: "Have you not discovered, have I never betrayed, what a narrow doctrinaire I am, under a thin disguise of levity? The Duke of Orleans nearly described my feelings when he spoke, testamentarily, of his religious *flag* and his political *faith*. Politics come nearer religion with me, a party is more like a church, error more like heresy, prejudice more like sin, than I find it to be with better men."[2] Acton's standpoint was not in the least denominational. He wrote to Gladstone in 1888:

> You insist, broadly, on belief in the divine nature of Christ as the soul, substance and creative force of Christian religion. You assign to it very much of the good the Church has done; you urge the consent of ages; and you say that people have

---

[1] *Corr.*, pp. 54–56. Acton's personal Catholic piety was profound. He always maintained that his religion was dearer than life itself.
[2] *L.M.G.*, p. 199.

no right to deny this fundamental dogma. All this with little or no qualification or drawback. . . .

Enter Martineau, or Stephen, or Morley (unattached), and *loq*.—Is this the final judgment of the chief of Liberals? The pontiff of a church whose Fathers are the later Milton and the later Penn, Locke and Bayle, Toland, Franklin, Turgot, Smith, Washington, Jefferson, Bentham, D. Stewart, Romilly, Jeffrey, B. Constant, Tocqueville, Channing, Macaulay, Mill? These men and others like them disbelieved that doctrine, established freedom, and undid the work of orthodox Christianity. They swept away that appalling edifice of intolerance, tyranny, cruelty, which believers in Christ built up, to perpetuate their belief. There is much to deduct from the praise of the Church in protecting marriage, abolishing slavery, preventing war, and helping the poor. No deduction can be made from her evil-doing towards unbelievers, heretics, savages, and witches. Here her responsibility is more undivided, her initiative and achievement more complete.

Now the common run of Liberals are used to look on these transactions as the worst of all crimes. The assassins did not kill in masses. The Terrorists generally inflicted a painless death. The Christian Church superadded the cruelty of Red Indians, by the use of torture and fire.

It was the negation not only of religious liberty, which is the mainspring of civil, but equally of civil liberty, because a government armed with the machinery of the Inquisition is necessarily absolute. So that, if Liberalism has a desperate foe it is the Church, as it was in the West, between 1200 and 1600 or 1700. The philosophy of Liberal history which has to acknowledge the invaluable services of early Christianity, feels at the same time rather more strongly the anti-Liberal and anti-social action of later Christianity, before the rise of the sects which rejected, some the divinity of Christ, others, the institutions of the Church erected upon it.[1]

Early in life Acton became convinced that there was a philosophy of politics implicit in the Christian religion and in the principles of the British constitution, and that they completed each other. As he wrote to Simpson, "I think the true notion of a Christian State, and the true latent notion of the constitution coincide and complete each other."[2] To Acton the New

---

[1] *Corr.*, pp. 216–217.   [2] *Gasquet*, p. 3 (1858, *aetat.* 24).

Testament marks a revolution in politics and economics as well as in ethics.[1] The ethical revolution is contained in the Beatitudes and the Sermon on the Mount. The most fundamental principles of economics are self-reliance and self-denial, and they are written as plainly in the Gospels as in Adam Smith. In politics, the injunction "Render unto Caesar the things that are Caesar's, and unto God the things that are God's" constitutes the fundamental charter of freedom—the preservation of immunity from the State of the supreme sphere of conscience, an immunity which was made the perpetual charge and supreme responsibility of the most energetic institution and the most universal association in the world.

The ultimate principle of the British constitution is self-government, the principle underlying its growth. Everything follows from the principle of distributive justice *suum cuique*: "I understand by political science the development of the maxim *suum cuique* in the relation of the State with other States, corporations and individuals."[2] Self-government means the self-government of real communities, of corporations possessing coporate personality.[3] (The House of Commons is the house of communities—*communitates*—that is, of those communities that are towns and those that are counties.) Political authority is federal in its roots, just as, in some of the most developed communities, it is also federal in structure.[4]

Political science is the one science which is deposited by the stream of history, like grains of gold in the sand of a river.[5] True science and true religion cannot conflict.[6] Both science and religion come under the law of development. This was first expounded by Leibniz, and was the common element in his anticipation of Hegel and his anticipation of Darwin. For scientific politics and scientific ethics an ultimate principle, beyond development, is required. This is the sanctity of human life. A war, unless unavoidable for the sole cause of liberty, is only wholesale murder.[7] The essential object is liberty. It means

---

[1] *Gasquet*, p. 258; *H.F.*, p. 29.
[2] *Gasquet*, pp. 129–130 (1860). [3] *Ibid.*, p. 235.
[4] Cf.: "It would be hardly too much to say that, for some generations, the English legislature was rather Federal than Imperial in its essential character.—Brodrick, *Local Government*, 7." (Add. 4945.)
[5] *L.M.H.*, p. 2. [6] *Gasquet*, p. 223.
[7] *Corr.*, p. 249.

freedom of conscience, that is, of what is highest and best in man. Liberty is the "growing point," the concrete development: "Liberty is not a gift, but an acquisition; not a state of rest, but of effort and growth; not a starting point, but a result of government; or at least a starting point only as an object, not a *datum*, but an aim. . . . liberty is the result of the principle *suum cuique* in action."[1] Acton expressed the same idea thirty-five years later in his lectures on the French Revolution, where he states that it was not realised that liberty is a goal to achieve, not a capital to invest.[2]

The sanctity of human life is not only the ultimate ethical principle. It is also the scientific principle which alone can give objectivity to political and historical judgments. The marrow of history is ethical, not metaphysical. And the ethics of political science and history cannot be denominational. Writing to Mary Gladstone in 1887 Acton referred to "a science of political ethics."[3] In 1892 he said: "Murder, as the conventional low-watermark, is invaluable as our basis of measurement. It is the historian's interest that it shall never be tampered with. If we have no scientific zero to start from, it is idle to censure corruption, mendacity, or treason to one's country or one's party, and morality and history go asunder."[4]

A philosophy of politics and history is also a theology. Progress towards liberty, slow though it may be, is the justification of God to men. Acton realized, of course, that many people would reject this view: "Many persons, I am well assured, would detect that this is a very old story, and a trivial commonplace, and would challenge proof that the world is making progress in aught but intellect, that it is gaining in freedom, or that increase of freedom is either a progress or a gain."[5]

[1] *Gasquet*, p. 228. Cf. Add. 4941: "Liberty is the one common topic of ancient and modern history. Every nation, every epoch, every religion, every philosophy, every science."

[2] *F.R.*, p. 107. In 1861 (*aetat.* 27) Acton wrote: "All liberty is conditional, limited, and therefore unequal. The State can never do what it likes in its own sphere. It is bound by all kinds of law" (*Gasquet*, p. 234).

[3] *L.M.G.* (2nd ed.), pp. 180–183.

[4] *H.E.*, pp. 494–495. Cf. *H.E.*, p. 506: "The greatest crime is homicide. The accomplice is no better than the assassin; the theorist is worse."

[5] *L.M.H.*, p. 11 (1895).

Science involves fulness of knowledge[1] and sincerity. Sincerity means not resting content till we have constructed a stronger case for the view we reject than its supporters themselves can furnish. "In order to understand the cosmic force and the true connection of ideas, it is a source of power, and an excellent school of principle, not to rest until, by excluding the fallacies, the prejudices, the exaggerations which perpetual contention and the consequent precautions breed, we have made out for our opponents a stronger and more impressive case than they present themselves."[2] This maxim Acton himself applied systematically, so that the context of his words must always be studied with the utmost caution to avoid ascribing to him what is, in fact, his own scrupulously fair statement of the view he rejects. He was fond of a passage in Landor: "Few scholars are critics, few critics are philosophers, and few philosophers look with equal care on both sides of a question."

The key to the understanding of Acton is that his thought was always developing, and he himself stressed this point in his *Inaugural*, in which he said John Hunter spoke for all of us when he used the words: "Never ask me what I have said, or what I have written, but if you will ask me what my present opinions are, I will tell you." In the same passage he also quotes with approval the words of Faraday: "In knowledge, that man only is to be condemned and despised who is not in a state of transition."[3]

The best example of the development of Acton's thought is the change of emphasis in his opinion of Burke. At the age of twenty-five Acton regarded the later, i.e. the conservative, Burke as (in his own words) "the law and the prophets"— and especially the *Appeal from the New to the Old Whigs*.[4] At the age of forty-five and later, Acton regarded the later Burke as inconsistent, untrue to himself, mistaken in his interpretation of the Revolution of 1688. Writing to Gladstone in 1896 (*aetat.* 62)

---

[1] Cf. Add. 4940: "Get the heaviest available accumulation of authority"; and Add. 4947: "Study politics both as a national science and as a general science."

[2] *L.M.H.*, p. 18. In the Acton MSS. there are two further illustrations: (1) an error is not finally disposed of till it has received its most perfect expression (Add. 5470); (2) an idea not fully thought out is not a light but a will-o'-the-wisp (Add. 4916).

[3] *L.M.H.*, p. 21.   [4] *Gasquet*, pp. 4, 60.

he says: "Some day, I shall say to a pupil: Read Burke night and day. He is our best political writer, and the deepest of all Whigs—and he will answer: Dear me! I thought he broke up the party, carried it over to the Tories, admired the despotism of the Bourbons, and trained no end of men towards Conservatism? I shall have to answer: So he did. Both sayings are true."[1] In his lectures Acton said that Burke was mistaken in regarding the Revolution of 1688 as conservative: "All this was not restitution, but inversion," adding "it is the greatest thing done by the English nation."[2] To Mary Gladstone he wrote that Goldsmith's cruel line about Burke "And to party gave up what was meant for mankind" is literally true.[3] So too, Acton's attitude to democracy underwent a profound change. In early life he tended to identify the term with the reign of terror or Napoleon III's plébiscitary dictatorship. In 1888, reviewing Bright's history of the nineteenth century, he says (with a pleasant allusiveness) "democracy is the term which divides us least."[4]

Acton's method, apart from exhaustive research, comes out most clearly in a letter dated 1861. He writes: "I have studied politics very elaborately, and more as a science than people generally consider it, and therefore I am afraid of writing like a doctrinaire, or of appearing zealous to force a particular and very unpalatable system down people's throats... my plan has been from time to time to put forward a fragmentary view on one subject, and then another separate fragment, without pointing out the connection or interdependence of the two, and especially without trying to derive them from the fundamental general truths from which I believe them to proceed."[5]

After Acton's death a document was found among his papers recording in imaginative form the ideals at which he was aiming: "[he] said things that were at first sight grossly inconsistent, without attempting to reconcile them. He was reserved about himself, and gave no explanations.... He respected other men's opinions... and when forced to defend his own he felt bound to assume that everyone would look

---

[1] *Corr.*, p. 227 (1896).   [2] p. 231.
[3] *L.M.G.*, p. 49 (1880).   [4] *H.F.*, p. 473.
[5] *Corr.*, pp. 33–34. Cf. Add. 4947: "To be conversant with all political thinking, American, French, Swiss, German, English."

sincerely for the truth and would gladly recognize it. . . . Being quite sincere, he was quite impartial, and pleaded with equal zeal for what seemed true, whether it was on one side or on the other. He would have felt dishonest if he had unduly favoured people of his own country, his own religion, or his own party, or if he had entertained the shadow of a prejudice against those who were against them, and when he was asked why he did not try to clear himself from misrepresentation, he said that he was silent both from humility and pride. At last I understood that what we had disliked in him was his virtue itself."[1]

Acton maintained that politics should be studied "with the chastity of mathematics." "Science is valueless unless pursued without regard to consequences or to application. . . . I think our studies should be all but purposeless. They want to be pursued with chastity, like mathematics. This, at least, is my profession of faith."[2] And again: "We ought to learn from mathematics fidelity to the principle and the method of inquiry and of government."[3] The view Acton rejected is well shown in a passage in a letter to Mary Gladstone written in 1881: "My life is spent in endless striving to make out the inner point of view, the *raison d'être*, the secret of fascination for powerful minds of systems of religion and philosophy, and of politics, the offspring of the others, and one finds that the deepest historians know how to display their origin and their defects, but do not know how to think or feel as men do who live in the grasp of the various systems. And if they sometimes do, it is from a sort of sympathy with the one or the other, which creates partiality and exclusiveness and antipathies."[4]

Fundamentally it is a moral question that is at the bottom of politics.[5] Politics is the art of doing, on the largest scale, what is right.[6]

Writing in 1881, Acton gave a short sketch of the evolution of one part of his thinking:

> Being refused at Cambridge, and driven to foreign universities, I never had any contemporaries, but spent years in looking for men wise enough to solve the problems that puzzled me, not in religion or politics so much as along the

[1] *H.F.*, pp. xxxviii–xxxix.   [2] *Gasquet*, p. 57.   [3] *Ibid.*, p. 222.
[4] *L.M.G.*, p. 60.   [5] *Ibid.*, p. 96.   [6] *Ibid.*, p. 81.

wavy line between the two. So I was always associated with men a generation older than myself, most of whom died early —for me—and all of whom impressed me with the same moral, that one must do one's learning and thinking for oneself, without expecting short cuts or relying on other men. And that led to the elaborate detachment, the unamiable isolation, the dread of personal influences, which you justly censure.[1]

Later Acton adds: "Though I am very suspicious of early impressions and of doctrines unaccounted for, I know I am much more favourable to the great Whig connection, to the tradition of Locke and Somers, Adam Smith, and Burke and Macaulay, than Mr. Gladstone would like. Yet it would seem dust and ashes, but for him. . . . The idea that politics is an affair of principle, that it is an affair of morality, that it touches eternal interests as much as vices and virtues do in private life, that idea will not live in the party."[2] To the same correspondent Acton wrote: "There is no constructive power among the Whigs. There is some among the Democrats, because their principles have been thought out, and provide legislation for generations."[3] It is by a consistent evolution that Acton reaches his final view, a belief in the divine right of free men; and what that involves.

One of his colleagues at Trinity said that Acton really regarded the whole of history as political science. Acton himself, as already noticed, put the matter somewhat differently, comparing political science to grains of gold deposited by the stream of history.[4] He made the same point again in the same lecture where he says that political science is not identical with history.[5] At the same time it is true that Acton believed that some twenty or thirty supreme forces, most of them religions or substitutes for religion, had produced the society of his own day. And he regarded political science as involving all the other social sciences, political and social theory, institutions, ethics, economics, historical jurisprudence, philosophy, theology, and education. For Acton political science includes international law and international relations also. Freedom, he wrote in his

---

[1] *L.M.G.*, p. 105.   [2] *Ibid.*, p. 107.   [3] *Ibid.*, p. 117.
[4] In Add. 4941 he writes: "What is political science? The secret of the progress of the world."   [5] *L.M.H.*, p. 11.

French Revolution, depends on innumerable conditions. Liberty is an idea which has two hundred definitions.[1]

As an illustration we may take theology. The first of human concerns, writes Acton, is religion. Liberty means freedom of conscience—and the claims of conscience are the indestructible soul of revolution. Christianity means primarily ethics. It is not a system of metaphysics which borrowed its ethics elsewhere. It is rather a system of ethics which borrowed its metaphysics elsewhere.[2] It was speculations touching the nature of conscience which promoted a nobler and more spiritual conception of the liberty that protects it.[3] The close study of the psychology of conscience in the thirteenth century led men to speak of it as the audible and infallible voice of God.[4] It was the theological dogma of toleration held by the Independents in the seventeenth century that was responsible for the victory of political freedom in the modern world. Acton regarded theology as a still developing science. He devoted three years to its study, and though he explicitly disclaimed any theological mastery, he believed he knew the difference between a real theologian and a merely learned writer on theology.[5]

Again, historical jurisprudence Acton regarded as the real demonstration of the law of development, which he sees as a major clue to the understanding of the British constitution, Christianity, the history of ideas, and the growth of knowledge.

Philosophy is needed to elucidate the meaning of freedom, international law helps to illustrate the difference between public and private morality, and the study of political institutions and of history is needed to understand what are the necessary constitutional safeguards of freedom. Political science involves the entire history of political doctrine, a history in which, Acton writes, almost every chapter has still to be written. Finally, economics and ethics are the foundation stones of Acton's whole philosophy of politics.

The history of every social science is the prerequisite of its fruitful study. In economics, for example, he studied the ideas

---

[1] *L.M.H.*, p. 12. [2] Letter to Creighton, *H.E.*, p. 504.
[3] *L.M.H.*, p. 13. [4] *Ibid.*, p. 31.
[5] In the Acton MSS. there are, for example, interesting references to Kierkegaard, whom Acton must have been one of the earliest Englishmen to notice, just as he was one of the first to realize the importance of Marx.

of Raleigh in the seventeenth century, as well as Turgot and Adam Smith in the eighteenth, and Roscher, Cournot, Marx, and Marshall in the nineteenth. When Acton refers to Rousseau, he also has in mind the doctrine of Alcuin of York, a thousand years earlier, that the voice of the people is the voice of God, the mediaeval idea that the Christian faith is safeguarded in the conscience of the masses, and the appeal to the conscience of the people by the prophets of the Old Testament.

Acton did not mistake learning for wisdom. It was one of his maxims, though he was by universal consent the most learned Englishman of his time, that solidity of criticism is better than plenitude of erudition. But he regarded it as unscientific to write with anything less than complete mastery of existing knowledge. This was one of the reasons for his relatively small output, though his collected writings fill seven volumes and his uncollected writings are as much again.

More than once Acton explained that his elaborate study of the entire literature of political theory was due to his desire to understand his own age and to find principles which, in public life, he could, as he expressed it, stand to. The same motive, he told Gladstone, inspired the collection of his enormous library: "The whole collection was made with a single view to understanding the public life of the time, and the world I lived in."[1] Only exhaustive, impartial, and disinterested study could yield that quintessence of history which is political philosophy. As he put it in one of his early essays, what matters is "that disinterested spirit of investigation" which applies "to moral science something of the patient self-denial and closeness of observation which belongs to natural philosophy."[2]

In Acton's view the foundations of politics are economics and ethics. Power follows property. This is a law that was discovered by Harrington.[3] President Adams regarded it as the greatest discovery since the invention of printing, and Acton always ranked Harrington extremely high. In a reference to

[1] *Corr.*, p. 232 (1890).

[2] *Rambler*, 1861, p. 300. Cf. Add. 4941: "Whether a man devoted himself to the study of politics, to public life, or to the literature of his age, or to history, the result is nearly the same. One must master much the same topics of learning—and cultivate the same faculties. Let us suppose all three united—."

[3] *L.M.H.*, p. 204.

Sieyès, himself a close student of Harrington, Acton says, "In the little band of true theorists, composed of Harrington and Locke, Rousseau and Jefferson, Hamilton and Mill, the rank of Sieyès is very far from being the lowest."[1] This was Acton's mature estimate, and it is a view he repeatedly stressed. The point is so fundamental in Acton's (and any) philosophy of politics that it is worth while to illustrate it fully. In his Cambridge lectures Acton said:

> Harrington is the author of what Americans have called the greatest discovery since the printing press. For he has given the reason why the great Rebellion failed, and was followed by the reaction under Charles II. He says that it failed because it omitted to redistribute the property of the kingdom. The large estates constituted an aristocratic society, on which it was impossible to construct a democratic state. If the great estates had been broken up into small ones, on a definite plan, the nation would have been committed to the new order of things, and would have accepted the law of equality. Poverty would have been diminished on one side, and nobles would have been abolished on the other. A timorous conservatism and legal scruples made this impossible, and government, by a law of nature, took its shape from the forms and forces of society.[2]

Twenty years earlier, Acton wrote, "England, seething with the toil of political thought, had produced at least two writers who in many directions saw as far and as clearly as we do now.... But Harrington and Lilburne were laughed at for a time and forgotten."[3] In the famous study of German schools of history occurs the following passage:

> [Treitschke] had attacked, and it was thought had refuted the notion of a separate science of society, as the sphere of religion, morality, economy, and knowledge, as a vast community, organically distinct from the State, and able to control it. The idea, which comes from Harrington, and was pronounced by John Adams the greatest discovery in politics, had been made by Lorenz von Stein the key to the Revolution, in a work exposing the economic cause of political science, with Hegelian formalities which contrast unhappily with Treitschke's gleaming style.[4]

[1] *H.E.*, p. 492.
[2] *L.M.H.*, pp. 204–205.
[3] *H.F.*, p. 50.
[4] *H.E.*, p. 380 (1886).

In 1882 Acton wrote to Mary Gladstone: "[Monarchy] was restored because Presbyterians would not stand being oppressed by Congregationalists; and for another reason which was discovered by Harrington, and may still be discovered in his Works."[1] In his *French Revolution* Acton notes, "Harrington, a century before, had seen that the art of government can be reduced to system"; [Harrington wrote of the American colonies] "they are yet babes, that cannot live without sucking the breasts of their mother-cities; but such as I mistake if, when they come of age, they do not wean themselves; which causes me to wonder at princes that like to be exhausted in that way."[2]

Harrington was the modern pioneer in the economic interpretation of politics, familiar though it was to Aristotle and Thucydides. He overestimated the importance of landed property, and he underestimated the influence in England of wealth derived from trade, though he realized that in commercial communities, such as Holland or Genoa, power would follow the distribution of capital. Harrington's importance was not generally appreciated till the present century.[3]

A. L. Smith, quoting from the younger Matthew Wren, Harrington's acutest critic, has argued that the contention between Hobbes and Harrington, whether it is power or property that is the basis of society, is immaterial, as the one comes to the other.[4] A. L. Smith goes on to note the renascence of Harrington's other ideas in the constitution of the United States (rotation in office, residential qualification, division of powers, indirect electoral bodies, belief in popular government). A. L. Smith concludes: "Yet there had been withal a strong aristocratic element in Harrington's republicanism; everything depended, he thought, on the natural aristocracy within a democracy being allowed to rule, and it was to secure this that he had insisted so much on a universal national education, and on complete liberty of individual religious opinions."

[1] *L.M.G.*, p. 139.   [2] *F.R.*, pp. 11, 20.
[3] See Russell Smith, *Harrington*, Gooch, *Bacon to Halifax*, and the same writer's *English Democratic Ideas in the Seventeenth Century*, Liljegren's great Heidelberg edition of the *Oceana* (1924), Professor Tawney's British Academy lecture(1941), and Liljegren's edition of a French Draft Constitution of 1792 based on Harrington's *Oceana*.
[4] *C.M.H.*, VI, pp. 797–798.

INTRODUCTION

Hume called Harrington's the only rational model of a commonwealth, and Coleridge ranked Harrington with Thucydides. The constitutions of Carolina, New Jersey and Pennsylvania in the seventeenth century showed Harrington's influence. Harrington's works have been called the political bible of Otis and John Adams. Jefferson's copy has been preserved in the Library of Congress. Harrington was translated into French during the Revolution, and supplied Sieyès with many of his ideas. Harrington also advocated family allowances and double taxation of the unmarried.[1] "A Commonwealth," wrote Harrington, "is nothing else but the National Conscience."

As Lecky noted,[2] Harrington perceived very clearly that political liberty cannot subsist where there is not absolute religious liberty, and that religious liberty does not consist simply of toleration, but implies a total abolition of religious disqualifications. "Where civil liberty is entire it includes liberty of conscience. Where liberty of conscience is entire, it includes civil liberty."[3]

As we shall see later, Acton did not disregard these other ideas of Harrington's. But it was the economic foundation of politics, which Acton took from Harrington, that he was fond of stressing, both in the form it takes in Harrington and also in the writings of the French Physiocrats, and in Adam Smith.

Discussing Turgot, Acton says:

> [Turgot] found his home among the Physiocrats, of all the groups the one that possessed the most compact body of consistent views, and who already knew most of the accepted doctrines of political economy, although they ended by making way for Adam Smith. They are of supreme importance to us, because they founded political science on the economic science which was coming into existence. Harrington, a century before, had seen that the art of government can be reduced to system; but the French economists precede all men in this, that holding a vast collection of combined and verified truths on matters contiguous to politics and belonging to their domain, they extended it to the whole, and governed the constitution by the same fixed principles that governed the purse. They said: A man's most sacred property is his labour. It is anterior even to the right of

[1] *Prerogative of Popular Government*, p. 97.   [2] *Rationalism*, Vol. II, p. 76.
[3] Harrington's *Political Aphorisms*, pp. 23–24.

property, for it is the possession of those who own nothing else. Therefore he must be free to make the best use of it that he can. The interference of one man with another, of society with its members, of the State with the subject, must be brought down to the lowest dimension. Power intervenes only to restrict intervention, to guard the individual from oppression, that is, from regulation in an interest not his own. Free labour and its derivative free trade are the first conditions of legitimate government. Let things fall into their natural order, let society govern itself, and the sovereign function of the State will be to protect nature in the execution of her own law. Government must not be arbitrary, but it must be powerful enough to repress arbitrary action in others.[1]

The same line of thought is also expressed in a letter to Mary Gladstone:

> Adam Smith set up two propositions—that contracts ought to be free between capital and labour, and that labour is the source, he sometimes says the only source, of wealth. If the last sentence, in its exclusive form, was true, it was difficult to resist the conclusion that the class on which national prosperity depends ought to control the wealth it supplies, that is, ought to govern instead of the useless unproductive class, and that the class which earns the increment ought to enjoy it. That it is the foreign effect of Adam Smith—French Revolution and Socialism. We, who reject that extreme proposition, cannot resist the logical pressure of the other. If there is a free contract, in open market, between capital and labour, it cannot be right that one of the contracting parties should have the making of the laws. . . . Justice required that property should—not abdicate, but—share its political supremacy.[2]

The disinterested study of the classical economists gave rise in Germany to the school known as the "academic socialists", who captured most of the Professorships in German universities in the last quarter of the nineteenth century: "The better part of him [Henry George], with more moderation and philosophy, and a wider induction, may be found in the writings of the academic socialists, who, in the last ten years, have occupied almost all the chairs of Germany."[3] Acton reverted to the same

[1] *F.R.*, pp. 11–12.   [2] *L.M.G.*, p. 92.   [3] *Ibid.*, p. 170 (1883).

point the following year: "In their writings [i.e. of the academic socialists], inspired by the disinterested study of the classical economists, one finds most of the ideas and illustrations of Mr. George. . . . This makes him less new . . . but . . . I do believe that he has, in a large measure, the ideas of the age that is to come."[1]

Acton wrote more fully on the same topic in other letters: "Within the last ten or twelve years there has been a wonderful change in political economy in the direction of which Laveleye, Ingram, Cliffe Leslie are popular exponents. . . . The essential point is the history and analysis of property in land. . . . Two volumes contain all that it is necessary to read: Roscher, *National Oekonomik des Ackerbaus*, and Wagner's *Grundlegung der Volkswirtschaft*."[2] Later he wrote: "Wagner's *Grundlegung* is an exceedingly able, bold, and original book, and the author occupies, at Berlin, the first chair of Political Economy in Germany."[3] In the same connection Acton discusses Laveleye:

> Laveleye has a great knowledge of Political Economy and of politics, and his peculiarity is that he does not think of party, or power, or wealth, but is thoroughly anxious about the condition of society. That separates him from orthodox Economists (Lowe, Mallet, Newmarch), who do not attend to the problem of Distribution, and are not made sleepless by the suffering and sorrow of the poor. He is slightly heterodox, what Germans call Kathedersozialist, and what even Maine would call downright Socialist. His chief work is an account of early forms of property, an indirect and rather confused plea for common property in land. Ingram, Cliffe Leslie nearly represent him in England.[4]

As previously noticed, Acton said that political economy was as much an ethical as a material science, that its fundamental principles were self-reliance and self-denial, and that these were as clearly legible in the New Testament as in the *Wealth of Nations*. He adds a quotation from the *Anti-Dühring* of Marx-Engels, "Political Economy is a historical study."

"The form of government and the condition of society must always correspond. Social equality is therefore a postulate of pure democracy."[5] "Democracy is a gigantic current which

---

[1] *L.M.G.*, p. 175 (1884).   [2] *Ibid.*, p. 90 (1881).
[3] *Ibid.*, p. 97.   [4] *Ibid.*, pp. 75–76.   [5] *H.F.*, p. 265 (1862).

has been fed by many springs. Physical and spiritual causes have contributed to swell it. Much has been done by economic theories, and more by economic laws."[1] "A people averse to the institution of private property is without the first element of freedom."[2] The essentials of free government, Acton writes, include emancipation of slaves, freedom of trade, and relief of poverty. "Liberal progress aims at a point where the public is subject to no restrictions but those of which it feels the advantage."[3]

Political, social, and economic science rest upon the observation of laws, and the regularity with which like causes produce like effects.[4]

Acton repeatedly emphasized "the connection between the doctrine of Adam Smith, that labour is the original source of all wealth, and the conclusion that the producers of wealth virtually compose the nation, by which Sieyès subverted historic France."[5] Adam Smith provided a scientific backbone to liberal sentiment.[6] To Mary Gladstone he wrote: "I quite agree with Chamberlain that there is latent socialism in the Gladstonian philosophy."[7]

The entire history of economic theory Acton regarded as essential for political philosophy. Thus he notes "the studies of Roscher and Laspeyres on the English, the German, and the Dutch economists of the sixteenth and seventeenth centuries."[8] Acton valued Raleigh as an economist, as well as for his *History of the World*. Locke, by his labour theory of value, was, he notes, the father of Adam Smith.[9] He studied Marshall as well as Marx; and Cournot he quoted repeatedly in the notes to his *Inaugural*. On the same occasion he said, "The mean duration of life is the most compendious test of improvement. Life is prolonged by all the chief agents of civilization, moral and material, religious and scientific, working together, and depends on preserving at infinite cost, which is infinite loss, the crippled child and the victim of accident, the idiot and the madman, the pauper and the culprit, the old and infirm, curable and incurable."

---

[1] *H.F.*, p. 62.   [2] *Ibid.*, p. 297.   [3] *Ibid.*, p. 23.
[4] *Ibid.*, p. 233.   [5] *Ibid.*, p. 57.
[6] *Hawarden Letters*, p. 188.   [7] *L.M.G.*, p. 212 (11 Nov. 1885).
[8] *Chronicle*, 1 June 1867, p. 235.   [9] *Corr.*, p. 230.

INTRODUCTION

Acton's treatment of the economic factor in history forms the subject of an appendix. Here a few preliminary examples may be noted. The whole of history has been occupied by attempts to prevent properly balanced constitutions, attempts made in the interests of land, money, or numbers.[1] For the ancient doctrine that power goes with land Pericles introduced the idea that power ought to be so equitably diffused as to afford equal security for all.[2] The discovery of the New World "reversed the conditions of production, wealth, and power."[3] "The Dutch Republic was, in fact, a trade association. Its leading politicians were the chiefs of the East India Company" (Add. 4937). "For the divine right of kings, it [the Revolution of 1688] established, in the words of Defoe, the divine right of freeholders."[4] It confined power to them.[5] Though the Revolution of 1688 is the greatest thing done by the English nation, it involved no transfer of power from the aristocracy to the people, and it brought the National Debt, the Bank of England, the growth of the moneyed interest. But the agrarian interest still largely predominated, and the landlords, as the ruling class, required, and in the form of the Corn Laws received, a reward for their share in the elevation of William.[6] It is the very meaning of the French Revolution that the producers of wealth should control the State.[7] But rights are founded on duties. The rights of man on earth are the consequence of the rights of God in Heaven. The ultimate object of politics is freedom, that is, freedom of conscience. It means freedom to avoid sin.[8] Ethics includes politics. These are Acton's primary postulates and must be illustrated first. Morley, Acton writes, "sees nothing in politics but higher expediency and no large principles. As there are, for him, no rights of God, there are no rights of man—the consequence, on earth, of obligation in Heaven."[9] As he put it in his *Inaugural*, "duties are the cause of rights."[10] A generation earlier Acton wrote: "Liberty is not the power of doing what we like, but the right of being able to do what we ought."[11]

[1] *H.F.*, p. 10. [2] *H.F.*, p. 79. [3] *L.M.H.*, p. 4.
[4] *H.F.*, p. 54. [5] *Ibid.*, p. 83. [6] *L.M.H.*, p. 230.
[7] *F.R.*, p. 1. Cf. Add. 4951: "Property, not Conscience, is the basis of liberty. For the defence of Conscience need not arise. Property is always exposed to State interference. It is the constant object of policy."
[8] Add. 4870.   [9] *L.M.G.*, 2nd ed., p. 179.   [10] *L.M.H.*, p. 13.
[11] *Rambler*, Jan. 1860, p. 146.

"Liberty enables us to do our duty—unhindered by the State, by society, by ignorance and error."[1] In a later manuscript note he writes: "We don't learn our duty from the State. The ancients did."[2] As early as 1858 (*aetat*. 24) Acton said, "The feeling of duty and responsibility to God is the only arbiter of a Christian's actions."[3] The emphasis on moral duty as the ultimate foundation of political theory is the unvarying element in Acton's thought. In 1862, for example, he wrote, "Our connection with the race is merely natural or physical, whilst our duties to the political nation are ethical."[4] The State "is an authority governing by laws, imposing obligations, and giving a moral sanction and character to the natural relations of society."[5] But, Acton adds, "the man who prefers his country before every other duty shows the same spirit as the man who surrenders every right to the State. They both deny that right is superior to authority."[6] The establishment of liberty for the realisation of moral duties is the end of civil society.[7] The growth of liberty is to be identified with the cause of morality, and is the condition of the reign of conscience.[8] Morality is involved in questions of political right.[9] "Leibniz was bitterly opposed to that political atheism which denies all public obligations, sets up the arbitrary will of man above the will of God."[10] Authority is essentially an ethical term, but when separated from liberty it is nothing but force.[11] The State has a moral nature and purpose.[12]

Christianity means primarily ethics. It is (it must be repeated) not a system of metaphysics which got its ethics elsewhere. It is rather a system of ethics which borrowed its metaphysics elsewhere.[13] Ethics does not mean expediency, as Burke and Morley maintain. The doctrine of expediency is a negation of a science of political ethics.[14] Ethics is, in fact, an independent discipline, to which even churches, as well as states, are subject. The ethics of political science cannot be denominational. The moral code, in its main lines, is not new, it has long been known, it is

[1] Add. 4870, p. 1. [2] *Ibid.*, p. 10. [3] *H.F.*, p. 203.
[4] *H.F.*, p. 292. [5] *Ibid.*, p. 293. [6] *Ibid.*
[7] *Ibid.*, p. 298. [8] *Ibid.*
[9] *H.F.R.*, Jan. 1863, p. 253. [10] *Ibid.*, Oct. 1862, p. 545.
[11] *Ibid.*, Oct. 1863, p. 717. [12] *Ibid.*, April 1864, p. 723.
[13] *H.E.*, p. 504. [14] *L.M.G.*, 2nd ed., pp. 180–183.

not universally accepted in Europe even now, the difference in moral insight between past and present is not very large. The principles of public morality are as definite as those of the morality of private life; but they are not identical."¹ The principle of judgment is, not the orthodox standard of any religious, philosophical, or political system, "but according as things promote, or fail to promote the delicacy, integrity, and authority of Conscience."²

Plato and Aristotle, who gave the primacy to ethics, are the writers from whom, says Acton, we can learn most about the principles of politics, more especially the *Laws* of Plato, and the *Politics* of Aristotle.³ Before them the inspired men who prophesied against the tyrants of Israel appealed to the healing forces that slept in the uncorrupted conscience of the masses, and all freedom has been won by the two-fold appeal to tradition, and to the higher law,⁴ that is, the principle that political authority is subject to natural law. Natural law is the law of reason and of God.

It was the Stoics who bridged the gap between pagan and Christian ethical thinking.⁵ Zeno led men to the very Gate of Christianity.⁶ The Stoics looked for the principles that ought to regulate the lives of men and the existence of society. They taught that there is a will superior to the collective will of men and principles that can be traced to a higher legislator. What we must obey, they said, is the eternal law of God Himself.⁷

The great question, in their view, is to discover, not what governments prescribe, but what they ought to prescribe, for no prescription is valid against the conscience of mankind. Before God there is neither Greek nor barbarian, neither rich nor poor, and the slave is as good as his master, for by birth all men are free. They are citizens of that universal commonwealth which embraces all the world, brothers of one family, and

---

[1] *H.E.*, p. 506. As these references show, Acton's ultimate principle is duty to God. This may be contrasted with, for example, Bosanquet's famous judgment in the *Philosophical Theory of the State*: "the freewill that wills the freewill—this is the root of political obligation." For Acton this is a heresy, involving substituting the will of man for the will of God, unless the freewill is thoroughly conscientious. Acton's position is, of course, much closer to that of T. H. Green.

[2] *H.E.*, p. 505. [3] *H.F.*, p. 22. [4] *Ibid.*, p. 5.
[5] *Ibid.*, p. 24. [6] *Hawarden Letters*, p. 187. [7] *H.F.*, p. 24.

children of God. The true voice is the voice of God who dwells in our souls.

The New Testament marks an ethical and political revolution, ethical in the Beatitudes and the Sermon on the Mount, political in the text "Render unto Caesar."

The Stoic doctrines were adopted and applied by the great jurists of the Empire.[1] The law of nature, they said, is superior to the written law. Slavery contradicts the law of nature. These are also the views of Cicero, Seneca, and of Philo of Alexandria. Philo believed in liberty and thought a limited democracy the most perfect government.[2]

There is hardly a truth in politics, says Acton, that was not grasped by the wisest of the ancient writers.[3]

The mediaeval theory of politics, Acton writes, is that the unwritten law reigns supreme over the municipal law.[4] In the age succeeding Machiavelli, men "saw that public morality differs from private, because no government can turn the other cheek, or can admit that mercy is better than justice."[5] Nobody in the sixteenth century sincerely thought of politics as a law for the just and the unjust, or tried to find out a set of principles that should hold good alike under all changes of religion. "Hooker's *Ecclesiastical Polity* stands almost alone."[6]

Charron, in a passage almost literally transcribed from Aquinas, "describes our subordination under a law of nature, to which all legislation must conform; and he ascertains it not by the light of revealed religion, but by the voice of universal reason, through which God enlightens the consciences of men. Upon this foundation Grotius drew the lines of real political science."[7] From that time it became possible to make politics a matter of principle and conscience.[8]

The erection of ethics into a separate study was accomplished in successive stages by the following: Erasmus, Rabelais, Montaigne, La Boétie, L'Hospital, Pibrac, Bodin, Duvair, Charron. They all "agreed in making morality independent of religion."[9] The same point is made in one of Acton's manuscript notes: "How higher views came to prevail—L'Hospital, Pasquier, Thuanus, Casaubon, Grotius,"[10] and more fully in his lectures:

[1] *H.F.*, p. 25. [2] *Ibid.*, p. 26. [3] *Ibid.*, p. 27.
[4] *L.M.H.*, pp. 80–81. [5] *H.F.*, p. 40. [6] *Ibid.*, p. 45.
[7] *Ibid.*, p. 46. [8] *Ibid.* [9] *N.B.R.*, July 1870, p. 540. [10] Add. 4870.

a new heresy, the political heresy, had been discovered, which Cardinal Baronius, the foremost of the Roman divines, denounced as the most damnable of all heresies. By that was meant the notion of a science of politics limiting the ecclesiastical domain; an ethical and political system deriving its principles elsewhere than from the Church, and setting up a new and rival authority, yet to be defined, ascertainable in no book, and not accepted by the nations. Those amongst us who deny the existence of a political science, and believe that ethics cannot be made to include politics, have ardent supporters in the Roman clergy of three centuries ago.[1]

Socinus in the sixteenth century, and the Independents in the seventeenth century, required religious toleration, while Grotius founded international law on the law of nature. Burke, in his liberal phase, and the American writers such as Otis, regard the law of reason as supreme. Otis identified the British constitution with the law of nature, as Montesquieu called the Civil Law written reason.[2]

"It was from America," writes Acton, "that the plain ideas that men ought to mind their own business, and that the nation is responsible to Heaven for the acts of the State . . . burst forth like a conqueror upon the world they were destined to transform, under the title of the Rights of Man."[3] As he put it in one of his letters: "the universal, abstract, ethical character of the American Rights of Man."[4]

So too among the heralds of the French Revolution:

> [The Jansenist lawyer Domat] insisted that law shall proceed from common-sense, not from custom, and shall draw its precepts from an eternal code. The principle of the higher law signifies Revolution. No government founded on positive enactment only can stand before it, and it points the way to that system of primitive, universal, and indefeasible rights which the lawyers of the Assembly, descending from Domat, prefixed to their constitution.[5]

Sieyès himself may be quoted:

> Sieyès understood politics as the science of the State as it ought to be, and he repudiated the product of history, which

---

[1] *L.M.H.*, p. 173. [2] *F.R.*, p. 23. [3] *H.F.*, p. 55.
[4] *Corr.*, pp. 272–273. [5] *F.R.*, p. 2.

is things as they are. No American ever grasped more firmly the principle that experience is an incompetent teacher of the governing art. He turned resolutely from the Past, and refused to be bound by the precepts of men who believed in slavery and sorcery, in torture and persecution.[1]

The method of modern progress has been revolution rather because of the attraction of ideal right than by reason of provocation by actual wrong. Hence the Dutch, English, American and French Revolutions.

As we have seen, according to Acton the true theorists are Harrington, Locke, Rousseau, Sieyès, Jefferson, Hamilton, and Mill.[2] That judgment shows the importance Acton attached to the ethical criterion. It is supplemented by what he says of Plato and Aristotle, and by his remark that the greatest writers of the eighteenth century were Burke and Hamilton, of the nineteenth Tocqueville and Roscher. Acton also rated especially highly Vinet, who "made Conscience and Liberty a law in Church and State,"[3] and "the illustrious Trendelenburg", who founded his system of politics on the principles of ethics. Similarly Acton supremely valued the ethics of Rothe, whom he regarded as the greatest moral theologian of modern times, and the sociology of law as represented by Ihering, whose insight and dialectics he thought keener and deeper than Hegel's.

Freedom of conscience is the root of self-government, individually and collectively, for both depend on moral responsibility. To political and moral science the same patience, self-denial, and closeness of observation should be applied as in the natural sciences.[4] The cause of liberty is the cause of morality, of duty and rights, for its meaning is freedom of conscience. "The moral law is written on the tablets of eternity."[5] A true principle is more sacred than the most precious interest.[6] "Political obligation is determined, not by arbitrary maxims of expediency, but by definite and consistent principles."[7] The political law is founded on the divine.[8]

Acton summarizes all history when he speaks of the "great

---

[1] *F.R.*, p. 159.   [2] *H.E.*, p. 492.   [3] *Hawarden Letters*, p. 189.
[4] *Rambler*, 1861, p. 300 (aetat. 27).   [5] *L.M.H.*, p. 27.
[6] *Rambler*, Sept. 1861, p. 295.
[7] *N.B.R.*, 1 July 1869, quoted in *Corr.*, pp. 313–314.
[8] *H.F.R.*, Oct. 1863, p. 681.

controversy" of all ages as the controversy between reason and custom. Reason means primarily ethics. Over long periods there is an advance of moral over material influence, and slow progress in the direction of humanity, rational persuasion, and the appeal to common, simple and evident maxims.[1]

The supremacy of ethics, which is true in the theory of politics, should be consistently reflected in practical politics. Liberalism is founded on conscience. Practical politics is an affair of principle, of morality. Liberalism means that morality and the ethical purpose and standard are supreme.[2] But to many people the idea is repugnant that there is a moral question at the bottom of politics.

Acton regretted that George Eliot "refused to admit that political differences are, what religious differences are not, founded on an ultimate diversity of moral principles."[3] In the essay on German Schools of History, Acton remarks: "The belief that men carry about them the knowledge of good and evil is the very root of revolution."[4] And he adds: "the growth of ethical knowledge has become . . . the supreme object of history."[5] It is the office of historical science "to maintain morality as the sole impartial criterion of men and things, and the only one on which honest minds can be made to agree."[6] The ethics of history cannot be denominational.[7]

Ethics is the essence of Whiggism.[8] Writing to Gladstone in 1890 Acton said "it will not do to act as if the moral question was not the supreme question in public life, and, in a sense, the *vera causa* of party conflict."[9] Earlier, he wrote to Mary Gladstone: "We have to keep the national conscience straight and true, and if we shrink from doing this because we dare not cast obloquy on class or party or institution, then we become accomplices in wrongdoing, and very possibly in crime."[10]

One of the best examples Acton gives of the practical application of the ethical criterion is what he says of the decline of Athens:

> The causes which ruined the Republic of Athens illustrate the connection of ethics with politics rather than the vices

[1] *L.M.H.*, p. 33. [2] *Corr.*, pp. 54 ff. [3] *H.E.*, p. 300.
[4] *Ibid.*, p. 355. [5] *Ibid.*, p. 362. [6] *Ibid.*, p. 437.
[7] *Ibid.*, p. 505. [8] *H.F.R.*, Jan. 1863, p. 253. [9] *Corr.*, p. 257.
[10] *L.M.G.*, p. 95.

inherent to democracy. . . . The short triumph of Athenian liberty, and its quick decline, belong to an age which possessed no fixed standard of right and wrong. An unparalleled activity of intellect was shaking the credit of the gods, and the gods were the givers of the law. It was a very short step from the suspicion of Protagoras, that there were no gods, to the assertion of Critias that there is no sanction for laws. If nothing was certain in theology, there was no certainty in ethics and no moral obligation. The will of man, not the will of God, was the rule of life, and every man and body of men had the right to do what they had the means of doing.[1]

In the Middle Ages Aquinas taught that the whole nation, as a matter of right, ought to have a share in governing itself, and Marsilius taught that laws derive their authority from the nation and have no validity without its assent.[2] It is an ethical appeal that underlies modern revolutions.

Acton's most elaborate vindication of the ethical criterion in practical politics is given in a long passage in the second edition of the *Letters to Mary Gladstone:*

> The great bulk of cultured men in our day do not believe that politics are a branch of Moral Science. They think that politics teach what is likely to do good or harm, not what is right or wrong, innocent or sinful. If I say: "I owe this man half-a-crown. He is sure to get drunk on it; shall I pay him?" They will answer—Certainly; you must do your duty, in private life, and wherever the plain rules of morality or the applicable laws extend, regardless of consequences. But they would not admit a like obligation in politics. America cannot be taxed because it is not represented. Civil disabilities for religion must be abolished. Slavery must be put down. The tyranny of Indian princes must be repressed, etc., etc., etc. Such propositions they would deny absolutely. They would say: "It is highly desirable—not obligatory. We must consider consequences, balance probabilities, estimate forces, choose the lesser evil. Until it can be shown that oppression, repression, suppression, damage the interests of the State, there is no good reason to interfere with them. If the State would be greater, stronger, richer, by restraining labour, by working children to death in factories, by wars for prestige, etc., etc., etc., then those things are lawful by the only test known to politics. You must keep your promises and pay the

---

[1] *H.F.*, p. 70.   [2] *Ibid.*, pp. 36–37.

public debt, because the law of common morality goes as far as that. But the law of common morality is silent as to questions that exist only in a political shape. Those can only be treated experimentally, by the Baconian methods. There is no code of political morality distinct from or beyond the limits of private. There is no such thing as political science; men do not lose their souls by political, as they do by domestic, error. Whoever does not see this is a doctrinaire, a fanatic, an unfit survival from the dogmatising and abstract epoch, before the reign of Induction.

Thus Maine, Stephen, Dilke, all men who live in diplomacy, all men concerned with India, all men belonging to the Services. Above all, this is part of the teaching of Burke, and from him Morley has adopted it.

Newman and Keble are the two types. When Newman moaned and murmured at the Disestablishment[1] policy, Keble said, "But isn't it just?" Newman must have thought that the good man was getting a little weak. At Christmas 1885, when Bryce came to Cannes and talked about Home Rule, I said, "Remember, it will break up the Liberal Party." I could not have said such a thing to Morley, or Newman, or Maine. They would have replied, "You cannot be sure that this policy will succeed in Ireland; you are persuaded that it will grievously injure political life in England. What else have you to go upon?" Bosworth Smith spoke to me in almost these very terms, and evidently felt that he had said what could not be answered.

But this negation of a science of political ethics, this repudiation of political principle, does not depend on men's attitude to religion. Political Economy and Criminal Law were the first branches of practical politics that assumed a scientific form. The founders of the former, Hume, Quesnay, Smith, Turgot, were all unbelievers. So were the reformers of Criminal Law, Beccaria, Morellet, Bentham. Jefferson, who wrote the American *Rights of Man*, Lafayette and Sieyès, who composed the French, were all alike unbelievers.

There is a very strong tendency to substitute for a religious system another system of obligations, equally determined and absolute, but not at all religious. Especially nowadays when unbelief in the shape of doubt is yielding to unbelief in the shape of certain conviction.

And in these things the influence of religion is by no means

---

[1] In Ireland.

certain. It has often been opposed to the theory of the divine right of man. As the history of persecution, of slavery, shows, quite naturally. The New Testament, which deals so largely with private morality, deals very little with public, and introduced only one political idea beyond the Hellenic horizon. If, therefore, we admit the authority of a binding system, independent of religion, we raise up a rival power, in morals as in science. Our conduct becomes subject to a law which is not that of the Church, which may deviate from it, and which, at certain points, inevitably collides with it. We live under a divided reign. Christianity becomes an influence instead of an authority, a prop, but not a sufficient guide. The surrender of one bit of its domain to the mathematicians, of another to the economists, of a third to the politicians, may be followed by further encroachment from biologists, and Monistic philosophers.

That is the line of reasoning which makes religious belief a weak security for political principle, unless the faith of men is thoroughly sincere, and even men thoroughly sincere may object that they know not which political theory or which system of the Rights of Man is so surely the right one that, where it commands, they must prefer it to their religion. No consensus, no Vincentian Rule, exists that can decide this question.

Therefore, although I fully admit that political Rights proceed directly from religious duties, and hold this to be the true basis of Liberalism, I do not mean to say that there is no other foundation for a system of rights for men who know of no relations between man and God. Indeed I gathered that Burke and Austin had deleteriously influenced Morley in this respect, and that he easily submitted to their influence, having no conception of certain rights that are divine.

Let me add, as I am disparaging Burke, that he is not consistent, and there is another strain in his web. But if he had not taken the lower level in the American question, he would have been forced into an attitude on Irish questions, and perhaps on parliamentary reform, which would have isolated him and alienated his friends, who were also his patrons, in the British aristocracy.[1]

As Acton succinctly put the same point in his letter to Creighton: in judging men and things ethics comes before

[1] *L.M.G.*, 2nd ed., pp. 180–183.

dogma, politics, or nationality;[1] and in the *Inaugural:* "I exhort you never to debase the moral currency or to lower the standard of rectitude."[2]

Ethics furnishes the criterion and objective of politics, practical as well as theoretical, international as well as national, and the principles of public as well as of private morality. It is for ethical reasons that the supreme object of politics is liberty, that is, freedom of conscience, the security of the weaker groups, and its necessary securities.[3] Its outward signs are representation, the extinction of slavery, and the reign of opinion.[4] Liberty is not negative, it is the active and creative principle, the motive and source of all life, the name which conscience takes when it emerges to model society in accordance with the dictates of reason.[5] Liberty is a thing that grows and is not a primitive or natural condition.[6] "Why is the advance of liberty so slow? Because it depends on the advance of so many other things. They go before."[7] Before turning to Acton's analysis of conscience, on which his idea of freedom turns, it will be convenient to illustrate further his general conception of freedom, and subsequently to examine his theory of toleration, and of the relation of Church and State, which is bound up with it.

Acton said that liberty resembled the camel in having more definitions than any other object in nature. His own definition involves certain conditions: (1) long and arduous experience, (2) a rampart of tried convictions, (3) accumulated knowledge, (4) a fair level of general morality, (5) education, (6) courage, (7) self-restraint.[8] "Liberty is the assurance that every man shall be protected in doing what he believes his duty against the influence of authority and majorities, custom and opinion."[9] Liberty is the delicate fruit of a mature civilization.[10] It depends on innumerable conditions.[11] It is the essential condition and guardian of religion, which is the first of human concerns.[12] Liberty is not a means to a higher political end. It is itself the

[1] *H.E.*, p. 505.
[2] *L.M.H.*, p. 24 (1895). Professor Woodward regards this as Acton's supreme merit. *Politica*, Sept. 1939, p. 265.
[3] *L.M.H.*, p. 13 (1895).   [4] *Ibid.*
[5] *Ibid.*, p. 327.   [6] *H.F.R.*, April 1863, p. 656.
[7] Add. 4916, p. 6.   [8] *L.M.H.*, p. 13.
[9] *H.F.*, p. 3 (1877).   [10] *H.E.*, p. 596; *H.F.*, p. 1.
[11] *F.R.*, p. 107.   [12] *L.M.H.*, p. 8.

highest political end. It is required not for the sake of good public administration, but for security in the pursuit of the highest objects of civil society, and of private life. But it is not the sum or the substitute of all the things men ought to live for. To be real it must be circumscribed, and the limits of circumscription vary. Liberal progress aims at a point where the public is subject to no restrictions but those of which it feels the advantage. The supreme political object ought sometimes to be postponed to still higher moral objects.[1] True freedom means obeying God. The injunction "Render unto God the things that are God's" was the true inauguration of freedom and the repudiation of absolutism.[2] Nations that lack the self-governing force of religion are unprepared for freedom.[3] The best things that are loved and sought by men are religion and liberty. The essence of the English system of government is liberty founded on inequality, as contrasted with the ideal of the French Revolution which was liberty founded on equality. The true equality is the equal claim to be free: "Liberty should be alike for all. Liberty and security. That is its connection with equality."[4] Private property is the first condition of freedom.[5] What the poor need if the liberal movement in politics is not to be a mockery is comfort.[6]

In short—liberty is a goal, not a starting-point.[7] It is a faculty to be acquired, not a capital to invest.[8] Sieyès was a true liberal, for he thought liberty was the object of government.[9] The most certain test of whether a country is really free is the amount of security enjoyed by minorities.[10] For liberty, it is as necessary that democracy should restrain itself as that oligarchy should be restrained. As Constant said, "The will of a whole people cannot make just that which is unjust."[11] Government by the whole people requires institutions that will protect the people against itself, and uphold the permanent rule of law against arbitrary revolutions of opinion.

The equal claim of every man to be unhindered by man in the fulfilment of duty to God is a doctrine laden with storm and

---

[1] *H.F.*, pp. 22–23, i.e. liberty pre-supposes justice. Acton praises Sieyès for the same view.   [2] *H.F.*, p. 29.   [3] *F.R.*, p. 6.
[4] Add. 4941.   [5] *H.F.*, p. 297.   [6] Add. 5487.
[7] *Gasquet.*   [8] *F.R.*, p. 107.   [9] *Ibid.*, p. 161.
[10] *H.F.*, p. 4.   [11] *L.M.H.*, p. 342.

havoc, is the secret essence of the Rights of Man, and the indestructible soul of Revolution.¹

From 1858, when Acton was twenty-four, to 1901, the year before his death, when he was sixty-seven, that is, for a space of forty-three years, the idea of freedom is the guiding star of Acton's thought. "He that deems he can advocate the cause of religion without advocating at the same time the cause of freedom, is no better than a hypocrite and a traitor."² "The outward forms, in which the substance of Liberty does not necessarily reside."³ "According to the prevailing doctrine, which derives power from the people, and deposits it ultimately in their hands, the State is omnipotent over the individual, whose only remnant of freedom is then the participation in the exercise of supreme power; while the general will is binding on him. Christian liberty is lost where this system prevails."⁴ State-absolutism is the modern danger against which neither representative government nor democracy can defend us.⁵ "All liberty consists *in radice* in the preservation of an inner sphere exempt from State power. That reverence for conscience is the germ of all civil freedom, and the way in which Christianity served it. That is, liberty has grown out of the distinction (separation is a bad word) of Church and State."⁶ A kind of superstition is required in all men who are not free.⁷ "It is liberty acknowledged as a principle, not liberties obtained by compromise and concession, that generates toleration."⁸ Before the American Revolution, Pennsylvania was almost the only example of freedom.⁹ It is only men without fastidiousness in their political tastes who "imagine that liberty flourished under Alfred, under Charlemagne, or . . . in the Hercynian forest."¹⁰ As "that refined essence which draws sustenance from all good things it [liberty] is clearly understood as the product of civilization, with its complex problems and scientific appliances, not as the elementary possession of the noble savage, which has been traced so often to the primeval forest."¹¹

[1] *L.M.H.*, pp. 10–11 (1895).
[2] *Rambler*, Dec. 1858, p. 422.
[3] *Ibid.*, p. 425.
[4] *Ibid.* See the chapter on Democracy, below, for Acton's distinction between true and false democracy.
[5] *Ibid.*, March 1860, p. 397.
[6] *Gasquet*, pp. 253–254 (1862).
[7] *H.F.R.*, April 1863, p. 656.
[8] *Chronicle*, 20 July 1867, p. 395.
[9] *H.F.*, p. 84 (1878).
[10] *H.E.*, p. 468 (1888).
[11] *H.F.*, p. 596 (1895).

"The true apostles of toleration are not those who sought protection for their own beliefs, or who had none to protect; but men to whom, irrespective of their cause, it was a political, a moral, and a theological dogma, a question of conscience involving both religion and policy. Such a man was Socinus."[1] The heralds of the French Revolution were called Liberal: "Montesquieu, because he was an intelligent Tory; Voltaire, because he attacked the clergy; Turgot, as a reformer; Rousseau, as a democrat; Diderot, as a freethinker. The one thing common to them all is the disregard for liberty."[2] Sieyès defined liberty as "that which makes men most completely master of their faculties, in the largest sphere of independent action.... In the history of political doctrine, where almost every chapter has yet to be written, none will be more valuable than the one that will show what is permanent and progressive in the ideas which Sieyès originated."[3]

"We have no thread through the enormous intricacy and complexity of modern politics except the idea of progress towards more perfect and assured freedom, and the divine right of free men."[4]

---

[1] *L.M.H.*, p. 10 (1895). [2] *F.R.*, p. 19 (1895). [3] *Ibid.*, pp. 161, 164.
[4] *L.M.H.*, p. 202 (1901). Cf. Add. 4939: "Liberty and morality. How they try to separate them—to found liberty on rights, on enjoyments, not on duties. Insist on their identity. Liberty is that condition which makes it easy for conscience to govern. Liberty is government of Conscience—Reign of Conscience."

I

THE THEORY OF CONSCIENCE

Acton's conception of freedom hinges on the idea of conscience. For this, among other reasons, he gave an important place in the history of political doctrine to Bishop Butler. Acton believed that Kant's doctrine of the infallibility of conscience was derived from Butler, and Butler's from Sarasa—a seventeenth-century Jesuit whose chief work was entitled *Ars semper gaudendi*. But Acton's writings are studded, from start to finish, with references to conscience; and in the Acton MSS. at Cambridge there are two boxes of notes on conscience[1] which further elucidate his views. There is valuable ancillary material in the folders containing his notes on Vinet (5495), Burke (5389), and Grotius (5434).

One of the papers on conscience in the Acton MSS. gives a rough sketch plan of how Acton thought the topic ought to be treated. It runs as follows:[2]

> Plan
> Growth of the notion of Conscience (Ethics)
> Growth of Securities and Machinery
> Notions of property
> Growth of scientific methods
> Progress of religious knowledge.

In this chapter it is with the first of these that we shall be primarily concerned.

"Butler," Acton notes, "when he deified Conscience followed Socrates. When Socrates declared that he would obey God rather than man, he meant God manifest within—with no oracle, no sacred book, no appointed minister—with no organ but within."[3] But the "notion of Conscience had to be fully developed. This did not happen till the eighteenth century."[4]

---

[1] Add. 4901 and Add. 5395. [2] Add. 5395, p. 85.
[3] *Ibid.*, p. 152. [4] *Ibid.*, p. 1.

Conscience is unknown in the religions of the East.[1] "The word Conscience does not occur in the O[ld] T[estament]."[2] In the Old Testament "the heart holds the place of conscience. ... The word is wanting, but not the thing."[3] "Conscience depends on, or is parallel with, clear notions of ethics."[4] "It comes into play in Sophocles, Euripides, Socrates. At the turning of Greek life, at the breakdown of mythology and the rise of Democracy. Its first appearance [is] in Periander—7 Wise men."[5] "First, instead of sacred tradition, present authority of general consent. This led to the extreme of democracy. Reaction against this, in the third stage, Conscience, or the appeal to personal autonomy—Socrates."[6] In the New Testament 'Conscience' occurs 32 times.[7]

The Stoics, who led the way to freedom, said that what we must obey is the eternal law of God Himself. The true guide is the Voice of God who dwells in our souls.[8]

The Fathers describe Conscience as sufficient and unerring. "But then [according to them] differences of opinion cannot be conscientious, at least not in things regarding salvation."[9] One page of Acton's notes is worth quoting in full.[10]

> Importance of S. Thomas's use of the term [Conscience].
> Why, then, did he not apply it to religion?
> Because he denies that religious error is conscientious.
> So long, there was no liberty.
> If the State excludes all that, it does what it likes.
> Extend the domain of Conscience to religious error, and then only is liberty possible.
> How was that great step taken?
> St. Augustine's view. S. Thomas. Reformation.

Aquinas made the passage in Romans xiv. 23 the basis of a theory of conscience.[11] "Was it known before him, or was that his discovery? If so, it was a great step in the ways of freedom." Another note runs:

> S. Thomas. As to penal laws, he went with his generation. For half a century, when he wrote, not a voice had been

---

[1] Add. 5395, p. 5. But in Add. 4901 (which is later) Acton cites the *Laws of Manu*, VIII, 91–92, "on the voice of Conscience" (p. 299).
[2] Add. 5395, p. 35.   [3] *Ibid.*, p. 37   [4] *Ibid.*, p. 43.   [5] *Ibid.*, p. 44.
[6] *Ibid.*, p. 46.   [7] *Ibid.*, p. 66.   [8] *H.F.*, p. 24 (1877).
[9] Add. 4901, p. 3.   [10] *Ibid.*, p. 1.   [11] *Ibid.*, p. 8.

THE THEORY OF CONSCIENCE

raised for toleration. He strengthened a view which could hardly be stronger. But in respect of conscience he innovated. He went farther than all his time in proclaiming its authority. This was peculiarly his own idea—set out by him, and gifted with power, in time, to overcome the other.[1]

The growth of the notion of Conscience had been interrupted by dogmatic controversy in the twelfth century.[2] In his Lectures, speaking of Conscience, Acton wrote:[3]

> Its psychology was first closely studied late in the thirteenth century,[4] and it began to be said that conscience is the audible Voice of God which never misleads or fails. It ought to be obeyed always, whether enlightened or darkened, right or wrong. With the decline of coercion the claims of conscience rose. It was seen that knowledge of good and evil was not the exclusive prerogative of states, nations or majorities. Conscience was defined and regarded as something divine in human nature. Its effect was to limit power by causing the sovereign voice within to be heard above expressed will and settled custom. The soul became more sacred than the state, because it receives light from above, as well as because its concerns are eternal, and out of proportion with the common interests of government.[5]

> To men ignorant of Greek, like the first generation of the Renaissance, the fourteenth-century men, much in ancient philosophy was obscure. But one system, that of the Stoics, they studied deeply, and understood, for they had the works of Seneca. For men craving for self-help and the complete training of the faculties, eager to escape from the fixed types of mediaeval manhood, minted by authority, and taught to distrust conscience, when it was their own, and to trust it only in others, Seneca was an oracle. For he is the classic of mental discipline, vigilant self-study, and the examination of conscience.[6]

Acton notes a passage in *Doctor and Student* in the time of Henry VIII: "Conscience never resisteth the law nor addeth to it, but only when the law is directly in itself against the law of God, or law of reason."[7] "Conscience depends on, or is

---

[1] Add. 4901.
[2] *Ibid.*, p. 23. The idea of conscience is found in the twelfth century in John of Salisbury.   [3] Pp. 31–32 (1901).   [4] [Aquinas and Eckhart.]
[5] *L.M.H.*, pp. 31–32.   [6] *Ibid.*, 73 (1901).   [7] Add. 4901, p. 9.

parallel with, clear notions of ethics. Obscure ethics indicate imperfect conscience. Therefore obscure ethics imply imperfect liberty. For liberty comes not with any ethical system, but with a very developed one. Therefore liberty was imperfect in M[iddle] A[ges], from want of means, but also from weakness of [idea of] conscience proceeding from a confusion of ethics."[1] "The first emancipators of ethics were two men who were as near union as any of their time: Grotius and Calixtus."[2] It was Grotius who separated religion and politics.[3]

Grotius founded real political science on the universal principle of our subordination to a law of nature, to which all legislation must conform, that is to say, the voice of universal reason, through which God enlightens the consciences of men. Politics are therefore a matter of principle and conscience.[4]

The Jesuit Sarasa preceded Butler in proclaiming the infallibility of conscience.[5] Butler borrowed this doctrine from Sarasa and it is indefensible.[6] Kant took his doctrine of conscience from Butler.[7] Sarasa is the link between conscience and progress.[8] It is by conscience that religion has served the cause of freedom.[9]

It appeared to the seventeenth-century sects that governments and institutions are made to pass away, like things of earth, whilst souls are immortal; that there is no more proportion between liberty and power than between eternity and time; that, therefore, the sphere of enforced command ought to be restricted within fixed limits, and that which had been done by authority, and outward discipline, and organized violence, should be attempted by division of power, and committed to the intellect and the conscience of free men.[10]

There were some among the Puritans who enforced, though they did not discover, the... principle, that a man's conscience is his castle, with kings and parliaments at a respectful distance.[11]

Conscience was "connected with Quakerism as Penn under-

---

[1] Add. 5395, p. 43.
[2] Add. 5434, p. 42. George Calixtus was a Protestant theologian.
[3] *Ibid.*, p. 1.   [4] *H.F.*, p. 46 (1877).
[5] *L.M.H.*, p. 116 (1901).   [6] *Corr.*, pp. 79–80.
[7] *Ibid.*, pp. 224–225.   [8] Add. 4901, p. 264.   [9] *Ibid.*, p. 357.
[10] *L.M.H.*, p. 10 (1895).   [11] *Ibid.*, p. 143 (1901).

stood it."¹ "It had assumed, in one of the Sects, a very peculiar shape. The doctrine of the inner light.² Quakers [were] not originally liberal." "But the inner light struggled vigorously for freedom. In the very days in which the theory of Consc[ience] reached its extreme term, W[illiam] Penn proclaimed L[iberty] of C[onscience] as the teaching of his sect. And so it became the basis of Pennsylvania—Voltaire's best government."³ In the eighteenth century conscience "became not only judge but lawgiver, the exclusive C[onscience] both of men and nations."⁴ The eighteenth-century tendency to exalt conscience culminated in Kant.⁵ He believes that Conscience proves God, when reason cannot. "Rousseau develops conscience so that he concludes from it that man is originally good, and is only corrupted by outward influences—the inward influence, which is the man himself, is right and good."⁶

"Towards the end of the eighteenth century, Conscience was developed as a substitute for religion—*Vicaire Savoyard*, etc. At the same time, scientific methods [i.e. economics, with Adam Smith⁷] came in. This developed individualism."⁸

Kant stands on the shoulders of the *Analogy* when he elevates the probability into a substitute for proof; and on those of the Sermons, when he makes the infallible Conscience the basis of certainty and the source of the Categorial Imperative. "And my point," writes Acton, "is that he hails really from Butler, directly or indirectly, and not as they say, and he seems himself to imply, from Rousseau."⁹

---

¹ Add. 4901, p. 338.   ² *Ibid.*, p. 355.   ³ *Ibid.*
⁴ *Travers Twiss*, quoted in Add. 5395, p. 52.
⁵ Add. 5395.   ⁶ Add. 4901, p. 19.
⁷ *Hawarden Letters*, p. 188: (re Adam Smith) "scientific backbone to Liberal sentiment."
⁸ Add. 4901, p. 19. Puritan individualism in the seventeenth century, e.g. in Robinson, Acton terms "atomism" (*Hawarden Letters*, pp. 187–189). This is because Acton believes that practical freedom must be based on real communities (Cf. letter to Simpson in *Gasquet* where he writes: "What you most want for your theory of liberty is a definition of corporations and then the constant distinction between States founded on corporations—where they are therefore political—and States which tolerate corporations in the social department, but which are not founded by them." *Gasquet*, p. 235). Cf. Maitland, *Collected Papers*, Vol. 3. See also Lord Lindsay's article on individualism in *E.S.S.*
⁹ *Corr.*, p. 226.

"Although Newman, in spite of Development, cared little for the pedigree of ideas, it was curious to see how, towards the end, the Butler of early life coalesced with Kant, whom he only got to know very late."[1]

The supreme development is in Vinet. "The theory of conscience did not secure liberality in its teachers—Butler, Rousseau, Kant, Fichte, were not liberals. It is Vinet who wrought that alliance and drew that consequence.[2] Vinet made Conscience and Liberty a law in Church and State.[3]

Before giving his own judgment Acton proceeds to marshal all the arguments *against* conscience: "Opposition to Conscience: It is not infallible. It often is obscure and misleading. It is a product of society—the echo of others, not the Voice of God. It is incapable of being defined, and should be neglected. It does not exist at all. There is no free will."[4]

Acton adds: "The ablest moral theologian of modern times, Rothe, ejects the term itself from his theological vocabulary."[5]

Acton notes Leslie Stephen's definition in his *Science of Ethics* (p. 351): "Conscience is the utterance of the public spirit of the race, ordering us to obey the primary conditions of its welfare."[6] Among the "enemies of Conscience" Acton lists Locke, Adam Smith, James Mill, Feuerbach, Strauss and Treitschke.[7]

Acton's conclusions are: "The Christian notion of conscience imperatively demands a corresponding measure of personal liberty. The feeling of duty and responsibility to God is the only arbiter of a Christian's actions. With this no human authority can be permitted to interfere. We are bound to extend to the utmost, and to guard from every encroachment, the sphere in which we can act in obedience to the sole voice of conscience, regardless of any other consideration."[8]

---

[1] *Corr.*, pp. 225–226. (3 Oct. 1892.)

[2] Add. 4901, p. 282. Cf. *Ibid.*, p. 350: "Theory of conscience led up to its supreme development in Vinet. Catholic, Protestant, Deist, Rationalist, Sceptic all co-operated to make it supreme among the divisions, and the ruins of Churches and authority."

[3] *Hawarden Letters*, p. 189. This is said with special reference to Vinet's *Manifestation des Convictions religieuses*.

[4] Add. 4901, p. 93.

[5] *Ibid.*, p. 186. This refers to the *second* edition of Rothe's *Theological Ethics*.

[6] *Ibid.*, p. 280.   [7] *Ibid.*, p. 332.   [8] *H.F.*, p. 203.

THE THEORY OF CONSCIENCE

Conscience is "the great resource of unbelief. It came to the front about 1700."[1] "Conscience [is] only a capacity. [It is] capable of being extinguished, as in some nations. [It is] capable of being immensely developed, as in others. [It is] dependent on cultivation. [It is] higher in [the] higher nations."[2] "The more men understood individual responsibility, the more they strove for freedom. At last came the idea of collective responsibility."[3] "Rationalism taught that Reason suffices without dogma. It followed that they encouraged the inner light also in ethics. The guide to truth is in the mind, not outside."[4] "A developed conscience claims more liberty, and can use it. The more developed the more free."[5] "Conscience grows more perfect, both in our lives, and by process of ages."[6] "Conscience becomes more enlightened . . . gains in force and distinction, by experience, and new trials and tests; and by the light of Christianity, of the new law. This discovery opposed by those who appealed to antiquity, or to authority, or to the letter of revelation."[7] "It was setting up a power superior to all these—motion where they were fixed."[8] The reason "Conscience cannot prevail in politics without science [is] because [in politics] it is a different system of morals from private morals.[9] The obstacles to liberty [are] real, not mere error."[10] "Liberalism [is] ultimately founded on [the] idea of conscience. A man must live by the light within—prefer God's voice to man's.[11] So Liberalism flourished in the golden age of conscience—Butler, Rousseau, Kant, Fichte, Channing, Vinet, Rosmini, Passavant, Renouvier, Shaftesbury, Ramsay, Kierkegaard, Gizycki. How that epoch is threatened now. Formerly, by external authorities—now by theories—Stephen, Spencer, J. S. Mill, Guyau, Wundt, Hartmann."[12] "The doctrine of the sovereignty and finality of Conscience . . . promoted toleration, . . . the doctrine of its infallibility . . . promoted all liberty."[13]

---

[1] Add. 5395, p. 10.
[2] Ibid., p. 12.
[3] Ibid., p. 22.
[4] Ibid., p. 28.
[5] Ibid., p. 34.
[6] Ibid., p. 48.
[7] Ibid., p. 85.
[8] Ibid.
[9] Add. 5434, p. 91. Cf. Add. 4939: "Difference of public and private ethics: Partly because the State stands as trustee for others. Partly because it has power of making war, and the same thing applies, to prevent war."
[10] Add. 5434, p. 92.
[11] Add. 4901, p. 20.
[12] Ibid.
[13] Ibid., p. 98.

"Our conscience exists and acts for ourselves. It exists in each of us. It is enough for oneself, not for another. It respects the consciences of others. Therefore it tends to restrict authority and to enlarge liberty. It is the law of self-government."[1] "Men must not be condemned for obeying their consciences. Conscience becomes more and more enlightened by experience, and the discipline of history."[2] "The theory of Conscience brought over religion to the cause of freedom. It was the underlying principle."[3]

It follows that toleration is the heart of Acton's political philosophy. Liberty is the supreme object, and liberty means security for the rights of conscience. On toleration Acton regards Locke as the principal classic. But before the time of Locke he notices that it was Asoka, the first of the Buddhist kings, in 250 B.C., who was the first in history to enact religious toleration.[4] In Christian times in a theological but pregnant sense, divines of the second century insist on liberty, and divines of the fourth century on equality. In the fifteenth century persecution had languished, and there was abundant ground for believing that toleration would prevail. But it was Socinus, in the sixteenth century, who first demanded the separation of Church and State and universal toleration.

Socinus was followed by the English independents who made religious toleration a fundamental religious doctrine. In 1644 we learn "Godwin . . . is openly for a full liberty of conscience, to all sects, even Turks, Jews, Papists." The author of the tract, *What the Independents would have*, says that he thinks it a sin either to follow an erring conscience or to go against it; but to oppose it the greater sin, for he that will do the least sin against conscience is prepared in disposition to do the greatest.[5] Acton accepts the doctrine of the "erring conscience," as also, as already noticed, does Mr. Carritt.[6]

Locke has a place in Acton's "little band of true theorists." As the philosopher of the English Revolution, which Acton

---

[1] Add. 4901, p. 254.   [2] *Ibid.*, p. 258.   [3] *Ibid.*, p. 353.
[4] Acton says: "The first of human concerns is religion." Compare Collingwood: "Religion is the heart of a civilization," and Toynbee, *A Study of History*, throughout.   [5] *L.M.H.*, p. 206.
[6] *Ethical and Political Thinking* (Oxford, 1947), Chap. II.

regarded as the greatest thing done by the English nation, it might have been expected that Acton would view him with almost uncritical admiration. This is far from being the case. "John Locke is always reasonable and sensible, but diluted and pedestrian and poor."[1] But when Acton speaks of Locke's influence, and especially of his writings on toleration, a different note is struck:

> It is hard on Locke to attribute his success so much to opportunity and current. In the history of thought, especially of thought bearing on action, he is, not the greatest certainly, but the largest of all Englishmen, looming tremendously, and filling an immense space. The *Lettres sur les Anglais*, which put England into continental circulation, dealt most with him and Newton, and he is the master of Voltaire and Condillac. As the—unscientific—inventor of the division of power, he is the master of Montesquieu. By his theory of education and the Social Contract, he is the master of Rousseau, the most powerful political writer that ever lived. By his political economy he is the master of Adam Smith, and, in a sense, of Turgot. He gave to Whiggism whatever general ideas it mixed with the specific national elements, and is the theorist of government by the great families. Lastly, in the Catena of tradition on Toleration, he is very nearly the principal classic.[2]

In the *Letters Concerning Toleration* Locke writes:

> I esteem it above all things necessary to distinguish exactly the business of civil government from that of religion, and to settle the just bounds that lie between one and the other . . . No man can so far abandon the care of his own salvation, as blindly to leave it to the choice of any other, whether prince or subject, to prescribe to him what faith or worship he shall embrace. For no man can, if he would, conform his faith to the dictates of another. . . . Laws are of no force at all without penalties, and penalties in this case are absolutely impertinent: because they are not proper to convince the mind.
> . . . [The theory of persecution involves that] men would owe their eternal happiness or misery to the places of their nativity. . . . [A Church is] a free and voluntary society. . . .

---

[1] *L.M.H.*, p. 217.   [2] *Corr.*, p. 230.

> The Gospel frequently declares that the true disciples of Christ must suffer persecution. . . . The Church itself is a thing absolutely separate and distinct from the Commonwealth . . . God Himself will not save men against their wills. . . . If I take a wrong course in regard to the life to come . . . it is not in the magistrate's power to repair my loss. . . . No way whatsoever that I shall walk in against the dictates of my conscience, will ever bring me to the mansions of the blest.

Acton once explained to a correspondent that all his life he had specially studied the problems which lie on the "wavy line" between Church and State,[1] and elsewhere he writes that the theory of toleration is bound up with the general problem of the relation of Church and State.

The heralds of the French Revolution had not studied this problem and were unaware that it had any general solution. The French Revolution, in the Civil Constitution of the Clergy, went to pieces because of its failure to deal with it. It was the French Doctrinaires of the nineteenth century who held the solution of the problem of the relation of Church and State.

Acton ends his lecture on the Civil Constitution of the Clergy with these words:

> I have repeatedly pointed to the jealousy of the executive as a source of fatal mischief. This is the greatest instance of the harm it did. That the patronage could not be left in the hands of the King absolutely as it was by the Concordat of Leo X was obvious; but if it had been given to the King acting through responsible ministers, then much of the difficulty and the danger would have been overcome, and the arrangement that grew out of the Concordat of Napoleon would have been anticipated. That idea was constantly rejected, and, stranger still, the idea of disestablishment and separation was almost unperceived. A whole generation later, under the influence of American and Irish examples, a school of Liberals arose among French Catholics, who were as distinct from the Gallicans, as from the Ultramontanes, and possessed the solution for the perpetual rivalry of Church and State. For us, the great fact is that the Revolution

---

[1] Passage cited in the Introduction.

produced nothing of the sort, and went to ruin by its failure in dealing with the problem.[1]

The solution here referred to is that of the Doctrinaires, of whom Royer-Collard is the best example.[2] (The others are Guizot and Constant.) Royer-Collard insisted on religious freedom. In his view any Church is a power in the State, and is a potential danger to the State if its freedom is not fully allowed. A privileged Church is a cause of discontent, and a theocracy is the most dangerous form of absolutism. If the sanctions of religion are added to the power of the State, the intelligence of men is taken captive. On the other hand a Church whose freedom has been guaranteed is a permanent safeguard of the freedom of the individual, for it involves the admission that no institution can absorb the whole allegiance of man. Such religious freedom makes the individual realize the duty he owes to his intelligence, which is also his duty to humanity. It involves the freedom of the individual soul. It necessitates the development of the individual conscience. It makes possible the refusal to submit to wrong by establishing a criterion of right independent of the State. At the same time it safeguards individuality by compelling the citizen to understand his perpetual responsibility for political judgment. The individual is saved from absolute power.

Royer-Collard insists that if a Church is free it is an association of consciences, an association which by that very fact sets limits to the demands the State may make upon its members. If a Church is united with the State the essential condition of freedom vanishes. It becomes officialized. And those who govern the Church are tempted to divert its influence to their own purposes. Similarly, the support of the Church dangerously increases the authority of the State, by giving a religious sanction to the behests of the State. This increases the danger of

---

[1] *F.R.*, p. 173.
[2] See Faguet, *Politiques et Moralistes du 19ième Siècle*, Vol. I, 1890, which Acton regarded as the really important book on the Doctrinaires, Laski, *Authority in the Modern State*, Acton, *Correspondence*, and E. L. Woodward's study of Guizot in *Studies in European Conservatism* (1929). Acton included Constant in the Swiss school, cf. Add. 4942: "The Swiss School: De Staël, B. Constant, Dumont, Sismondi, Cherbuliez, Vinet." Elsewhere he includes Rossi, and the whole school he termed "The seven champions of [Lake] Leman."

despotism. In these conditions the Church will require privileges, and will not respect any conscience not its own. By putting itself under the protection of secular authority it will allow the State to decide who is to govern the Church. It loses its independence, and its supreme purpose becomes temporal instead of eternal. "Let a religious organization," said Royer-Collard, "be exclusive or even dominant and one may rest assured that its ministers will be rich and important in political life, that they will exercise a vast dominion and intervene without cessation in civil life to bring it under their own control."[1] The choice is not between infidelity and theocracy. The choice is between the use of an illegitimate weapon for wrongful purposes and the admission that the function of religion does not enter into the field of politics.[2]

Religious independence and freedom of the Press are necessary to create the atmosphere in which political power can be adequately restrained. Religious independence refuses to permit the complete absorption of the individual in the State, quickens the public conscience and opposes an institutional barrier against absolutism. For this purpose there must also be the safeguard of the irremovability of magistrates. Security of tenure of judicial office is the necessary recognition that not even the State may transgress the principles of justice. The judge is the guardian of the natural and social rights of man.

The implications of Royer-Collard's view of the right relationship of Church and State come close to Acton's philosophy. Royer-Collard had learned from experience that power is poison to those who exert it.

Faguet,[3] writing of Royer-Collard, says: Political science is a science. It is infinitely complex. Royer-Collard knew almost all the secrets of this science and almost all the resources of this art. His good old political grammar, like the educational works of Port-Royal which he loved so much, we should consult with attention, and it can only be with profit. He found his philosophy in Thomas Reid. He found another in 1815, when he saw the whole of his political philosophy in the Charter.

---

[1] Barante, "Life," II, 101.
[2] Laski, *op. cit.*, p. 296. I take this to mean metaphysics, not ethics.
[3] *Politiques et Moralistes*, Vol. I.

The only question is, Where is the sovereignty? The answer is, 'There is no sovereignty.' "*Il n'y a pas de souveraineté, voilà tout l'esprit politique de Royer-Collard.*"

Freedom of religion is a limiting power. Free churches are liberties. Parliamentary government is the greatest guarantee of liberty and the most powerful limiting power.

His system was not at all metaphysical. There are four liberties—Press, religion, parliament, judges. His was a system due to circumstance, which is high praise. He had, no doubt, a narrow and incomplete conception of liberty—an aristocratic conception.

Of Guizot, Faguet says that he wanted not only the *Juste milieu* but also educational freedom. The supernatural, Guizot thought, we can neither prove nor not believe. He believed in the middle class—though his middle class was in fact an aristocracy. Guizot stressed *opinion* which is not always the general will. Opinion is what one says. History according to Guizot is the emergence of the middle class. Social groups multiply. *Reason*, said Guizot, ought to be sovereign. The two legitimate things are reason and history. Civilized society is the foundation of personal liberty. Government should be penetrated by the citizen. The middle class respects liberty of conscience.

Of Constant, Faguet writes that his philosophy is a fetishism of the self. His ideal is the minimum of government. He believes in liberalism and the divine right of man and his moral personality. Man is sacred: he is a temple. He has a divine right because in him is a divine thing—Conscience.

In his *Studies in European Conservatism*, Professor Woodward writes:

> In an unpublished fragment on political philosophy[1] Guizot said that men were wrong in looking for the principle of sovereignty where sovereignty did not even exist. "Any kind of sovereignty attributed to men, to one man, many men, or all men, is a lie and an iniquity." Reason alone is sovereign. Any attempt to find an objective, unalterable sovereign legitimate of itself, and always commanding obedience, must end in the establishment of a tyranny. "Man has attempted to set up sovereignty on earth, as he has tried to set up

[1] See Pouthas, *Guizot pendant la Restauration: préparation de l'homme d'état* (1814–1830) (Paris, 1923), pp. 313–321.

divinity . . . He has been no more successful in fixing, irrevocably, and without limit, his obedience, than in localising his faith.[1]

So far Guizot had but borrowed the sovereign reason of the ideologues. Yet reason was not to him, as to them, only that utilitarian good sense which defined good and bad according to human interest or desire. Nor was Guizot thinking of the autonomous reason laboriously expounded by Kant. Reason was the recognition of a rule; the rule was the will of God. Here Guizot spoke as a Christian. Government was the instrument of reason; therefore government and sovereignty could not be the same. Government exists where society exists; society exists where men have recognised the need for a rule, the need for reason, and therefore the need for some power to watch over the observation of the rule. This power is government. Government is not the rule of force, nor the result of contract, but the consequence of the recognition that man must obey the will of God.[2]

This is almost pure Acton. The difference is that Acton would say the *rule* is supplied by *ethics*, that is, the ethics of politics, the conditions necessary for liberty, which *means* self-government. Self-government means individual and collective moral responsibility: "the common root from which [civil and religious liberty] derive their sustenance, is the right of self-government. The modern theory, which has swept away every authority except that of the State, and has made the sovereign power irresistible by multiplying those who share it, is the enemy of that common freedom in which religious freedom is included. It condemns, as a State within a State, every inner group and community, class or corporation, administering its own affairs, and, by proclaiming the abolition of privileges, it emancipates the subjects of every such authority in order to transfer them exclusively to its own. It recognizes liberty only in the individual, because it is only in the individual that liberty can be separated from authority, and the right of conditional obedience deprived of the security of a limited command."[3] Acton's view of conscience resembles that of

[1] In Add. 4916 Acton takes a parallel passage from Guizot's *History of Representative Government* (I, 93): "*Ce que je dis, c'est que le gouvernement représentatif n'attribue la souveraineté de droit à personne.*"
[2] P. 135.   [3] *H.F.*, p. 151 (March 1862; *aetat.* 28).

William Penn, whom he described as the most liberal mind of his time, the greatest historic figure of the age.[1] As Adam Smith pointed out, the theory of conscience crystallized in opposition to Hobbes, whom Marx called "the father of us all." The doctrine of Hobbes Acton regarded as political atheism.

[1] Cf. "Theory of Liberalism, as the Unity of History" (Add. 4953); "Difference of Whig and Liberal. Locke and Fox or Penn and Harrington. Property is the most sacred of men's rights—or Conscience" (Add. 4953); "Definition. Liberty is the reign of conscience" (Add. 4941).

II

THE IDEA OF DEVELOPMENT

IN Acton the idea of development means continuity and progress.¹ Professor Herford, who acknowledges his indebtedness to Acton, analyses the idea as it appears in the jurists and others, as a compound of the ideas of organism and progress.² In its modern form the idea of development was effectively due to four men, Petavius, Leibniz, Mabillon, and Robinson. The most striking of these was Leibniz, of whom Acton once said that the fertility of his genius was such that the harvest could never be completely gathered.³ I will begin with Acton's view of Leibniz.

"The *lex continui* was a central idea with Leibniz, who discovered it, for it was the point in common between his anticipation of Darwin and his anticipation of Hegel. In the same double sense it was renewed by Haller, and obtained some superficial acceptance through Herder, until it came to govern entirely the Hegelian notion of history."⁴ From Leibniz Acton also took the idea that history is the true demonstration of religion, that is, that slow but sure progress in the direction of liberty is the justification of God to men. This view occurs repeatedly in Acton's writings, and most notably in his *Inaugural*, and the notes attached to it:

> We can found no philosophy on the observation of four hundred years, excluding three thousand. It would be an imperfect and fallacious induction. But I hope that even

¹ Add. 4965. But in Add. 4952 he writes: "Progress if not organic, is nothing but change."
² *Germany in the Nineteenth Century* (Manchester University Press, 2nd ed., 1912), p. 56. Herford traces the idea in Hegel (philosophy of history), Schleiermacher (philosophy of religion), Savigny (law), Niebuhr (history), Gregorovius (town-biology), Burckhardt (history of ideas).
³ *N.B.R.*, July 1870, p. 551. The philosophical work in this field is still unfinished.
⁴ *H.E.*, p. 361.

this narrow and disedifying section of history will aid you to see that the action of Christ who is risen on mankind whom He redeemed fails not, but increases; that the wisdom of divine rule appears not in the perfection but in the improvement of the world; and that achieved liberty is the one ethical result that rests on the converging and combined conditions of advancing civilisation. Then you will understand what a famous philosopher said, that History is the true demonstration of Religion.[1]

The famous philosopher is Leibniz: *Historiae ipsius praeter delectationem utilitas nulla est, quam ut religionis Christianae veritas demonstretur, quod aliter quam per historiam fieri non potest.*[2] Twice Acton noticed the influence of Leibniz on Döllinger, his own teacher: "He knew Leibniz chiefly in his letters, and was perceptibly affected by his law of continuous progression, his general optimism, and his eclectic art of extracting from men and books only the good that is in them; but of monadology or pre-established harmony there was not a trace."[3] And again, "The assistants were countless, but the masters were few, and he looked up with extraordinary gratitude to men like Sigonius, Antonius Augustinus, Blondel, Petavius, Leibniz, Burke, and Niebuhr, who had opened the passes for him as he struggled and groped in the illimitable forest."[4]

Petavius was one of the first to give an evolutionary account of the development of doctrine. In his lectures Acton wrote: "Petavius first described the evolution of dogma, and cast every system into the melting-pot of history."[5] This statement Acton slightly amended in one of the essays:

When it [the idea of development] was put forward, in guarded, dubious, and evasive terms, by Petavius, the indignation was as great as in 1846. The work which contained it, the most learned that Christian theology had then produced, could not be reprinted over here, lest it should supply the Socinians with inconvenient texts. Nelson hints that the great Jesuit may have been a secret Arian, and Bull stamped upon his theory amid the grateful applause of Bossuet and his friends. Petavius was not an innovator, for the idea had long found a home among the Franciscan masters: . . .

L.M.H., p. 12.
[2] Leibniz, *Opera*, ed. Dutens, vi, 297, cited by Acton, *L.M.H.*, p. 328.
[3] *H.F.*, p. 381.   [4] *Ibid.*, p. 393.   [5] *L.M.H.*, p. 117.

Cardinal Duperron said nearly the same thing as Petavius a generation before him . . . All this does not serve to supply the pedigree which Newman found it so difficult to trace. Development, in those days, was an expedient, an hypothesis, and not even the thing so dear to the Oxford probabilitarians, a working hypothesis.[1]

Mabillon was "one of the best and best-known names in the line of discoverers, from Valla and Sigonius to Borghesi and Morgan, who have made history a science."[2] It was Mabillon who first studied the development of documents.

Robinson glimpsed the idea of development in his farewell to the pilgrims: "I am very confident that the Lord has more truth yet to break forth out of His holy Word."[3] But it was Turgot who made the idea of development and progress familiar:

> From Lucretius and Seneca to Pascal and Leibniz we encounter a few dispersed and unsupported passages, suggesting advance towards perfection, and the flame that brightens as it moves from hand to hand; but they were without mastery or radiance. Turgot at once made the idea habitual and familiar, and it became a pervading force in thoughtful minds, whilst the new sciences arose to confirm it. He imparted a deeper significance to history, giving it unity of tendency and direction, constancy where there had been motion, and development instead of change.[4]

In the National Assembly, in 1789, "very dimly, ideas which rose to power in other days and evolved the great force of nationality, were at work."[5]

Burke was the intellectual ancestor of the conservative school of historians, jurists, and philosophers who made the idea of development triumph in the nineteenth century. "All the successions of thought during three generations constitute the shaft whose shining point is made" by the conservative school of historians.[6] Acton continues: "They are the legitimate dynasty . . . inheritors of the line that comes down from Burke to the last stage of evolution and selection, who have set up the reign of imperishable moral forces for an intermittent

---

[1] *H.F.*, pp. 591–592.   [2] *H.E.*, p. 460.   [3] *Ibid.*, p. 592.
[4] *F.R.*, p. 10.   [5] *Ibid.*, p. 103; especially the idea of development.
[6] *H.E.*, p. 383.

Providence, the play of passion, and the blind will of man."[1] This judgment does not conflict with Acton's liberal philosophy: "If the nation is the source of law, it is reasonable to infer that national consent is a normal element in legislation, and that the State ought legitimately to take its limits from the nation. Niebuhr, in unguarded moments, drew one of these inferences, and Dahlmann the other."[2]

In Acton's account of Hegel there is a superb appreciation of his significance in the history of the idea of development:

> The tendency of the nineteenth-century German to subject all things to the government of intelligible law, and to prefer the simplicity of resistless cause to the confused conflict of free wills, the tendency which Savigny defined and the comparative linguists encouraged, was completed in his own way by Hegel. He displayed all history by the light of scientific unity, as the manifestation of a single force, whose works are all wise, and whose latest work is best. The *Volksgeist* of the new jurisprudence was less dazzling than the *Weltgeist* of the new philosophy, with the smallest allowance of hypothesis for the largest quantity of phenomena. Science was propitiated with visions of unity and continuity; religion by the assurance of incessant progress; politics by the ratification of the past. Liberty and morality were less well provided; but it was the epoch of the Restoration.
>
> An ambiguous use of terms concealed the breach between pantheism and Christianity. . . . The breach with experimental science betrayed itself by the contempt for Newton in which Hegel was of one mind with Goethe and Schelling and Schopenhauer; but there were scientific men who, to the disgust of Humboldt, accepted the *Naturphilosophie*. Its defects were visible when Hegel's lectures appeared after his death, and the system went down under the assault of inductive science. But his influence on historical study has not gone down, and it is the one thing on which he retains his grasp. The *lex continui* was a central idea with Leibniz, who discovered it, for it was the point in common between his anticipation of Darwin and his anticipation of Hegel. In the same double sense it was renewed by Haller, and obtained some superficial acceptance through Herder, until it came to govern entirely the Hegelian notion of history.

[1] *H.E.*, p. 383.   [2] *Ibid.*, p. 348.

Hegel did not shine in expounding public transactions, excepting cases like the French Revolution, where the individual is swallowed up by the logic of events. ... The quest of the *vera causa* failed with men, but it was beyond measure successful away from the world of sense, in explaining the action and succession of ideas.

The history of philosophy had taken rise before Hegel was born, and was secreted in books not destitute of plodding merit, but unreasonably dead and dull. Under the magic wand systems fell into an appointed and harmonious order. ... The progress of speculative thought has been made, by less systematic and coercive successors, one of the luminous spots in literature, to the damage and exclusion of more essential things. For the marrow of civilised history is ethical, not metaphysical, and the deep underlying cause of action passes through the shape of right and wrong. Hegel did not promote the study of morals, and Germany fell behind the French eclectics, until, in the revolt of the last ten years against utilitarians and materialists, the growth of ethical knowledge has become, for the first time, the supreme object of history.[1]

But it was the jurists whose work in this field was the most fruitful. According to Savigny the sovereign legislator is not the government, but the nation. Law, like language, proceeds from its primitive nature and its experience and is part of its identity. Laws are found, not made, and are determined by what is latent in the public conscience. Learning and eloquence, Acton comments, long effectually concealed the logical effect of this doctrine. It predominated for half a century and yielded only slowly to the deeper philosophy of Ihering.[2] It was the historical school who, having abolished, as they supposed, the law of nature, which was the motive of 1789, instituted the law of nationality, which became the motive of 1848.[3] "The generation of 1830, which in a variety of converging ways assigned the property of growth undetermined by will or wit of man, of development without forfeiture of identity, to the civil law, the academic philosophy, and the Aryan grammar, was not tempted to deny an analogous prerogative to Christianity."[4]

The revived study of history was the supreme manifestation

---

[1] *H.E.*, pp. 360–362 (1886).   [2] *Ibid.*, p. 347.
[3] *Ibid.*, p. 348.   [4] *Ibid.*, p. 368.

of the idea of development, and Acton, who early in life had described it as a movement in the world of thought as important as the Renaissance, at the end of his life described it as more important than the Renaissance. In 1861 he could write: "The present day is much more strongly marked by the discoveries in the moral than in physical science. The science of history and the science of language, and the philosophical study of jurisprudence, are all new discoveries of this century."[1] Later he noted an historian's view that Darwinian evolution was merely an application of the historical method.[2]

In middle life Acton wrote: "I should have wished . . . to relate by whom, and in what connection, the true law of the formation of free States was recognized, and how that discovery, closely akin to those which, under the names of development, evolution and continuity, have given a new and deeper method to other sciences, solved the ancient problem between stability and change, and determined the authority of tradition on the progress of thought."[3] And in the *Inaugural*: "The jurists brought us the law of continuous growth which has transformed history from a chronicle of casual occurrences into the likeness of something organic."[4]

Acton notes without comment the notion of the Tübingen school of the growth of truth (*Das Werden der Wahrheit*). He comments on Baur with grim humour: "According to Baur the business of history is not so much with facts as with ideas; and the idea, not the fact, of the Resurrection is the basis of the Christian faith. Doctrines are developed out of notions, not out of events. Whether or no the belief is true, he refuses to inquire. In the most characteristic passage ever written by a German historian, he declares that it is a question beyond the scope of history."[5]

As an unnamed philosopher wrote, "It is then in the change to a higher state of form or composition that development differs from growth. We must carefully distinguish development from mere increase; it is the acquiring, not of greater

---

[1] *Gasquet*, p. 193. [2] *Inaugural*. [3] *H.F.*, p. 58 (1877).
[4] *L.M.H.*, p. 21. In another place Acton writes of Savigny: "His theory of continuity has this significance in political science, that it supplied a basis for conservatism apart from absolutism and compatible with freedom" (*H.F.*, p. 594). [5] *H.E.*, p. 369.

bulk, but of new forms and structures, which are adapted to higher conditions of existence."[1]

Cournot noticed that no idea among those that refer to the order of nature comes nearer to the category of religious ideas than the idea of progress or is more suited to become the principle of a kind of religious faith for those who have no other.[2]

Acton himself wrote: "Universal history is a continuous development; it is not a burden on the memory but an illumination of the soul."[3] "The notion of progress is not a pagan notion . . . The impelling force at the bottom of all progress, the striving to know and to love God."[4]

In the Acton MSS. there is a notebook, written by one of Acton's children, recording the substance of a conversation in 1890, in which Acton laid it down that the New Testament rests upon tradition, and that it was by tradition that it was decided that the canonical Gospels should be received, and that the remainder of the fifty narratives of the Gospel story should be rejected.[5] The famous formulation of the principle of tradition by St. Vincent of Lérins—a principle already ancient in his time—*quod semper, quod ubique, quod ab omnibus*—was used by Lamennais to mean Christianity as old as the Creation. "The development he meant led up to the Bible, and ended at the New Testament instead of beginning there."[6]

The illustrations Acton gives of the working of the principle of development fall into three divisions: development in ideas, in knowledge, and in history.

Discovery and the development of knowledge are the vital spark in history.[7] Science is invincible.[8]

"It has come to be understood," wrote Acton in 1867, "that philosophy must proceed like other sciences, by the accumulation, not the rediscovery of truth; that, instead of beginning *de novo*, and breaking it off again with each successive thinker, it must take up the problems that have been handed down, and start anew from the point already attained."[9] Or as he put it six months later:

[1] *H.F.*, p. 407.
[2] *Ibid.*, p. 589.
[3] *L.M.H.*, p. 317.
[4] *Chronicle*, 1 Feb. 1868, pp. 107–108.
[5] Add. 4871.
[6] *H.F.*, p. 593.
[7] *Inaugural*.
[8] *Ibid.*
[9] *Chronicle*, 4 May 1867, p. 140.

Philosophical discussion must remain barren and profitless as long as the terms in dispute are considered without reference to the history of their origin. It is only when we become acquainted with history that we are able to appreciate them at their worth. We are saved from a rough and ready rejection of metaphysical abstractions when we find that the physical sciences themselves are based on metaphysical abstractions derived from the early philosophy of Greece.[1]

Reviewing Erskine May's *Democracy in Europe* Acton wrote: "There are links in the argument, there are phases of development which he leaves unnoticed, because his object has not been to trace out the properties and the connection of ideas, but to explain the results of experience ... The great mass ... do not care to be told ... what connection there was ... between Penn and Rousseau, or who invented the proverb *Vox Populi Vox Dei*."[2]

A liberal, says Acton, "who thinks his thought out to the end without flinching is forced to certain conclusions which colour to the root every phase and scene of universal history. He believes in upward progress because it is only recent times that have striven deliberately, and with a zeal according to knowledge, for the increase and security of freedom."[3]

A further illustration of the working of the principle of development in the field of knowledge as it occurs in Acton's writings is: "the inexhaustible tradition of the teaching of our Lord ... the full exposition of truth is the great object for which the existence of mankind is prolonged on earth ... This growth in knowledge ... is a conquest of the Christian mind in its conflict with the phases of untruth."[4]

The idea of development underlies Acton's whole conception of history. But, he wrote in 1868, "free agency [is] the factor which distinguishes history from any necessary process, whether natural or logical."[5] History is the knowledge of things that live and move:[6]

> Laws are part of a thing's nature. Law is national, growing on a particular soil, suited to a particular character and

[1] *Chronicle*, 30 Nov. 1867, p. 859.
[2] *H.F.*, p. 99. [The connection between Penn and Rousseau is the appeal to conscience. The inventor of the proverb was Alcuin of York.]
[3] *H.F.*, pp. 400–401.   [4] *H.F.R.*, July 1863, pp. 162–163.
[5] *Chronicle*, 18 Jan. 1868, p. 69.   [6] *H.E.*, p. 367.

wants. Legislation should grow in harmony with the people
—should be based on habits as well as on precepts. It should
be identified with the national character and life. On this
depends growth and progress. The people cannot administer
a law not their own. This is the reverse of self-government,
which proceeds not from a code but from custom, is learnt
not from books but from practice, is administered by the
people themselves. However good the code may be, if it
comes from *aliunde* than from national life and history, it
destroys self-government ... even if its forms are liberal ...
it is for this reason that it has never been possible to export
more than phantoms of the British Constitution.[1]

The idea of development is the clue to the nature of the
State: it belongs as much to the primitive essence of a nation
as its language.[2] Or as Acton put it at the age of twenty-four,
"Our institutions are part and parcel of the nation itself, not
a garment that can be imitated by a skilful workman. What
they can teach foreign statesmen is, to cling in every political
change to the traditions and character of their own people."[3]
In the development of Europe something was wanted that
antiquity lacked—"Something was wanted beyond all the gifts
of reflection and experience—a faculty of self-government and
self-control, developed like its language in the fibre of a nation,
and growing with its growth."[4] Our indigenous constitution,
"not made with hands or written upon paper, but claiming to
develop by a law of organic growth."[5] The principle of development is the secret of English history:

> Every appeal against oppression was to the hereditary
> rights; the only protection which the Englishman knew was
> in the traditional laws of his country. By means of the per-
> petual recurrence to old principles, and of the gradual con-
> trivance of new forms in which to secure their action, the
> English people conquered their freedom. The intensity of
> their conservatism was an impulse as well as a guide to their
> progress ... The one thing that saved England from the fate
> of other countries was ... the consistent, uninventive, stupid
> fidelity to that political system which originally belonged to
> all the nations that traversed the ordeal of feudalism.[6]

[1] *Gasquet*, pp. 245–256.
[3] *Ibid.*, Dec. 1858, pp. 424–425.
[5] *Ibid.*, p. 593.
[2] *Rambler*, March 1860, p. 397.
[4] *H.F.*, p.31.
[6] *H.F.R.*, Oct. 1863, p. 174.

This view, in a modified form, reappears thirty years later. Discussing the Puritan Revolution, Acton writes:

> Long before, political observers like Commynes and Fortescue recognized the distinctive character and superiority of the insular institutions, but these were not strong enough to withstand the Tudors, and the work had to be begun over again. It was begun, upon the ancient ways, with tradition and precedent; and when that was found to be not quite convincing, it was pursued by means of new, general, and revolutionary principles. The combination, or alternation, of these methods of policy is the peculiar note of the times before us.[1]

Acton concluded his second lecture on freedom with the following words:

> I do not like to conclude without inviting attention to the impressive fact that so much of the hard fighting, the thinking, the enduring that has contributed to the deliverance of man from the power of man, has been the work of our countrymen, and of their descendants in other lands. . . . All these explanations lie on the surface, and are as visible as the protecting ocean; but they can only be successive effects of a constant cause which must lie in the same native qualities of perseverance, moderation, individuality, and the manly sense of duty, which give to the English race its supremacy in the stern art of labour, which has enabled it to thrive as no other can on inhospitable shores, and which (although no other people has less of the bloodthirsty craving for glory . . .) caused Napoleon to exclaim, as he rode away from Waterloo, "It has always been the same since Crécy."
>
> Therefore, if there is reason for pride in the past, there is more for hope in the time to come. . . . Anomalies and defects there are, fewer and less intolerable, if not less flagrant than of old.
>
> . . . the dreary and heartbreaking course by which men have passed to freedom . . . the light that has guided us is still unquenched, and the causes that have carried us so far in the van of free nations have not spent their power; because the story of the future is written in the past, and that which hath been is the same thing that shall be.[2]

---

[1] *L.M.H.*, p. 195.   [2] *H.F.*, pp. 59–60.

That eloquent tribute to the element of continuity in development is paralleled by the conclusion of Acton's last lecture at Cambridge. The subject was the American Revolution:

> The Federal Constitution did not deal with the question of religious liberty. The rules for the election of the President and for that of the Vice-President proved a failure. Slavery was deplored, was denounced, and was retained. The absence of a definition of State Rights led to the most sanguinary Civil War of modern times. Weighed in the scales of Liberalism, the instrument, as it stood, was a monstrous fraud. And yet, by the development of the principle of Federalism, it has produced a community more powerful, more prosperous, more intelligent, and more free than any other which the world has seen.[1]

The doctrine of development Acton more than once expressed in a generalized form. Two passages in particular must be quoted. The first is taken from an early article in the *Home and Foreign Review*:

> The Romans, as well as the Greeks and the Christian nations, held that God is the first lawgiver; and that the political law is founded on the divine. But it is peculiar to an organism to develop according to the laws of its nature, and to escape the control even of that from which it received its origin and impulse. It is faithful to its origin if it is true to its own inherent law, but it cannot obey any external influence. The morality which regulates the aims of private life is unable to deal with the very different objects and situations of civil society. It has a negative influence on government as on medicine, but it is as little adapted to manage the government of States as to compass the cure of disease.[2]

The second occurs towards the end of the study of freedom in Christianity:

> The acquisition of real definite freedom is a very slow and tardy process. The great social independence enjoyed in the early periods of national history is not yet political freedom. The State has not yet developed its authority, or assumed the functions of government. A period follows when all the action of society is absorbed by the ruling power, when the

[1] *L.M.H.*, p. 314.   [2] *H.F.R.*, Oct. 1863, p. 681.

licence of early times is gone, and the liberties of a riper age are not yet acquired. These liberties are the product of a long conflict with absolutism, and of a gradual development, which, by establishing definite rights, revives in positive form the negative liberty of an unformed society. The object and the result of this process is the organisation of self-government, the substitution of right for force, of authority for power, of duty for necessity, and of a moral for a physical relation between government and people.[1]

Yet much later in life he noted that development was still a confused and unsettled chapter in the history of modern knowledge.[2] Since then Professor Macmurray and Mr. Joseph have discussed some of these difficulties.[3]

Acton believed that there were occasions on which the law of development was profoundly modified—the beginning of modern history, the English Revolution and the American Revolution.[4] There is one absolute exception—the injunction Render unto Caesar. But, in a higher series, all history is a continuous development—not a burden on the memory but an illumination of the soul.

Acton did not share the idolatry of material progress. In a very early essay he noticed that Macaulay was the great partisan of the theory of material progress. By this standard moral greatness is of very little real use. "Hence the worship of intellect rather than virtue, and especially of that kind of intellect which manifests itself in tangible results—the genius of Newton, Watt, or Arkwright . . . All the books that are written to celebrate our age at the expense of those which have preceded it, will in a few years become obsolete and ridiculous. Future generations will have a keen eye for our failings when they have corrected them, and will not be dazzled by our discoveries when they have been surpassed."[5]

---

[1] *H.F.*, pp. 59–60.   [2] *Ibid.*, p. 591 (1895).
[3] Professor Macmurray's *Inaugural* as Grote Professor, University of London, and Mr. Joseph's Romanes Lecture on Evolution, reprinted in his *Essays*.
[4] The numerous momentous changes in the generation 1490 to 1520 "sapped the ancient reign of continuity"; the English Revolution was "inversion" not "restitution"; of the American Revolution Acton writes, "here or nowhere we have the broken chain."
[5] *Rambler*, July 1858, pp. 63–65 (*aetat.* 24).

For Acton the criteria of real progress were ethical and political. As he put it in middle life:

> Progress depends not only on the victory, the uncertain and intermittent victory, of Liberals over Conservatives, but on the permeation of Conservatism with Liberal ideas, the successive conversion of Tory leaders, the gradual desertion of the Conservative masses by their chiefs—Fox, Grenville, Wellesley, Canning, Huskisson, Peel—Tory ministers passing Emancipation, Free Trade, Reform—are in the order of historic developments.[1]

Acton's mature view was that "progress is along diagonals,"[2] because compromise is the soul, if not the whole of politics, and is the resultant of forces that pull in different directions, for example, class interests on one side and political and social ideals on the other. Acton indicated his philosophy of development by a quotation from William Harrison: "Nothing but a thorough knowledge of the social system, based upon a regular study of its growth, can give us the power we require to affect it."[3]

The idea of development epitomizes the two sides of Acton's thought—continuity *and* progress. And though he always laid greater stress on the element of moral and political advance, he never forgot the vital element of continuity, which was one of the essential bases of his political and constitutional philosophy. Thus he was wont to condemn what he regarded as the contempt of the Radical for fact and of the Conservative for principle. But he recognized that historical jurisprudence had provided a basis for conservatism compatible with freedom. Acton made it a main rule to plead for what seemed to him the truth whether on one side or the other.[4]

Acton's deepest thought on development is in his manuscript notes on Burke. These are as follows:[5]

---

[1] *L.M.G.*, p. 200 (1884; *aetat.* 50). Cf. Add. 4950: "The strongest of all the obstacles to progress, the reign of the dead."
[2] *H.E.*, p. 489 (1888).   [3] *L.M.H.*, p. 319.   [4] *H.F.*, p. xxxix.
[5] Add. 4965. This section consists of extracts from these manuscripts. I have inserted connecting words, e.g. in the first half of the first paragraph the original reads: "Canon of constitutional government. Set up by Montesquieu. Burke developed this—not independent enough to go straight. Invented the value of history. This was a new canon. It was the antirevolutionary principle in its perfection."

The canon of constitutional government, set up by Montesquieu, was developed by Burke. Burke had not a speculative mind; and he invented the value of history. This was a new canon, the anti-revolutionary principle in its perfection. "He wished to find the genuine voice of English tradition, not merely laws, expedients, forms, but germs [and] principles—a subtler essence than law—Constitution."

Burke had an "intensity of religion." It was this that "inclined him to adopt the Leibnitzian theory of continuity[1]— Look to the deposit of ideas—Develop what underlies—Disregard the superimposed work of men." But, "if Montesquieu is right," "it is applicable everywhere," "not national, not a partial truth." "Then," says Acton, "it is identical with truth itself," and "can be found elsewhere than in history."

"Burke went further. It is good, he said, because it is ours. Its value is national. Try to learn its laws of growth. Help it in its natural course. Don't be wiser."

Burke stands between Montesquieu and Bentham.[2]

"Was Burke's idea of historic constitutionalism derived from ... his studies in Roman law ... The idea of the constitution of Solon in Thucydides and Demosthenes. What it wanted to be full-blown [was (1) the idea of] continuity, [which came with] Leibniz, [(2) the idea of] progress, [which was chiefly due to] Turgot. [The idea of] development ... combines the two, [and results in] nationality, Savigny, [and, especially] Hegel.[3] [Account has also to be taken of] Herderism and Wolf [and] Lessing's *Education of the World*. Examine Meyer's theory that Savigny was anticipated by the Dutch jurists."

"Burke ... failed," [because he produced] "no principle to reconcile national and universal—continuity and Revolution. He thought France ought to make the best of institutions which had slumbered for ages."

"[There is] no security that the laws of a particular moment

---

[1] Cf. "Did Burke get his idea of continuity from Bolingbroke, whom he studied so much, and who taught Pope Leibniz?" (Add. 4965); and "Knowledge of the past is knowledge of religious forces—knowledge of the present is study of forces that are not religious. One sails without gas—the other without ballast" (Add. 4941).

[2] The MS. reads: "So Montesquieu leads to Bentham. Burke stands between."

[3] MS. reads: "Development really Hegel."

will be right. [There is] no canonical epoch. But [there is] some security that what always was, either developed, or striving to develop, will be right. Men can err. But their conscience will resist, and the constancy of the resisting force will make itself felt. We don't judge by men's acts, but by the sense of right which underlies their acts. That is Burke's idea—what all men hold, what a nation has always held. But the views of the moment have no sanction or security.

"What changes is the will of the nation. What endures is its conscience. Catch what is permanent, disregard what is momentary. For what is continuous is not will, but conviction. The will of the moment is therefore limited and checked by the constant notions of right. The nation cannot do what it likes. [It is] bound by its past, not by the single enactments, but the long current."

Under Bacon's influence and the Whigs English thought had been inconclusive, indefinite, in character:[1] "Butler, explaining the supremacy of Conscience, stops half-way, [Adam] Smith founds society on self, and or symp[athy, he] knows not which, Warburton on Church and State. Just like this was Burke, refusing to inquire about the Rights of Man, or about the virtues of Marie Antoinette. He thought one-fifth of grown-up Englishmen were Jacobins."

"Burke [from] 1770 to 1780 [is the] culmination of Whiggism—that development was under [the] influence of America, not of France."

"Brougham [stated[2] of the later Burke:] "Mr. Wilberforce told me that Mr. Burke avowed to him that he had once been favourable to the abolition of the slave trade, but that he had altered his opinion, and could only consider it to be a shred of the accursed web of Jacobinism."

"For half a century after Burke's death our political writers lived on his ideas, Canning on one side, Brougham on the other, Mackintosh, successively, on both sides, Macaulay wavering between them. Austin and Mill, starting from Bentham, went farther. Mill's great merit was the defence of the minority, [and of the rights of minorities]."

---

[1] MS. reads: "Inconclusiveness, indefiniteness, a character of English thought under Bacon's influence and the Whigs."

[2] 26 Feb. 1828, *Hansard* 775.

"H[erbert] Spencer, [in the] *Classification of the Sciences* . . . [writes]: The social mechanism does not rest upon opinions, but almost wholly upon character. Hence, [says Acton] Burke prefers men to measures, as the basis of party."

"Burke [is an] example, in politics, of the same kind as Roscher in economics."

"Keep Burke in two—Burke as a Liberal—Burke as a continuist."

"Burke's intolerance in 1773-1791 amounted to this—don't tolerate those who would establish intolerance. It is perfectly true."

"Burke breaks up his party—votes against Emancipation, and [the] abolition of the slave trade, backs the old régime, and obtains, without having ever been a minister, for these party services therefore, a pension equal to the salary of a dozen German professors."

"Burke forgot that [the Revolution of] 1688 came after the experiment of 1640. France could not do at once what took us fifty years. Besides, in England the institutions survived, and the revolution preserved them. In France the monarchy had destroyed them. Democracy was historic in one country as aristocracy was in the other."

Acton's formula, the sovereignty of the developed conscience, is the attempt to solve the problem Burke failed to solve, to provide a principle that will reconcile national and universal, continuity and revolution. It means the sovereignty of the conscience developed by experience and knowledge, ideally the conscience enlightened by the totality of knowledge. This notion may be criticized as ideal, oracular, ambiguous and formalistic. But it does what it sets out to do, that is, to state the answer in terms of a principle, the principle of right. It means permanent and tested convictions resting on a basis of certain knowledge. The growth of knowledge develops conscience. The great example is the historical method itself.

III

THE ENGLISH AND AMERICAN POLITICAL TRADITIONS

IN his lectures Acton wrote:

The Commonwealth is the second stage on the road of revolution, which started from the Netherlands, and went on to America and France, and is the centre of the history of the modern world. Seen from a distance the value of that epoch is ... in the prodigious wealth of ideas which it sent into the world. It supplied the English Revolution, the one that succeeded, the American, the French, with its material. And its ideas became efficacious and masterful by denying their origin. For at first they were religious, not political theories. When they renounced their theological parentage, and were translated into the scientific terms of politics, they conquered and spread over the nations as general truths, not as British exports.[1]

The most important of these ideas are four: Freedom of conscience, separation of Church and State, self-government, diminution of inequalities of wealth.[2]

In Acton's view, it was the Whigs, from the Trimmers to Gladstone, who were the party of real freedom.[3] They were lacking in originality, deficient in ideas, prone to compromise, often taken in tow by others, frequently in the wrong. But they are the central feature in that great progressive chapter in the human mind, still unfinished, which begins with Grotius, Bacon, and Descartes.[4] They took their rise in the age which

---

[1] *L.M.H.*, p. 205.

[2] Harrington said that economic inequality was the obstacle to democracy in England.

[3] This section is based on Acton MSS. Add. 4955. Its relation to the original manuscript is fully analysed in Appendix VII, p. 229. (In the analysis it has sometimes been necessary to alter slightly the added words there given in square brackets.) I believe this to be the most important of all Acton's manuscripts.

[4] Cf. Add 4944: "It [Liberty] depends on Toleration and the theory of

saw the beginnings of modern science and modern philosophy. That climate of thought must be understood first. Its dominant idea is the idea of clearness of thought.

The doctrine of clearness took deep root in the seventeenth century, and, though most familiar in its Cartesian form, it was an idea that was generally current. It entered into the view of Whig philosophy and proved the greatest source both of power and of error. The remarkable fact that so many of the greatest Englishmen of that age inclined to Socinianism—Milton, Locke, Newton—is another sign of the same influence. And one of its results was that it reduced the dogmatic quality of the State religion. The doctrine of clearness was also necessary for popular action. The masses only understand what is quite clear. If they are to decide, things must be made clear—and only such things submitted to them. This was one cause of the limitation of Whig doctrine. Science goes on clearing things up. The domain of certainty extends, and also the domain of evidence. Later, the doctrine of clearness was to be applied by Say, and by Bastiat. But truths that are obvious to children are good only for children. The principles of the wealth of nations lie rather deeper. The danger of the doctrine of clearness is that it gives the victory to those things which nobody can fail to see over those which belong to the intelligent.

Another of the philosophical ideas then in the air was the idea of progress, represented by Bacon, Descartes, Malebranche, Pascal and Leibniz.[1] This is the doctrine that the Moderns are not inferior to the Ancients, that progression is not in a circle, that the world is not gradually getting worse and worse, that God is stronger than the devil, and the spirit than the flesh. The two principles, tradition and progress, are met in all countries and all ages. Each attracts certain natures, certain ages, certain classes. Party divided the Whigs from the Conservatives, gave them one-sidedness, and made them more

Conscience, on International Law, on the predominance of Science, on the notion of Progress, on the refuge beyond the sea—All this is the work of that generation which begins with Galileo, Bacon, Grotius, Descartes, Pascal. From 1610 to 1665."

[1] Cf. Add. 4948: "Progress, part of the Whig scheme—and progress essential to Christianity. Christ did not die in vain—Continues his work among men. His action increasing in power—new organs—bent the world to it."

familiar with their liberal half. So they never combined the two sides properly, continuity and progress. Locke has no notion of development. That came with Leibniz, of whose ideas on the subject Locke shows no knowledge. Before Leibniz the appeal to the past was traditional. Then comes the idea that not the law is permanent, but the principle of the law. This is Conservatism spiritualized. It is the idea which Lessing, Herder, Humboldt, Savigny, Hegel and Baur made a patrimony of the Germans. Though the Whigs did not combine the ideas of progress and continuity properly, the principle of continuity was due to them, though they did not fully grasp its underlying law.[1] But the real force and value of tradition in society was known at that time to none, not even to Leibniz.

Newton's philosophy of nature, the philosophy of observation, also had its influence on Whiggism. Later that influence was revived and increased by Scottish philosophy, by Hutcheson, Reid, Ferguson, Brown, Playfair, Stewart, Mackintosh, Jeffrey, Napier, by the *Edinburgh Review*. The three greatest Whigs were Scotsmen—Brougham, Macaulay, and Gladstone.

The contributory currents were many—beyond experimental science, with Newton, Boyle, and Sydenham, and Bacon, and beyond Cartesian philosophy, there were the Cambridge Platonists, such as More and Whichcote, independent thinkers such as Cumberland, the lawyers, Selden and Pym, the Puritans, Milton, Marvell and Penn, Churchmen like Leighton, Chillingworth, Hales and Burnet, and revolutionary thinkers such as Harrington and Lilburne. It was the age of mechanics, of mathematics. Those were the prevailing discoveries. Not the formation of languages, physiology, ethnology, the forms and laws of growth. The mechanism, not the organism. But Harvey had thrown the deepest discredit on the ancients—for they had been so near it, and had not seen it.

To the Whigs, politics was an experimental and progressive

[1] That is to say, the Revolution of 1688 was carried out without breach of continuity. Cf. Add. 4945: "Whigs, by Compromise, were in touch with the opposite party, and possessed as much of conservative elements as were justified—they claimed to supersede Tories in the traditionalism of politics —They could go as far as any, almost, in a conservative direction—also in a radical direction. But would never allow the improving purpose to prevail without check, or restraint—never obeyed one principle alone."

science—not to be shut up in the formulas of doctrinaires. They perceived that the State cannot judge Dogma, and need not. It requires only moral convictions. But there are exceptions: (1) the unity of mankind, (2) immortality. Science pointed to cosmopolitanism. The sources of error most to be guarded against are national pride and prejudice, ambition, and the interests of classes, Churches, and races. Before then politics alone had been insufficient. Religion had always been needed to stimulate men, and to cause progress. Now there was a purely political force at work. Even without religious impulses political theory made its own way.

Certainty had just begun, and people learned to see clear. This was shown not only by Newton in astronomy, Sydenham, Boyle and the Royal Society; Mabillon had done it with history, Bentley with the classics, not to speak of Henschen, and Holstenius. England had more than her share of all this. At the same time political economy was beginning.

The idea of the Whigs was that there is such a thing as political science, that it is clear and certain, that it is as sacred as morality, that it is imperfect, progressive, and increasing, as essential to the welfare of society as religion or private morals, and as demonstrable as the truths of science. But the Whigs might also say that although there is a science of politics, it is not yet determined, the elements do not exist. Criminal law, international law, political economy were all in their infancy. So the past retained a hold, which it was destined to relax. Things might be gradually determined. Codes might develop themselves, practice and experience might be reduced to theory. Meanwhile, the Whigs accepted things as they were, without respect or authority, for want of certainty. Political science travels slowly. It was not treated scientifically, any more than political economy or criminal law at that time. The Whigs had not a very energetic system of ideas. Algernon Sidney's supply of information was very scanty. Locke was tolerably superficial. Burnet, Hoadly, Addison, Toland were all on the surface. But the Whigs began the emancipation of politics from religion—at least it was the first party that lived on purely political considerations. So it put religious arguments aside, and lost the sectarianism of 1641.

The Whigs lacked depth because they went back to no one

principle.[1] The Whigs took things as they found them, accepted the results of history, and decided to build from the foundations. If they had any principle it was what will practically promote freedom. Afterwards they canonized those inherited forms. This was the work of Montesquieu, who idealized them, and of Burke. This canon was shaken by the American Revolution.

Rationalism helped to prepare the way for the Whigs. And dreading the force of orthodoxy they relied a little on scepticism. Among the early influences have to be reckoned Lord Herbert of Cherbury, Spinoza, and Bayle. Religious unbelief is marked in Shaftesbury, Sidney, Halifax, Somers, Locke, Toland. Metaphysics do not decide against religion, for faith is stronger than metaphysics. But conscience is stronger than faith, so Whiggism put aside speculation, admitted only ethics. Penn was the most liberal mind of the age, and Coleridge thought that on toleration Penn was better than Locke. Though Locke is the Whig classic for propaganda, he is not the complete Whig, and he had a weak notion of the judiciary. There were other currents, including the idea of the supremacy of conscience.

Locke derived all knowledge from experience, as Leibniz did from intellect. The Whigs grew under the former influence. Rationalism rejected that method, claiming to produce everything from the reason. This is the revolutionary doctrine, distinguishing the French Revolution from the English Revolution. Lambert[2] and Kant corrected and combined the two. Grotius had produced the theory of doing without God, and it was on this basis that Locke constructed his theory. The eighteenth century developed the Whig ideas, worked on their lines and built up on their foundations. Voltaire, Montesquieu, Condillac, and Rousseau, who were the greatest forces, are only popularized Locke. Even Turgot and Adam Smith are largely founded on him, and also Hume and Kant and Lessing. It took long to make the Whigs scientific and to deliver them from their age. Locke displayed the metaphysical basis of Whiggism, Somers and Holt the legal, Burnet the ecclesiastical, Leibniz

[1] Cf. the distinction between Whiggism and Liberalism given in Add. 4950: "One is a policy aiming at a philosophy—the other is a philosophy seeking a policy."

[2] [For Lambert, see *Critique of Pure Reason*, passim.]

the universal. Later writers introduced deduction and *a priori* doctrines which were not indigenous to Whiggism. Mill, for instance, treats political economy as a deductive science.

The definition of Whiggism is morality applied to politics. Other parties represent class interests, or religions. They represent a principle, bound by no interest, attached to no class. Their rule was to consider the past, but to be ready, if need be, to break with it. Not one of their ideas was quite new. They desired the predominance of no class, of no religion, of no form. They obeyed at once experience, and the ideal. But both ideas were undeveloped. No part of the science of government was so well established as to make the ideal triumph. When that came, with Quesnay, and with Beccaria,[1] the ideal element gained strength from it. Nor was continuity, progress, or the method of growth ascertained. So that history was also, to them, an uncertain, unregulated force. So Whiggism was destined to be transformed.

The transition from the Roundheads to the Whigs is occupied by the Trimmers, who moderated the extremes of the former. The Shaftesbury party were in the right. Charles deserved to be deposed and James to be excluded. But the doctrine of aquiescence in forms had to prevail. They tried to make the throne, the Church, the aristocracy innocuous, and to make a king who should not oppress, a Church that should not persecute, a nobility that should not injure trade. If other men gave up enforcing their religion, the Whigs gave up more. They could not stand by other interests more firmly. So they were ready, for the sake of liberty, to see their faith suffer. In the same way, they had to sacrifice to Liberty their country and their class. The repudiation of class purposes was as strong in the Whigs as the repudiation of sectarianism. How could patriotism resist the contagion? Their rule was to promote whatever promoted liberty, and to prevent the domination of class. They adopted the idea of party, allowed what they claimed to others. This is the idea of being liberal—not to proscribe.[2]

Liberty regarded as security of property appears in Locke,

[1] [i.e. with economics and the reform of criminal law.]
[2] Cf. Add. 4947: "Party. Idea that it is better to spare error, and let it be free. This is a triumph of Liberalism."

Hume, and Fox. But this was not the character of the Revolution of 1688, which, in its essence, was spiritual. The Whigs were in the service neither of a particular Church, nor of any class, land, labour or capital. They were independent of special interests. They were not in the service of one part of society, at the expense of any others. At the time of the Revolution there were hardly any great towns. The poor were not represented, could not read, and were dependent on the preacher for ideas and on their employers for pay. Democracy was then without roots in England. Vane had been put to death, Baxter retracted, Harrington was in prison and forgotten, Prynne an eager royalist, Milton in obscurity. How completely democracy had disappeared became apparent afterwards. Yet Harrington's law that power follows property governed 1688 all the same. Somers, Locke, Davenant, Defoe, all proclaimed the dominion of land —the right divine of free holders.

The Whigs were the first party that made liberty its object. Therefore they opposed democracy. They desired the union of elements, the division of power. So far, there was a lurking tenderness for aristocracy. They sought liberty by ways propounded by others. So they were made to follow, not to lead— this is the story in the time of Adam Smith, Bentham, Mill, Gibbon Wakefield, Cobden, and O'Connell.

What was neither aristocratic nor puritan was somewhat general. The supreme principle was liberty—not anything else. The time might come when landed aristocracy would become obnoxious, when monarchy would stand stubborn in the way, when religion would be an obstacle to liberty. When that day came,[1] the foundations of the British Constitution would be dug up, for the sake of a principle which is above the nations, and does not depend on tradition. The Whig party subsisted on condition of not multiplying party dogmas and party tests. It accepted only what was common to Churchman, freeholder and capitalist. All this tended to detach them from the soil.

The fundamental principle and *raison d'être* of the Whigs was Liberty, and not for anybody in particular, but for the whole nation. This was the first time it was established. It is the beginning of that intense force—Liberty for its own sake. So it was

[1] The American Revolution.

for the sake of those who do not govern. Hence, Whig compromise and division of power, division, that is, between those who exercise power and those who do not. There was a tendency gradually to exalt the controlling forces outside, to gravitate towards the circumference. The forms of State tend to yield to the substance of the nation.

It was the idea of the Whigs to preserve the existing powers, to renounce speculation and radical improvement apart from tradition; to accept the results of history and make them tolerable—Crown, Church, aristocracy, army, judges, magistrates, corporations were all preserved, but not allowed to cause injury. All were brought under control, for the benefit of those outside. It was not the dominion of any favoured class or sect, but the safety of all those outside from all inside—of the governed from the governing elements, safety against privilege and power. And the meaning of that is liberty. They resolved to avoid extremes and to make King, Church, and Lords innocuous and acceptable. Land was the one thing untouched.

Every doctrine, to become popular, must be made superficial, exaggerated, untrue. We must always distinguish the real essence from the conveyance, especially in political economy. In the Whig view the people, the constituencies, were quite incompetent to decide a policy—the balance of power, the colonial trade, the Bank question, the currency question. They are not informed. There is no way to inform them. They must choose their members. Having chosen, they must let them act as they think best.

The people choose men—or have the choice of measures. The first is the Whig theory, the people have the choice only of men. As to measures, they can petition, they can hold meetings. But they cannot control their representatives. Therefore the debates were secret, there were no instructions, and the Lords were able to balance the Commons. Parliament might do what the nation did not wish. If all this disappears, then there is democracy, as in America, as in Switzerland. That divides Whigs and Democrats.

To be of one accord a community must be small. There are important passages in Waddington illustrative of this; the Independents, wiser than almost all their imitators, wished to deliver the individual, not to create an irresistible force for the collective individual. One democracy [i.e. the French] sets no limit to the general will. The Independents set the most definite limits. Defoe argued that all powers conferred by the people could be resumed. All depends [according to him] not on those who represent, but on those who are represented. The Act of Succession forbad the King to pardon a man accused by the Commons. They represented the people, and it must be assumed that they would undertake nothing unjust. This is very curious as a beginning of Infallibility.

As to the standing army, the Whigs said: If we cannot protect our liberties ourselves, we are not a free people.

The masses had no part in the Revolution of 1688. The Democracy of 1650 was theoretic. It came from Independency. It hardly grew on English soil. It was American.

The early Whigs were beaten by Charles II. It was the moderate party that survived. There is a great contrast between the two generations, the Roundheads and the early Whigs with their doctrine of Compromise, making the best of things, and progressing slowly. They came to subsist on condition of not multiplying party dogmas and party tests, accepting only what was common to Churchman and Nonconformist, royalist and republican, freeholder and capitalist. All this tended to detach them from the soil. As the Whig system was a delicate system of compromises, there was no eagerness to push enquiry to logical consequences—rather some reluctance. The Whigs took their lead from outside—never shut the door against ideas that would promote freedom, but would not open it with alacrity. They were always in tow, as witness negro slavery, American taxation, political economy, Bentham, Parliamentary Reform, Religious Liberty, the Colonies, Criminal Law, the Factory Laws, Grote, Mill.

The Whigs accepted existing forms without discussion. So far they were not scientific. Compromise between fact and theory was their object.[1] And they were driven to consider the essence, not forms—to leave these, and to decide what is good in principle, apart from forms. This meant the negation of

[1] Cf. Add. 4949: "The theory of Compromise involved party government. N.B."; and Add. 4952: "Party—Division of Power." Cf. also Add. 4942: "The Church was, in the Middle Ages—after the Carolingian epoch —the great divider of power."

Radicalism. It meant making the best of realities. So the Whigs were driven to find excuses for what they accepted. They canonized what they could not disturb. That is Burke. That is the glorification of country gentlemen, broad establishments, constitutional monarchy.

There is no Whig principle which the Whig party has not repudiated. Fox opposed Parliamentary Reform,[1] Walpole—the Dissenters, Chatham—America,[2] Russell—Free Trade, Grey—the Factory Laws, Fox—the French Treaty, Melbourne—the Charter, Palmerston—the Ballot.

The Whig want of system broke down in the end. America began it, with Camden and Chatham, France with Fox, Ireland with Grattan, Ricardo pushing forward Adam Smith, Bentham developing Beccaria. There was also the influence of independent thinkers—Grote, Wakefield, Mill, Cobden, Plunket. The Whig party was taken in tow and went reluctantly.

Whiggism was influenced by the economists, the liberals, the radicals, in succession. English Liberalism arose out of Adam Smith.

The rise of Liberalism in Europe, in France and Germany, followed the suppression of the Spanish Constitution in 1823. So an international system was gradually formed which was not Whig. Its basis was the inheritance, the lesson, of the French Revolution—the ideals of 1789 controlled by ten years—equal to centuries—of experience, together with the example—idealized—of England—and the practical example of America.

The term liberalism was first used about 1807—of Chateaubriand and of Madame de Staël. It is found in Spain in 1811. Other instances are the Irish members in the British Parliament, the *Edinburgh Review*, the influence of the Scots philosophy. It was an epoch of little faith. The general tendency is proved, outside of politics, by the poets—Schiller, Alfieri, Monti, the Freiheitsdichter, in Germany, even the Lake school at first, and Heine. Grün, Byron, Shelley, Landor, Tennyson, Browning, Swinburne, Campbell, Rogers, Moore, Quintana, Mickiewicz, Delavigne, Manzoni, Pushkin, Hugo.

Liberalism rose and spread, witness Jovellanos, Arguelles, Toreno, the Americans and South Americans, the English

---

[1] i.e. at one date.
[2] i.e. after France came into the war of American Independence.

opposition—Brougham, Romilly, Bentham, Dumont, Mill, Ricardo, Huskisson, Senior, Mill, Wakefield, Whately, Hare, Arnold, Cobbett, Frost, Charles Buller.

Continental Liberalism meant the residuum of the French Revolution—Daunou, De Staël, Constant, Broglie, Chateaubriand, Courrier, Fiévée, Foy; the Doctrinaires—De Serre, Royer-Collard, Guizot, Barante, Rossi, Rémusat; Comte, Thierry, and the recovery of the Saint Simonians, Chevalier, Say, Sismondi, Bastiat, Cousin, Thiers, Tocqueville, the representative school, the Socialist school, Comte's school; Lamennais.[1]

All these schools, towards 1848, combined together—when the lines of Lamennais, Chateaubriand, Daunou, S. Simon, Comte, Lafayette, Royer-Collard, Berryer, Sismondi, came to much the same general result, to a common ground, very near Constant, Rémusat, Tocqueville, Laboulaye, and others.[2] That idea is evidently very powerful. It has to be followed up, out of France, under French influence. It grew in Germany, Italy, Spain, Switzerland.

The stages of the progress of the ideas of Liberalism are marked by the following names: in France—Constant, Fiévée, Guizot, Sismondi, Rossi, Tocqueville, Le Play, Broglie, Cormenin, Bastiat, S. Simon; in Germany—Kant, Humboldt, Savigny, Hegel, Radowitz, Fröbel, Heine, Dahlmann, Vollgraff, Schmoller, Ihering.

The Tories might argue that Whig concessions would be limited by no principle. It might become democratic, revolutionary, Socialist. They would resist for a time, but not on principle. They would judge by expediency. There would be a period of incessant, indefinite change. Ideal Toryism was prepared by Burke's dislike of Parliamentary reform. Their great prize was the prize of tradition. According to ideal Toryism Burke was right in rejecting the French Revolution as the enemy of liberty. On this basis legitimacy arose on the Continent. Ideal Toryism opposed the new Poor Law and

[1] Cf. Add. 4942: "Large body of accepted truth, from Royer-Collard to Littré—that is the main stream of doctrine."

[2] Cf. Add. 4952: "Royer-Collard and Broglie praise Hallam above everybody. Rémusat thinks the Discontents [Burke's *Thoughts on the Present Discontents*] the best English political pamphlet. So the Doctrinaires distinctly associated themselves with the Whigs."

favoured the Factory Laws. The Tories had the common ground of Conservatism—government by tradition, by property, by religion, that is to say, acquired rights are sacred. Property, in their view, was the safest ruler, because property has the greatest stake in the country, also because the propertied classes are educated. They could argue that if political power is given without property, it will oblige property to follow it. Therefore, to avoid spoliation, power should be given to property.

But system means a view of only certain truths. What the Whigs represent is not a system, but a spirit. Liberty is one. It is the same cause always—but the opposition varies. But the desire of doing the enemy justice is a mark of scientific sincerity. The saying that the terms Whig and Tory belong to natural history was made by Jefferson and was adopted by Adams.

At one time the Whigs—Fox and Turgot, for example—admitted the supreme right of property. That was the liberty they most attended to. It is the old mediaeval view—the physical, not the moral basis of freedom.[1] It was revived by Locke—and it continued as long as toleration was not recognized. The insufficiency of it came out in the American Revolution. The right to tax was denied. The right to govern was admitted. This is the position of Chatham, Camden, Franklin. It was necessary to go one step further—and that was revolution. In reality, a Whig cannot think other governments legitimate. In him is a principle of revolution, if not of aggression. An attempt to upset governments resting on a basis he deems illegitimate must attract him.

There is not an absolute contradiction between liberal and conservative. It is a question of time and place and expediency. Liberals admit that men are not always ripe for freedom. Conservatives wish to preserve it lest it be imperilled. But Whigs and Tories really are contrary things, excluding each other. One wishes to preserve things for their own sake. The other will sacrifice every institution that does not stand the test of liberality.

Parties abroad have sometimes adopted Whig principles—Federalists, Feuillants, Cavour. But no constitutions have

[1] This does not represent the whole of Acton's view of course. Cf. Chap. VI below.

emulated the example of the Whigs. All have been drawn on French models—in Spain, Portugal, Holland, Belgium, Denmark, Austria, Prussia, Italy.

That they proposed the partition of Poland, maintained the penal laws, that they were responsible for the treatment meted out to the Dissenters, and to Ireland; their record in regard to slavery—that is the case against the Whigs.

As already noticed, Acton said that it was the ideas of the English thinkers of the Puritan revolution that supplied the American Revolution with its material. He defined his view of that event in the words, "They [the Americans] resolved to give up everything, not to escape from actual oppression, but to honour a precept of unwritten law. That was the transatlantic discovery in the theory of political duty."[1] And again, "The case was fought out on the ground of the Law of Nature, more properly speaking, of Divine Right. On that evening of 16 December 1773, it became, for the first time, the reigning force in History."[2] In the first of the two lectures on freedom given in February and May 1877, Acton referred to the same event in the words "scarcely a century has passed since nations, that knew the meaning of the term, resolved to be free." But in the same lecture he concluded that if a balanced constitution has succeeded anywhere "it has been in our favoured country and in our time; and we know not yet how long the wisdom of the nation will preserve the equipoise."[3] It was "by the development of the principle of Federalism, it [the Federal Constitution] has produced a community . . . more free than any other which the world has seen."[4] Acton was not idolatrous about the British Constitution. In the *Inaugural* he put his philosophy of history in the words: "It is suspicious of illusions in success, and though there may be hope of ultimate triumph for what is true . . . by the gradual exhaustion of error, it admits no corresponding promise for what is ethically right."[5]

Acton's view of the American Revolution reflects particularly well the two sides of his thought. As the matter is critical it will be convenient to give the evidence rather fully. In his lectures on the French Revolution Acton said: "When we speak in the gross of the American Revolution we combine

[1] *F.R.*, p. 24.   [2] *L.M.H.*, p. 311.   [3] *H.F.*, p. 20.
[4] *L.M.H.*, p. 314 (1901).   [5] *Ibid.*, pp. 25–26.

different and discordant things. From the first agitation in 1761 to the Declaration of Independence, and then to the end of the war in 1782, the Americans were aggressive, violent in their language, fond of abstractions, prolific of doctrines universally applicable and universally destructive . . . A change followed in 1787, when the Convention drew up the Constitution. It was a period of construction, and every effort was made, every scheme was invented, to curb the inevitable democracy. The members of that assembly were, on the whole, eminently cautious and sensible men. . . . Seward has pointed out the distinction between the revolutionary epoch and the constituent epoch that succeeded."[1] In a subsequent lecture Acton said: "The old European securities for good government were found insufficient protection against parliamentary oppression. The nation itself, acting by its representatives, had to be subjected to control. The political problem raised by the New World was more complicated than the simple issues dealt with hitherto in the Old. It had become necessary to turn back the current of the development of politics, to bind and limit and confine the State, which it was the pride of the moderns to exalt. It was a new phase of political history. The American Revolution innovated upon the English Revolution, as the English Revolution innovated on the politics of Bacon or of Hobbes."[2] Acton continues: "The dispute had been reduced to its simplest expression, and had become a mere question of principle. . . . By the rules of right, which had been obeyed till then, England had the better cause. By the principle which was then inaugurated, England was in the wrong, and the future belonged to the colonies."[3] "The Americans proceeded to give themselves a Constitution. . . . The powers of the states were limited. The powers of the federal government were actually enumerated, and thus the states and the union were a check on each other. That principle of division was the most efficacious restraint on democracy that has been devised; for the temper of the Constitutional Convention was as conservative as the Declaration of Independence was revolutionary. The Federal Constitution . . . by the development of the principle of Federalism . . . has produced a community . . . more free than any other which the world has seen."[4]

[1] *F.R.*, pp. 34-35. [2] *L.M.H.*, p. 309. [3] *Ibid.*, p. 311. [4] *Ibid.*

Earlier Acton had written: "It is in political science only that America occupies the first rank. There are six Americans on a level with the foremost Europeans."[1] And, "The anti-revolutionary temper of the Revolution belongs to 1787, not to 1776. Another element was at work, and it is the other element that is new, effective, characteristic, and added permanently to the experience of the world. . . . It teaches that men ought to be in arms even against a remote and constructive danger to their freedom."[2]

In 1878 Acton wrote: "American independence was the beginning of a new era, not merely as a revival of Revolution, but because no other Revolution ever proceeded from so slight a cause. . . . The greatest statesmen in England averred that it was just. It established a pure democracy; but it was democracy in its highest perfection, armed and vigilant, less against aristocracy and monarchy than against its own weakness and excess. Whilst England was admired for the safeguards with which, in the course of many centuries, it had fortified liberty against the power of the crown, America appeared still more worthy of admiration for the safeguards which, in the deliberations of a single memorable year, it had set up against the power of its own sovereign people. . . . Ancient Europe opened its mind to two new ideas—that Revolution with very little provocation may be just; and that democracy in very large dimensions may be safe."[3] In the previous year Acton said: "It was from America that the plain ideas that men ought to mind their own business, and that the nation is responsible to Heaven for the acts of the State—ideas long locked in the breast of solitary thinkers, and hidden among Latin folios—burst like a conqueror upon the world they were destined to transform, under the title of the Rights of Man."[4] Acton adds: "The principle gained ground, that a nation can never abandon its fate to an authority it cannot control. The Americans placed it at the foundation of their new government. They did more; for having subjected all civil authorities to the popular will, they surrounded the popular will with restrictions that the British legislature would not endure."[5]

It will be seen that in almost every case Acton supplements

[1] H.F., p. 578 (1888). [2] Ibid., p. 586. [3] Ibid., p. 84–5.
[4] Ibid., p. 55. [5] Ibid., p. 56.

the revolutionary principle by the constitutional. In this connection he used the metaphor of cutting and sewing. It is easy to "cut"; but "sewing" is a more difficult art. This distinction throughout is the perfect example of Acton's formula, the sovereignty of the developed conscience. Conscience may spell revolution; but the developed conscience, the conscience developed and instructed by experience and knowledge, insists on constitutional government.[1]

In a well-known passage in the *Inaugural* Acton said: "Achieved liberty is the one ethical result that rests on the converging and combined conditions of advancing civilization." In one of the notes to this passage there is a quotation from Renan which underlines its significance: "*Le libéralisme, ayant la prétention de se fonder uniquement sur les principes de la raison, croit d'ordinaire n'avoir pas besoin de tradition. Là est son erreur. L'erreur de l'école libérale est d'avoir trop cru qu'il est facile de créer la liberté par la reflexion, et de n'avoir pas vu qu'un établissement n'est solide que quand il a des racines historiques.* Acton believed that the natural rights the American revolution invoked had historic roots, and that its great achievement was to complement natural rights by a constitution that would prevent abuse of democratic power. But he did not ignore the special circumstances of America. The colonists, he pointed out, were "the heirs of boundless wealth," and they were fortunate in escaping many of the causes of difficulty in the old world, "popular ignorance, pauperism, the glaring contrast between rich and poor, religious strife, public debts, standing armies and war."[2] The French Revolution was the unsuccessful attempt, Acton wrote, to apply American principles in Europe. And in his manuscripts: "Our laws made the greatness of America"[3]; "Whigs: by their principles America made itself free."[4]

Acton explicitly recognized the economic factor in American history. He quoted with approval the judgment of an American: "The real foundation of the discontent that led to the Revolution was the effort of Great Britain, beginning in 1750, to

[1] Some of my reasons for differing from the conclusions in *J.M.H.*, Dec. 1949, are given in Appendix II.
[2] *H.F.*, p. 56 (1877). [3] Add. 4870.
[4] Add. 4955. Cf. Add. 4945: "Three main forms of Liberty—Historic—old English way, and German, Abstract—American, French, Religious—Reconciles them."

prevent diversity of occupation, to attack the growth of manufactures and the mechanic arts."[1] He refers tactfully to "the report that money prevailed at some of the turning-points of American history."[2]

[1] *F.R.*, p. 22. [2] *H.F.*, p. 578.

IV

THE STATE, GOVERNMENT, AND DEMOCRACY

THE State has a divine origin and purpose. "The Church and the State have the same origin and the same ultimate objects."¹ The true view of the origin and nature of the State "is that which recognizes in the State the same divine origin and the same ends as the Church, which holds that it belongs as much to the primitive essence of a nation as its language, and that it unites men together by a moral, not like family and society, by a natural and sensible bond."²

There is a difference between the Christian and the pagan State: "The difference between a Christian and a pagan monarchy, or between a Christian and a rationalist democracy, is as great, politically, as that between a monarchy and a republic."³ The great object is "by keeping the two spheres permanently distinct—by rendering to Caesar the things that are Caesar's, and to God the things that are God's—to make all absolutism, of whatever kind, impossible."⁴

The State is distinct from the Church. This distinction between religious and civil authority is denied by the pagan State.⁵ "The State aims at the things of another life but indirectly. Its course runs parallel to that of the Church; they do not converge."⁶ The State can give only indirect help to the individual by promoting the influence of that which is good—religion, education, and the distribution of wealth. Society also is distinct from the State: "Pray bring to bear upon your

¹ *Gasquet*, pp. 49–50.
² *Rambler*, March 1860, p. 397.
³ *H.F.*, p. 205 (1858).
⁴ *Ibid.*
⁵ *Gasquet*, p. 213. Cf. Lord Lindsay's chapter in *Voluntary Social Services* (Nuffield College Series), edited by A. F. C. Bourdillon.
⁶ *H.F.*, p. 251 (1862).

political speculations the distinction between State and society (unknown to the ancients, due to Christianity)."[1]

In his lecture on Freedom in Antiquity Acton wrote:

> When Christ said: "Render unto Caesar the things that are Caesar's and unto God the things that are God's," those words, spoken on His last visit to the Temple, three days before His death, gave to the civil power, under the protection of conscience, a sacredness it had never enjoyed, and bounds it had never acknowledged; and they were the repudiation of absolutism and the inauguration of freedom. For our Lord not only delivered the precept, but created the force to execute it. To maintain the necessary immunity in one supreme sphere, to reduce all political authority within defined limits, ceased to be an aspiration of patient reasoners, and was made the perpetual charge and care of the most energetic institution and the most universal association in the world. The new law, the new spirit, the new authority, gave to liberty a meaning and a value it had not possessed in the philosophy or in the constitution of Greece or Rome before the knowledge of the truth that makes us free.[2]

The Fathers did not fully understand the political consequences of Christianity which it was the business of the Middle Ages to evolve.[3] "It is quite wrong, but not heretical, to give the State a sinful origin, like war."[4]

The true theory of the State is to be derived from the principles of the Christian religion and of the British Constitution: "The true notion of a Christian State and the true latent notion of the [British] Constitution coincide and complete each other."[5] Acton adds: "The State in which freedom would be sufficiently secured against the government *and* against the people is ideal. England is the only example of the first."[6]

The State is organic: "If States would live, they must preserve their organic connection with their origin and history, which are their root and their stem; . . . they are not voluntary creations of human wisdom."[7] Growth is a characteristic

---

[1] *Gasquet*, p. 221 (1861). This distinction is also fundamental in Ihering's sociology of law (see *E.S.S.*).

[2] *H.F.*, p. 29 (1877).   [3] *Gasquet*, p. 49 (1859).   [4] *Ibid.*

[5] *Ibid.*, p. 3 (1858).   [6] *Ibid.*, p. 211 (1861).

[7] *H.F.*, p. 243 (1862). Later Acton preferred the term "the likeness of something organic" (*Inaugural*, 1895). This is, of course, a vital distinction.

feature of the State: "I cannot conceive a State in which reform should not be a normal condition of progress, that is, of existence. Growth need not be change."[1]

Acton elaborates his view as follows:

> The State could never grow out of society as its expression and fruit, unless society were organised and distributed into distinct classes and corporations, each enjoying social power in its own sphere; where this distribution is wanting, and the social mass comprehends no moral persons, but only physical units, society is atomic; and the State cannot be an organism, an expression or organ of society, but is supreme and absolute, whatever its form and constitutional pretences may be.[2]

"State absolutism is the modern danger."[3]

The nature of the State is seen in its historical development:

> The State is only ideally the original form of social life. Each particular State only gradually grew to be a power over the people. At first society was broken into pieces, self-sufficient; every group (not every man) for itself, and only God for all. There was no notion of sovereignty; the feudal lord was the highest authority. Hence feuds between them—the token of feudal life—the assumption of functions now devolved on the State, then discharged by every man for himself. This is one instance of the State not existing above society. It is the same in taxation: all local, none imperial, etc.[4]

> In that society out of which modern European States have grown, the corporation was the first thing, the sovereign State the second. But the State gradually gained ground, and took into its hands what was common to all.[5] . . . afterwards came Roman law (about the time of Frederic I) in which the State is the first thing; law comes downwards from the sovereign, does not grow upward from the people, as in the Teutonic State. This difference is not, however, in the original principle of the two legislations, but in this, that the

Intermediate is Add. 4941: "The State an organism. It follows that it is self-governing, and has a conscience."

[1] *Gasquet*, p. 214 (1860).

[2] *Rambler*, January 1861, p. 199 (*aetat.* 27). This judgment appears to antedate Gierke and Maitland.

[3] *Rambler*, March 1860, p. 397.   [4] *Gasquet*, pp. 231 ff. (1861).

[5] *Ibid.*

Roman law, which began to be studied, was that of a finished State, of a mature, an old people, of an empire that had developed the most extreme absolutism on the ruins of the *Populus*. The political ideas of the Theodosian or Justinian code are those of a society ground to atoms by the wheel of revolution, consisting, no longer of parts, but like sand or water, in which all life and power are in the sovereign. This is the very opposite of that society to which this system was introduced. Hence Frederic found men at Bologna who told him that all the property of the people was his and that he might take what he liked, that what he left was a concession on his part. The Germans were slow in realizing the State, so the legists clapped a pair of spectacles on their young noses, taught them to lean on a stick and to have the ills of ages. So they grievously overshot the mark, and introduced a dualism into European politics which went on increasing till now we [i.e. in Great Britain] stand alone on Teutonic ground.[1]

What you most want for your theory of liberty is a definition of corporations, and then the constant distinction between States founded on corporations—where they are therefore political—and States which tolerate corporations in the social department, but which are not founded by them.[2]

The purpose of the State is ethical, that is, liberty, which means freedom of conscience. Freedom is freedom to avoid sin.[3] The rights of man on earth are the consequence of the rights of God in Heaven. "The ends of science . . . are truth, . . . of the State . . . liberty."[4]

In another passage Acton writes: "Liberty . . . [is] the right of being able to do what we ought . . . general interests [cannot] supersede individual rights. . . . [the true theory] condemns, therefore, the theory of the ancient as well as of the modern State."[5] Referring to the sixth volume of Guizot's *Memoirs*, Acton says, "There is an excellent passage on the moral nature and purpose of the State, against those who treat it as a police organization for the protection of property."[6] Political science has a moral foundation: "I understand by political science the

[1] *Gasquet*, pp. 231–234 (1861).   [2] *Ibid.*, p. 235 (1861).
[3] Add. 4870.   [4] *Gasquet*, pp. 221–222 (Nov. 1861).
[5] *Rambler*, Jan. 1860, p. 146.   [6] *H.F.R.*, April 1864, p. 723.

development of the maxim *suum cuique* in the relation of the State with other States, corporations and individuals."[1] The criterion of the State is ethical. Political science is the science of the State as it ought to be.

As already noticed, Acton believes that political science is the one science which is deposited by the stream of history like grains of gold in the sand of a river.[2] The history of any science, and especially of political science, is the prerequisite of its fruitful study. Plato and Aristotle are the writers from whom we can learn most about the science of politics, more especially the *Laws* of Plato and the *Politics* of Aristotle.[3] The Stoics rightly judged the State by the law of nature, which the Middle Ages identified with the law of reason which is the law of God. Aquinas illustrates this point. Acton quotes from Aquinas, as the earliest exponent of the Whig theory of revolution, a passage in which occurs the following: "the whole nation ought to have a share in governing itself . . . all political authority is derived from popular suffrage, and all laws must be made by the people or their representatives."[4]

Marsilius of Padua he quotes as saying: "Laws derive their authority from the nation and are invalid without its assent. In obeying laws to which all men have agreed, all men in reality govern themselves."[5] Grotius laid down the lines of real political science.[6]

The true theorists according to Acton are Harrington, Locke, Sieyès, Rousseau, Jefferson, Hamilton, Mill.[7] Locke is "always reasonable and sensible," but, Acton adds, "diluted and pedestrian and poor."[8] Rousseau, Acton calls the author of the strongest political theory that had appeared amongst men. But his ideas are old friends, and may be found in Wolf, the Jesuit Casuists, Major of St. Andrews, Duplessis Mornay, and even in the early interpreters of the Aristotelian Politics which appeared just at the era of the first parliament.[9]

The theory of the democratic State is implicit in the account of Sieyès, who is Acton's democratic hero. In the ranks of the

---

[1] *Gasquet*, pp. 129–130 (1860). Also quoted in Introduction, *ante*.
[2] *Inaugural*, p. 2.   [3] *H.F.*, p. 22.
[4] *Ibid.*, p. 36.   [5] *Ibid.*, p. 37.
[6] *Ibid.*, p. 46.   [7] *H.E.*, p. 492 (1892).
[8] *L.M.H.*, p. 217 (1899–1901).   [9] *F.R.*, pp. 16–17 (1895–1899).

true theorists his place is very far from being the lowest.[1] "In the history of political doctrine, where almost every chapter has yet to be written, none will be more valuable than the one that will show what is permanent and progressive in the ideas that he originated."[2] In the debates of the National Assembly Sieyès used words that have added not a little to his moral stature, "They fancy that they can be free, and yet not be just."[3] Sieyès taught that the real national will proceeds from debate, not from election, and is the result not of crude arithmetic but of a refined intellectual operation.

Acton writes:

> Before coming to the conflict between Church and State, with which the legislation of 1790 closes, I must speak of a man memorable far beyond Mirabeau in the history of political thought and action, who is the most perfect representative of the Revolution. I mean the Abbé Sieyès. As a priest without a vocation, he employed himself with secular studies, and mastered and meditated the French and the English writers of the age, politicians, economists, and philosophers. Learning from many, he became the disciple of none, and was thoroughly independent, looking beyond the horizon of his century, and farther than his own favourites, Rousseau, Adam Smith and Turgot. He understood politics as the science of the State as it ought to be, and he repudiated the product of history, which is things as they are. No American ever grasped more firmly the principle that experience is an incompetent teacher of the governing art. He turned resolutely from the Past, and refused to be bound by the precepts of men who believed in slavery and sorcery, in torture and persecution. He deemed history a misleading and useless study, and knew little of its examples and its warnings. But he was sure that the Future must be different, and might be better. In the same disdainful spirit he rejected Religion as the accumulated legacy of childhood, and believed that it arrested progress by depreciating terrestrial objects.[4]

It is worth while at this point to notice Acton's other remarks about Sieyès. This is what he says:

---

[1] *H.E.*, p. 492. [2] *F.R.*, p. 164.
[3] *Ibid.*, p. 102. Freedom presupposes justice.
[4] *Ibid*, p. 159.

In the elections for the Constituent Assembly, Sieyès preferred to stand for the Third Estate at Paris, where he was elected last of all the candidates. One of his preliminary tracts circulated in 30,000 copies, and had promptly made him famous, for it was rich in consequences as the ninety-five theses of Wittenberg. His philosophy of history consisted in one idea. Barbarians had come down from Germany on the people of civilised and imperial Gaul, and had subjugated and robbed them, and the descendants of the invading race were now the feudal nobles, who still held power and profit, and continued to oppress the natives. This identification of privileged noble with conquering Frank was of older date; and in this [i.e. the nineteenth] century it has been made the master-key to modern history. When Thierry discovered the secret of our national development in the remarks of Wamba the Witless to Gurth, under the Sherwood oaks, he applied to us a formula familiar to his countrymen; and Guizot always defined French history as a perpetual struggle between hostile nations until the eighteenth century made good the wrong that was done in the fifth.

Right or wrong, the theory of Sieyès was adopted by his most learned successors, and must not be imputed to ignorance. His argument is that the real nation consisted of the mass of men enjoying no privilege, and that they had a claim for compensation and reprisal against those who had been privileged to oppress and to despoil them. The Third Estate was equal to the three Estates together, for the others had no right to be represented. As power exercised otherwise than by consent, power that does not emanate from those for whose use it exists, is a usurpation, the first two orders must be regarded as wrongdoers. They ought to be repressed, and the means of doing harm taken from them.

Although Sieyès neither wrote well nor spoke well, yet within a fortnight of his maiden speech he had vanquished the ancient order of things in France. The Court, the Church, and the *Noblesse* had gone down before the imposing coherence of his ideas.[1]

Sieyès was essentially a revolutionist, because he held that political oppression can never be right, and that resistance to oppression can never be wrong. And he was a royalist, not as believing in the proprietary right of dynasties, but because monarchy, justly limited and controlled, is one of

[1] *F.R.*, p. 160.

the many forces that secure the liberty which is given by society and not by nature. He was a Liberal, for he thought liberty the end of government, and defined it as that which makes men most completely masters of their faculties, in the largest sphere of independent action. He was also a democrat, for he would revise the constitution once in a generation; and he described the law as the settled will of those who are governed, which those who govern have no share in making. But he was less a democrat than a Liberal, and he contrived scientific provision against the errors of the sovereign nation. He sacrificed equality by refusing the vote to those who paid no taxes, and he preferred an elaborate system of indirect and filtered election. He broke the direct tide of opinion by successive renewals, avoiding dissolution. According to his doctrine, the genuine national will proceeds from debate, not from election, and is ascertained by a refined intellectual operation, not by coarse and obvious arithmetic. The object is to learn not what the country thinks, but what it would think if it was present at the discussion carried on by men whom it trusted. Therefore there is no imperative mandate, and the deputy governs the constituent. He mitigated democracy by another remarkable device. The Americans have made the guardians of the law into watchers on the lawgivers, giving to the judiciary power to preserve the Constitution against the legislators. Sieyès invented a special body of men for the purpose, calling them the constitutional jury.[1]

Thus, although all power emanates from the nation alone, and very little can be delegated to an hereditary and irresponsible monarch, he intended to restrict its exercise at every point, and to make sure that it would never be hasty, or violent, and that minorities should be heard. In his sustained power of consistent thinking, Sieyès resembles Bentham and Hegel. His flight is low, and he lacks grace and distinction. He seems to have borrowed his departments from Harrington, the distilled unity of power from Turgot, the rule of the mass of taxpayers over the unproductive class above them, from the notion that labour is the only source of wealth, which was common to Franklin and Adam Smith. But he is profoundly original, and though many modern writers on politics exceed him in genius and eloquence and knowledge, none equal him in invention and resource.[2] . . .

[1] *F.R.*, p. 161.   [2] *Ibid.*, p. 162.

Since I first spoke of Sieyès, certain papers have come to light tending to show that he was as wicked as the rest of them. They would not affect my judgment on his merit as a thinker.[1]

The limits Acton believed necessary in every form of government, and especially in a democracy, will be further illustrated in the course of the present chapter.

If the object of government is liberty, it is important to notice what, in Acton's philosophy, it is not. It is "not happiness, or prosperity, or power, or the preservation of an historic inheritance, or the adaptation of national law to national character, or the progress of enlightenment and the promotion of virtue."[2] The private individual should not feel the pressure of public authority, and should direct his life by the influences that are within him, not around him.[3] If any single definite object, other than liberty, is made the supreme object, the State becomes inevitably, for the time being, absolute.[4] This is contrary to Acton's first principle, the division of authority and power. Liberty alone demands for its realization the limitation of the public authority. Liberty is the only object which benefits all alike.[5]

The one thing common to all men is the universal and sovereign reason, which not all men perceive, but which, as Heraclitus said, is the only thing fixed and certain in the midst of change.[6] The great controversy of all ages is the conflict between custom and reason.[7] Burke said, "Only a sovereign reason should dictate."[8] D'Argenson thought the world ought to be governed by plain reason.[9] The Independents "inclined not only to liberty, but to equality, and rejected the authority of the past and the control of the living by the dead. The sovereignty of the yellow parchment fell before the light of reason."[10] Government is limited by reason and ethics. "The unwritten law reigns supreme over the municipal law."

The Socratic method, the appeal to each man's reason and

---

[1] *F.R.*, p. 164.   [2] *Ibid.*, p. 33.   [3] *Ibid.*
[4] *H.F.*, p. 288 (1862). This, I believe, is Acton's most original judgment.
[5] *Ibid.* "The ends of liberty are the true ends of politics, that is the one thing certain and known to all men" (*L.M.G.*, p. 216).
[6] *H.F.*, p. 22.   [7] *F.R.*, p. 357.   [8] *H.F.*, p. 156.
[9] *F.R.*, p. 10.   [10] *L.M.H.*, p. 200.

conscience is essentially democratic.[1] Among the Puritans there were some who enforced, though they did not discover, the principle that a man's conscience is his castle, with kings and parliaments at a respectful distance.[2] The substance of liberty does not necessarily reside in outward forms.[3] The essence of Whiggism is the acknowledgement of the supremacy of the higher law.[4] The self-government of free states requires the constant presence of dispassionate reason. Of this men must be deprived if they are to be governed by a revolutionary absolutism or an absolute democracy.[5] Christianity itself requires that all governments whatsoever should have only a limited authority.[6] Calhoun said: "I care not what the form of government is; it is nothing if the government is despotic, whether it be in the hands of one, or of a few, or of many men, without limitation."[7]

Legitimate government means self-government, based on individual and collective moral responsibility. The right of self-government is inherent, not only in the State, but in every legitimate association.[8] Burke said, "In all forms of government the people is the true legislator. The remote and efficient cause is the consent of the people, either actual or implied, and such consent is absolutely essential to its validity."[9] But self-government requires certain conditions: long and arduous experience, a rampart of tried conviction and accumulated knowledge, a fair level of general morality, education, courage, self-restraint.[10]

The underlying principle in self-government goes back to Socrates, as already noticed above. The passage in which Acton expresses this view needs to be quoted in full:

> The main point [writes Acton] in the method of Socrates was essentially democratic.

He continues:

> He urged men to bring all things to the test of incessant inquiry, and not to content themselves with the verdict of authorities, majorities, or custom; to judge of right and

---

[1] *H.F.*, p. 71.   [2] *L.M.H.*, p. 143.   [3] *Rambler*, 1858, p. 425.
[4] *H.F.R.*, Jan. 1863, p. 253.   [5] *Ibid.*, April 1863, p. 656.
[6] *H.F.*, p. 29. "The possession of unlimited power corrodes the conscience, hardens the heart and confounds the understanding" (*H.F.*, p. 11).
[7] *Rambler*, May 1861, pp. 48–49.   [8] *Gasquet*, pp. 221–222 (1861).
[9] *F.R.*, p. 29.   [10] *L.M.H.*, p. 13.

wrong, not by the will or sentiment of others, but by the light which God has set in each man's reason and conscience. He proclaimed that authority is often wrong, and has no warrant to silence or impose conviction. But he gave no warrant to resistance. He emancipated men for thought, but not for action. The sublime history of his death shows that the superstition of the State was undisturbed by his contempt for its rulers.[1]

Beyond the tradition of antiquity and all its gifts of reflection and experience, something additional was wanted—a faculty of self-government and self-control, "developed like its language in the fibre of a nation, and growing with its growth."[2] To develop this principle was the work of the thousand years we call the Middle Ages. The Church taught that power ought to be conferred by election: "The Councils of Toledo furnished the framework of the Parliamentary system of Spain, which is, by a long interval, the oldest in the world."[3] But the most healthy and vigorous growth of municipal liberties was in Belgium, "of all countries on the Continent, that which has been from immemorial ages the most stubborn in its fidelity to the principle of self-government."[4]

Aquinas and Marsilius both taught that the whole people should have a voice in governing itself.[5] The principle of representative government was everywhere recognized by the end of the Middle Ages.[6] But the victory of the idea in the modern world was due to the Puritans:

> The power of Independency was not in relation to theology, but to Church government. They did not admit the finality of doctrinal formulas, but awaited the development of truth to come. Each congregation governed itself independently, and every member of the Church participated in its administration. . . . The Church was governed, not by the State, or by bishops or by the presbytery, but by the multitude of which it was composed. It was the ideal of local self-government and of democracy.[7]

[1] *H.F.*, p. 71.   [2] *Ibid.*, p. 31.
[3] *Ibid.*, p. 34 (1877). Cf. Sir Ernest Barker's *The Dominican Order and Convocation*.
[4] *Ibid.*, p. 38.
[5] *Ibid.*, pp. 36–37.   [6] *Ibid.*, p. 39.
[7] *L.M.H.*, p. 200.

Acton proceeds: "The political consequences reached far. The supremacy of the people, being accepted in Church government, could not be repudiated in the State. There was a strong prejudice in its favour."

Acton adds:

> Seen from a distance the value of that epoch [the Commonwealth] is not in that which it created, for it left not creations but ruins, but in the prodigious wealth of ideas which it sent into the world. It supplied the English Revolution, the one that succeeded, the American, the French, with its material. And its ideas became efficacious and masterful by denying their origin. For at first they were religious, not political theories. When they renounced their theological parentage, and were translated into the scientific terms of politics, they conquered and spread over the nations as general truths, not as British exports.[1]

But the principle of limited authority receives its supreme illustration in the French Revolution:

> By right of the immense change they made in the world, by their energy and sincerity, their fidelity to reason and their resistance to custom, their superiority to the sordid craving for increase of national power, their idealism and their ambition to declare the eternal law, the States-General of 1789 are the most memorable of all political assemblies. They cleared away the history of France, and with 2,500 decrees they laid down the plan of a new world for men who were reared in the old. Their institutions perished, but their influence has endured; and the problem of their history is to explain why so genuine a striving for the highest of earthly goods so deplorably failed. The errors that ruined their enterprise may be reduced to one. Having put the nation in the place of the Crown, they invested it with the same unlicensed power, raising no security and no remedy against oppression from below, assuming, or believing, that a government truly representing the people could do no wrong. They acted as if authority, duly constituted, requires no check, and as if no barriers are needed against the nation. The notion common among them, that liberty consists in a good civil code, a notion shared by so famous a Liberal as Madame de Staël, explains the facility with which so many

---

[1] *L.M.H.*, p. 205. Also quoted above (Chapter III).

revolutionists went over to the Empire. But the dreadful convulsion that ensued had a cause for which they were not responsible. In the violent contradiction between the new order of things in France and the inorganic world around it, conflict was irrepressible.[1]

The principle of limitation of power means that there must be a constitution. It is supremely necessary in a democracy to protect the people against itself. Nothing but a constitution can avert arbitrary power.[2] The richest and most flexible of political forms is constitutional monarchy.[3] The object of a constitution is not to confirm the predominance of any interest, but to prevent it. All history has been occupied with the endeavour to upset the balance of power by giving the advantage to money, land or numbers.[4] All the ancient writers on politics were agreed that a mixed or balanced constitution was best. If it has succeeded anywhere, "it has been in our favoured country and in our time."[5]

What is a constitution? The best answers are those given by Hamilton and by Calhoun. Hamilton says: "There ought to be a principle in government capable of resisting the popular current. The principle chiefly intended to be established is this, that there must be a permanent will."[6] More elaborately, and with special reference to federal government, Calhoun expresses the idea as follows:[7]

> The powers which it is necessary for government to possess, in order to repress violence and preserve order, cannot execute themselves. They must be administered by men in whom, like others, the individual are stronger than the social feelings. And hence the powers vested in them to prevent injustice, and oppression on the part of others, will, if left

---

[1] *F.R.*, p. 199.
[2] *Ibid.*, p. 4. The judgment is Fénelon's. Acton accepts it.
[3] *Ibid.*, p. 104. As, for example, in England.
[4] *H.F.*, p. 10.   [5] *Ibid.*, p. 20 (1877).
[6] *H.E.*, p. 130. In the light of the examples given in Chapter II, it has not been thought necessary here to illustrate further Acton's insistence on the element of growth and development.
[7] The unique importance of this passage for Acton's thought is the reason for quoting from it so fully. Acton himself quoted it at much greater length. Cf. Add. 4950: "Constitutional: the sum of indirect influences which restrain the action of the Crown."

unguarded, be by them converted into instruments to oppress the rest of the community. That by which this is prevented, by whatever name called, is what is meant by constitution, in its most comprehensive sense, when applied to government. Having its origin in the same principle of our nature, constitution stands to government as government stands to security; and, as the end for which society is ordained would be defeated without government, so that for which government is ordained would, in a great measure, be defeated without constitution. . . . Constitution is the contrivance of man, while government is of divine ordination. . . . Power can only be resisted by power, and tendency by tendency . . . I call the right of suffrage the indispensable and primary principle; for it would be a great and dangerous mistake to suppose, as many do, that it is of itself sufficient to form constitutional governments. To this erroneous opinion may be traced one of the causes why so few attempts to form constitutional governments have succeeded; and why, of the few which have, so small a number have had durable existence. . . . So far from being of itself sufficient—however well-guarded it might be, and however enlightened the people—it would, unaided by other provisions, leave the government as absolute as it would be in the hands of irresponsible rulers, and with a tendency at least as strong towards oppression and abuse of its powers. . . . The process may be slow, and much time may be required before a compact or organized majority can be formed; but formed it will be in time, even without preconcert or design, by the sure workings of that principle or constitution of our nature in which government itself originates. . . . The dominant majority, for the time, would have the same tendency to oppression and abuse of power which, without the right of suffrage, irresponsible rulers would have. No reason, indeed, can be assigned why the latter would abuse their power, which would not apply with equal force to the former. . . . The minority, for the time, will be as much the governed or subject portion as are the people in an aristocracy, or the subject in a monarchy . . . The duration or uncertainty of the tenure by which power is held cannot of itself counteract the tendency inherent in government to oppression and abuse of power. On the contrary, the very uncertainty of the tenure, combined with the violent party warfare which must ever precede a change of parties under such governments, would rather tend to increase than diminish the tendency to oppression. It is manifest that this provision must be of a character calculated to prevent any one interest, or combination of interests, from using the powers of government to aggrandize itself at the expense of the others. . . . This too can be accomplished in only one way, and that is, by such an organism of the government—and, if necessary for the purpose of the community also—as will, by dividing and distributing the powers of government, give to each division or interest, through its appropriate organ, either a concurrent voice in making and executing the laws or a veto on their execution. . . . Such an organism as this, combined with the right of suffrage, constitutes, in fact, the elements of constitutional government. The one, by rendering those who make and execute the laws responsible to those on whom they operate, prevents the rulers from oppressing the ruled; and the other, by making it impossible for any one interest or combination of interests, or class, or order, or portion of the community, to obtain exclusive control, prevents any one of them from oppressing the other. . . . It is this negative power—the power of preventing or arresting the action of the government—be it called by what term it may, veto, interposition, nullification, check, or balance of power—which in fact forms the constitution. . . . It is, indeed, the negative power which makes the constitution, and the position which makes the government.[1]

Writing in 1861 at the age of twenty-seven, Acton said that Calhoun's arguments in this passage were the perfection of political truth.[2]

Acton expressed substantially the same view twenty years later, with reference to the House of Lords. Writing to Mary Gladstone, he said:

To "sweep away" the House of Lords would be a terrible revolution. The more truly the House of Commons comes to represent the real nation, the more it must fall under the influence of opinion out of doors. It has less and less a substantive and independent will of its own, and serves as a barometer to register the movement going on outside. Now the opinion of a whole nation differs from that of any limited or united or homogenous class by its inconstancy. It is not pervaded by one common interest, trained to the same level,

[1] *Rambler*, 1861, "Political Causes of the American Revolution" [i.e. Civil War].   [2] *Ibid.*

or inspired by one set of ideas. It is rent by contending motives, and its ideas cannot get a firm grip because there is nothing solid to lay hold of. The whole is not more sure to go wrong than a part, but it is sure not to go long the same way. This sort of fluctuation which is unavoidable in the nation has to be kept out of the State, for it would destroy its credit, its influence abroad, and its authority at home. Therefore the more perfect the representative system, the more necessary is some other aid to stability. Six or seven such aids have been devised, and we unite three of them in our House of Lords—Primogeniture, Established Church, and an independent judiciary. Its note is Constancy—the wish to carry into the future the things of the past, the capacity to keep aloof from the strife and aims of the passing hour. As we have none of the other resources proper to unmixed governments, a real veto, a federation of states, or a constitution above the legislature, we must treasure the one security we possess. A single assembly has an immense preponderance of authority and experience against it.[1]

Acton adds:

The worst anybody can imagine is a modification of the House of Lords, such as would make it less independent, less affected by tradition, less united in one interest, but more intelligent and, probably, more powerful. That seems to me possible, though difficult, and uncertain and hazardous in an infinite degree. I do not plead for this, but I cannot set myself absolutely and irrevocably against it. The House of Lords represents one great interest—land. A body which is held together by a common character and has common interests is necessarily disposed to defend them. Individuals are accessible to motives that do not reach multitudes, and may be on their guard against themselves. But a corporation, according to a profound saying, has neither body to kick nor soul to save. The principle of self-interest is sure to tell upon it. The House of Lords feels a stronger duty towards its eldest sons than towards the masses of ignorant, vulgar and greedy people. Therefore, except under very perceptible pressure, it always resists measures aimed at doing good to the poor. It has been almost always in the wrong—sometimes from prejudice and fear and miscalculation, still oftener from instinct and self-preservation. Generally, it does only a tem-

[1] *L.M.G.*, pp. 101–103 (1881).

porary injury, and that is its plea for existence. But the injury may be irreparable. And if we have manifest suffering, degradation, and death on one side, and the risk of a remodelled senate on the other, the certain evil outweighs the contingent danger. For the evil that we apprehend cannot be greater than the evil we know.[1]

As early as 1881 Acton wanted a reform of the House of Lords. This was promised in the preamble to the Parliament Act of 1911, and was further discussed by the leaders of the political parties in 1948.

It is a fundamental axiom of constitutional philosophy that the majority in an elected assembly are nearly always well-meaning. As Acton put it to Mary Gladstone: De Serre, the Restoration statesman, laid it down that "the bulk of a representative assembly is almost always well-meaning (an axiom of constitutional philosophy). Furious outcries from all the royalist benches interrupted him; shouts of '*Vous oubliez la Convention*!' He answered: 'Yes, even the Convention . . . and if the Convention had not voted under the terror of assassins, France would have been spared the most terrible of crimes.'"[2]

Liberty is not the right of doing all that you have the actual power to do. Liberty needs to be secured by certain unalterable rights founded on truths "which men did not invent and may not abjure."[3] This involves definite principles.

The first principle is the division and limitation of power. "Divided, or rather multiplied authorities are the foundation of good government."[4] The true natural check on absolute

---

[1] *L.M.G.*, pp. 101-103 (1881). The function of a constitution, in fact, is to provide for the supremacy of those permanent convictions which rest on certain knowledge. Cf. Add. 4945: "Protection of Property, the object of jurisprudence of Laws. Protection of Liberty, the object of Constitutions." Cf. also Add. 4947: "Notion of a National Conscience: Public opinion, when permanent, after public discussion, and decided, is decisive."

[2] *L.M.G.*, p. 75.

[3] *H.E.*, p. 132 (1866). Cf. *H.F.*, p. 47: "In the eighteenth century, the two ideas of Grotius, that there are certain truths by which every State and every interest must stand or fall, and that society is knit together by a series of real and hypothetical contracts, became, in other hands, the lever that displaced the world."

[4] *Gasquet*, p. 199 (1861). Cf. Add. 4954: "Liberty is partly participation in power—also, ideal limitation."

democracy is the federal system.[1] Legislation ought to be for the people and by the people,[2] as Aquinas rightly pointed out. That means representative[3] and responsible government.[4] But a legislature may be more dangerous than the executive.[5]

Representative democracy consults the electors as to men, not as to measures properly the result of debate.[6] Ideas and principles are the justifying cause of party: "If party is sacred to me as a body of doctrine, it is not as an association of men bound together, not by common convictions but by mutual obligations and engagements. In the life of every great man there is a point where fidelity to ideas, which are the justifying cause of party, diverges from fidelity to arrangements and understandings, which are its machinery."[7] Through Burke, and through American influence upon Burke, "the sordid policy of the Walpolean Whigs became a philosophy, and a combination of expedients was changed into a system of general principles."[8] Or, as Acton wrote elsewhere, "In their appeal to the higher law the Americans professed the purest Whiggism . . . By their closer analysis, and their fearlessness of logical consequences, they transformed the doctrine and modified the party . . . the era of compromise made way for an era of principle."[9] The Whig "seeks that which ought to be elsewhere than in that which is. His standing purpose is to effect change."[10] The Whig system "required that public opinion should control legislation. That could not be done without the liberty of the Press; and the Press was not free while it was forbidden to publish and to discuss the debates of Parliament."[11] The force which makes the law and is above the law is the logic of facts and the opinion of the nation.[12] The best safeguard of the constitution is the independence and the integrity of the judges.[13]

No conflict can be more irreconcilable than that between representation and direct democracy.[14]

[1] *F.R.*, p. 37.   [2] *Ibid.*, p. 2.   [3] *Ibid.*, p. 252.
[4] *Rambler*, 1861, "Political Causes of the American Revolution."
[5] *F.R.*, p. 8. As the French Revolution showed.
[6] *Ibid.*, p. 252.   [7] *L.M.G.*, p. 200 (1884).
[8] *L.M.H.*, p. 276. The American dispute "involved a principle, namely, the right of controlling government" (*H.F.*, p. 55).
[9] *F.R.*, p. 26.   [10] *L.M.H.*, p. 268.
[11] *Ibid.*, p. 276.   [12] *Ibid.*, p. 284.
[13] *H.F.*, p. 59.   [14] *F.R.*, p. 19.

Acton adopted and made his own the French proverb, "Centralization means apoplexy at the centre and paralysis at the circumference," adding that every statesman should have it ever in mind, and never forget that in politics apoplexy is called revolution.[1]

The scientific (i.e. exact) part of politics is economics: "It was the rise of political economy which suggested the idea of applying the methods of science to the art of government."[2] Adam Smith provided a scientific backbone for liberal sentiment.[3]

The principal puzzle in Acton's philosophy of government is, if the British Constitution is the supreme expression of the principle of self-government, why does he speak in even higher terms of American federalism? The answer is that Acton believed that the constitutional securities against democratic tyranny and popular dictatorship were greater and more effective in the American system than in the British. The dread of dictatorship was the deepest of Acton's political sentiments, and popular dictatorship on the Caesarean model had twice raised its ugly head in Europe in the nineteenth century— Napoleon I and Napoleon III. It was, in Acton's view, the danger in universal suffrage. Acton agreed with the unanimous conclusion of the ancient writers that the central problem of practical politics is constituted by (1) the right of the people to govern, (2) their inability to govern alone. The ancient writers correctly concluded that a mixed or balanced constitution was the best. But there is no example in history of such a balanced constitution lasting a century. If it has succeeded anywhere, it is in England—but "we know not yet how long the wisdom of the nation will preserve the equipoise."[4]

America saved liberty for the world in the eighteenth century,[5] and, in the federal system, had provided the solution for the most baffling practical problem in politics:

> [In the French Revolution] People were quite resolved to be oppressed no more by monarchy or aristocracy, but they had no experience or warning of oppression by democracy. The classes were to be harmless; but there was the new

---

[1] *H.F.R.*, April 1864, p. 725. [2] *H.F.*, p. 57.
[3] *Hawarden Letters*, p. 188. [4] *H.F.*, p. 20 (1877).
[5] Letter to Lady Blennerhassett, *Corr.*

enemy, the State. No European knew what security could be needed or provided for the individual from the collected will of the people. They were protected from government by authority or by minority; but they made the majority irresistible, and the plebiscite a tyranny.[1]

The answer to the problem came from America:

> The true natural check on absolute democracy is the federal system, which limits the central government by the powers reserved, and the State governments by the powers they have ceded. It is the one immortal tribute of America to political science, for State rights are at the same time the consummation and the guard of democracy.[2]

As he elsewhere wrote, "It is in political science only that America occupies the first rank. There are six Americans on a level with the foremost Europeans."[3]

Federal ideas had the sanction also of the greatest names in the political literature of France—Montesquieu, Rousseau, Necker, Mirabeau.[4]

Acton concluded his masterly article on Bryce's *American Commonwealth* with two quotations, one from Emerson, the second from Seward. Emerson wrote: "Institutions are not aboriginal, though they existed before we were born. They are not superior to the citizen. Every law and usage was a man's expedient to meet a particular case. We may make as good; we may make better."[5] Seward said: "The rights asserted by our forefathers were not peculiar to themselves, they were the common rights of mankind. The basis of the constitution was laid broader by far than the superstructure which the conflicting interests and prejudices of the day suffered to be erected. The constitution and laws of the federal government did not practically extend those principles throughout the new system of government, but they were plainly promulgated in the declaration of independence. Their complete development and reduction to practical operation constitute the progress which all liberal statesmen desire to promote, and the end of that

---

[1] *F.R.*, p. 104.   [2] *Ibid.*, p. 37.
[3] *H.F.*, p. 578. Five of these were secretaries of state, and one was secretary of the treasury.
[4] *F.R.*, p. 257.   [5] *H.F.*, p. 587 (1889).

progress will be complete political equality among ourselves, and the extension and perfection of institutions similar to our own throughout the world."[1]

Acton studied federal government for more than forty years.[2] It was the subject of one of his earliest important articles[3]—the article which led to his friendship with Gladstone. When he read this article, Gladstone wrote to Acton: "I have read your valuable and remarkable paper. Its principles of politics I embrace; its research and wealth of knowledge I admire: and its whole atmosphere, if I may so speak, is that which I desire to breathe."[4] The argument of the article was that sovereignty resided in the several States, and that by abuse of federal authority, south and north had each alternately attempted policies of economic victimization against the other. His mature view was that it was the absence of a really unambiguous definition of State rights which was the remote cause of the civil war.

The article which he wrote on Bryce's *American Commonwealth* best illustrates the extraordinary depth and range of Acton's study of federalism.[5] He pointed out that one of the very few propositions that Bryce had taken straight from Tocqueville was one of the few which a determined fault-finder would be able to contest. For both say that the need for two Chambers has become an axiom of political science. "But it may be urged that a truth which is disputed is not an axiom; and serious men still imagine a state of things in which an undivided legislature is necessary to resist a too powerful executive, whilst two Chambers can be made to curb and neutralise each other. Both Tocqueville and Turgot are said to have wavered on this

[1] *H.F.*, p. 587 (1889).
[2] Not only in its American form, but in Switzerland and in the Dominions; and he had been actually present at the debates in which one of the American States recast its constitution. So in his *Inaugural* he writes, "The discussions of constituent assemblies, at Philadelphia, Versailles and Paris, at Cadiz and Brussels, at Geneva, Frankfort and Berlin, above nearly all, those of the most enlightened States in the American Union, when they have recast their institutions, are paramount in the literature of politics."
[3] *Rambler*, 1861, "Causes of the American Revolution" [i.e. Civil War].
[4] *Corr.*, p. 158. The letter is dated 8 May 1861, from 11 Downing Street. Acton was twenty-seven at this time, Gladstone twenty years older.
[5] *H.F.*, pp. 575–587 (1889; *aetat.* 55).

point."[1] Acton goes on to compare Bryce's work with that of Holst, who spent twenty years on American debates and newspapers, and whose book, in several thousand pages, though not very well-designed or well-composed, is, "by the prodigious digestion of material, the most instructive ever written on the natural history of federal democracy."[2] Acton notes that Hamilton's argument against removals is mentioned by Bryce "but not the New York edition of *The Federalist* with the marginal note 'Mr. H. had changed his view of the constitution on that point.' "[3] Where Bryce speaks of the almost grotesque confidence of Americans in their constitution, Acton adds, "but this is a sentiment which comes down, not from Washington and Jefferson, but from Grant and Sherman."[4] We have "to distinguish what the nation owes to Madison and Marshall, and what to the army of the Potomac; for men's minds misgave them as to the constitution until it was cemented by the ordeal and the sacrifices of civil war."[5] Hamilton's merits, Acton writes, "can hardly be overstated." "Holst," he adds, "said that Hamilton was the foremost genius among public men in the new world, and Guizot told Rush that *The Federalist* was the greatest work known to him, in the application of elementary principles of government to practical administration."[6] Acton goes on to note that the development of the American constitution was largely the work of Marshall. After a long discussion of Hamilton, Acton concludes with a barbed comment:

> Hamilton stands higher as a political philosopher than as an American partisan. Europeans are generally liberal for the sake of something that is not liberty, and conservative for an object to be conserved; and in a jungle of other motives besides the reason of State we cannot often eliminate unadulterated or disinterested conservatism. We think of land and capital, tradition and custom, the aristocracy and the services, the crown and the altar. It is the singular superiority of Hamilton that he is really anxious about nothing but the exceeding difficulty of quelling the centrifugal forces, and that no kindred and coequal powers divide

[1] *H.F.*, pp. 575–576.
[2] *Ibid.*, p. 577.
[3] *Ibid.*, p. 578.
[4] *Ibid.*, p. 579.
[5] *Ibid.*
[6] *Ibid.*, p. 581.

his attachment or intercept his view. Therefore he is the most scientific of conservative thinkers, and there is not one in whom the doctrine that prefers the ship to the crew can be so profitably studied.[1]

In another place[2] Acton spoke of the arguments of Calhoun and Stephens as forming as essential a constituent in the progress of democratic thinking as Rousseau or Jefferson.

Acton concluded his last lecture at Cambridge with the words, "By the development of the principle of Federalism, it [the Federal Constitution] has produced a community more powerful, more prosperous, more intelligent, and more free than any other which the world has seen."[3]

As the foregoing illustrations have shown, Acton was a democrat with a difference. As he put it in 1888 (*aetat.* 54), "democracy, if not the most scientific notation, is the one that divides us least."[4] Not even a democracy must claim the things that are God's, as well as the things that are Caesar's. As we have also already seen, Acton valued the argument of Sieyès that the true national will proceeds from debate, not election, and the unanimity of ancient writers on the right of the people to govern and their inability to govern alone. The Middle Ages, which solved the great problems of principle, taught that government is illegitimate if it does not rest on consent.

Before illustrating further Acton's view of the true limits of democracy, we must notice that he borrows a distinction from Laboulaye:

> There are two kinds of democracy—the first is that "which obeys and flatters a master, and the next day knocks him down and insults him; such is the democracy of the Caesars, the ignorant and revolutionary democracy, the mob-rule of appetites and passions. The other is the Christian democracy, enlightened and industrious, wherein every individual is

[1] *H.F.*, p. 583. This also illustrates one of Acton's maxims, that an error is not finally disposed of until it has received its most perfect expression (Add. 5470).
[2] *H.E.*, p. 483.
[3] *L.M.H.*, p. 314 (1901). Acton was not ignoring the natural resources of the United States. Earlier he had spoken of the Americans as the heirs of boundless wealth.
[4] *H.E.*, p. 473.

taught from his infancy to govern himself, and to respect the rights of others, the law which protects individual rights, and the authority which guards the law. This is the democracy which the Liberal party loves; this it is which it desires to set up." ... The writer distinguishes between liberties which exist for themselves, and liberties which are the guarantees of the former class—individual and social liberties and political liberties.[1]

Absolute democracy Acton rejects because "absolute government contradicts the Divine law."[2] The self-government of free States requires the constant presence of dispassionate reason: "Of this men must be deprived if they are to be governed by a revolutionary absolutism or an absolute democracy."[3] Or, as he put it in the lecture on the American Revolution, "The nation itself, acting by its representatives, had to be subjected to control."[4] As Constant said, the will of a whole people cannot make just that which is unjust. Further, "No conflict can be more irreconcilable than that between representation and direct democracy."[5]

Liberty depends on the division of power. Democracy tends to unity of power. "To keep asunder the agents, one must divide the sources; that is, one must maintain, or create separate administrative bodies. In view of increasing democracy, a restricted federalism is the one possible check upon concentration and centralism."[6] Some nations are certainly quite unable to govern themselves, and liberty grows, and is not a primitive condition.[7] Democracy is "a part, one of three (or four) elements in the State, which in early undeveloped societies has no place at all, which it is the business of history to raise to its proper level and proportion, and the effort of the revolution to make sole and supreme. The solution is in self-government."[8] In 1862 Acton expressed his entire agreement with the following passage from Tom Paine's *Rights of Man*:

> It is not because a part of the government is elective that makes it less a despotism, if the persons so elected possess afterwards, as a parliament, unlimited powers. Election, in

---

[1] *H.F.R.*, April 1864, p. 725. [2] *Ibid.*, Oct. 1863, p. 691.
[3] *Ibid.*, April 1863, p. 656. [4] *L.M.H.*, p. 309.
[5] *F.R.*, p. 19. [6] *L.M.G.*, p. 124 (1882).
[7] *H.F.R.*, April 1863, p. 656. [8] *Gasquet*, pp. 222–228.

this case, becomes separated from representation, and the candidates are candidates for despotism.[1]

The American dispute "involved a principle, namely, the right of controlling government."[2]

Large constituencies make independent deputies. But experience proves that small assemblies, the consequence of large constituencies, can be managed by government.[3] Unequal electorates afford no security to majorities. Equal electorates give none to minorities. "Thirty-five years ago it was pointed out that the remedy is proportional representation."[4] In a bureaucratic State "everything that stirs independently of Government, and in the mass of the people as such, that is not in their organization, is virtually democratic."[5]

Though Acton regarded Rousseau's later writings as "loaded with sound political wisdom,"[6] he thought his influence was due to what was extreme and systematic and absolute, or as Sir Ernest Barker has recently put it, "totalitarian."[7] What Acton says of Rousseau illumines his own view as nothing else can. In his *French Revolution*, Acton writes:

> [According to Rousseau] There is an implied contract that no part shall ever be preferred to the whole, and minorities shall always obey. . . . The people necessarily sincere, and true, and incorrupt, cannot go wrong; . . . there is a right of resistance to all governments that are fallible, because they are partial, but none against government of the people by the people because it has no master and no judge, and decides in the last instance and alone: . . . insurrection is the law of all unpopular societies . . . and submission that of the only legitimate societies, based on the popular will; that there is no privilege against the law of nature, and no right against the power of all.[8]

Rousseau . . . faithful to Swiss precedent as well as to the logic of his own theory, was a federalist. In Switzerland,

---

[1] *Works*, II, 47.   [2] *H.F.*, p. 55.
[3] *Ibid.*, p. 96.
[4] *Ibid.*, p. 97 (1878). This was due to Hare, who got it from St. Just.
[5] *Gasquet*, p. 154 (1860).
[6] *F.R.*, p. 16 (1895).
[7] *The Social Contract* (World's Classics), Introduction.
[8] *F.R.*, p. 15.

when one half of a canton disagrees with the other, or the country with the town, it is deemed natural that they should break into two, that the general will may not oppress minorities. This multiplication of self-governing communities was admitted by Rousseau as a preservative of unanimity on one hand, and of liberty on the other. Helvetius came to his support with the idea that men are not only equal by nature but alike, and that society is the cause of variation; from which it would follow that everything may be done by laws and by education . . . Rousseau is the author of the strongest political theory that had appeared among men. . . . His books gave the first signal of a universal subversion, and were as fatal to the Republic as to the Monarchy. Although he lives by the social contract and the law of resistance, his later writings are loaded with sound political wisdom. . . . Rousseau's most advanced point was the doctrine that the people are infallible. . . . The maxim that the voice of the people is the voice of God is as old as Alcuin; it was renewed by some of the greatest writers anterior to democracy, by Hooker and Bossuet, and it was employed in our day by Newman to prop his theory of development. Rousseau applied it to the State.

In 1878 Acton eloquently expressed his own view as follows:

Recent experience has added little to the observations of those who witnessed the decline after Pericles, of Thucydides, Aristophanes, Plato, and of the writer whose brilliant tract against the Athenian Republic is printed among the works of Xenophon. The manifest, the avowed difficulty is that democracy, no less than monarchy or aristocracy, sacrifices everything to maintain itself, and strives, with an energy and a plausibility that kings and nobles cannot attain, to override representation, to annul all the forces of resistance and deviation, and to secure, by Plebiscite, Referendum, or Caucus, free play for the will of the majority. The true democratic principle, that the people shall not be made to do what it does not like, is taken to mean that it shall never be required to tolerate what it does not like. The true democratic principle, that every man's free will shall be as unfettered as possible, is taken to mean that the free will of the collective people shall be fettered in nothing. . . . Democracy claims to be not only supreme, without authority above, but absolute, without independence below; to be its own master, not a trustee.¹

But in his manuscript notes Acton copied out the following passage from a letter, dated 16 December 1859, from Cobden to Bright: "If the majority in a democracy injure me and themselves at the same time by unsound legislation, I have at least the consolation of knowing that they are honest in their errors, and that a conviction of their mistake will, for their own sakes, lead to a change."²

In 1891 Acton wrote to Gladstone: "I was, somehow, never compelled to make up my mind about Women's Suffrage . . . But, for many years, I inclined to favour the change . . . It now seems to me that there is no higher law deciding the question, and that it falls within the computation of expediency."³ Writing to Mary Gladstone, he said: "The men who pay wages ought not to be the political masters of those who earn them, for laws ought to be adapted to those who have the heaviest stake in the country, for whom misgovernment means not mortified pride or restricted luxury, but want and pain and degradation, and risk to their own lives and to their children's souls."⁴ Acton put the same essential point when he said of Harrington and Lilburne that in many directions they see as far as we do now.⁵

Acton sharply distinguished English and French democracy, preferring for English democracy the terms self-government, or constitutional monarchy. This is hardly surprising since, in France, universal suffrage had led to the twenty years' dictatorship of Napoleon III. Acton really judges democracy, subject to the qualifications already discussed, in the light of its history. He believed that there was a strong democratic ingredient in the early Whigs.⁶ In a Christian democracy the guarantees and constituent elements are universal suffrage, popular education, national representation, ministerial responsibility, a second chamber, equality before the law, freedom of the Press.⁷

Ideals in politics are never realized, but the pursuit of them determines history.⁸ The fate of every democracy, of every

---

¹ *H.F.*, pp. 93–94.
² Add. 4955.
³ *Corr.*, pp. 234–235.
⁴ *L.M.G.*, pp. 49–50.
⁵ *H.F.*, p. 50.
⁶ *H.F.R.*, Oct. 1863, p. 717.
⁷ *Ibid.*, April 1864, p. 725.
⁸ *Gasquet*, p. 133 (1860).

government based on the sovereignty of the people, depends on the choice it makes between these opposite principles, absolute power on the one hand, and on the other, the restraints of loyalty and the authority of tradition.[1] The point on which the ancient writers were most nearly unanimous is the right of the people to govern, their inability to govern alone, and therefore they adopted the theory of a mixed Constitution, of which Tacitus said that however admirable in theory it was difficult to establish and impossible to maintain. Acton thought that if the problem had been solved anywhere, it was in England in the last quarter of the nineteenth century. The true law of the formation of free States consists in development, evolution, and continuity. The nation, which is the source of its own organic institutions, should be charged with the perpetual custody of their integrity, and with the duty of bringing the form into harmony with its spirit.[2] But the ancient world lacked representative government, emancipation of slaves, liberty of conscience, and government by an elected body was even in theory unknown.

Mediaeval feudalism was the most absolute negation of democracy which has ever co-existed with civilization. The revival of democracy was due to the struggle of Church and State, for both sides appealed to the people. In this way arose the idea of the divine right of the people, an idea which ultimately became strong enough to resist both Church and State.[3] The Middle Ages solved the great question of principle, developed representative government, made taxation inseparable from representation, abolished slavery, and defined the right of insurrection against tyranny. Political authority became limited not only by representation, but by the universal recognition of the higher law which was defined as the law of reason which is the law of God.

In modern times the democratic element present in Calvinism, in the seventeenth-century sects, and in the Spanish Jesuits (Lessius, Molina, Mariana, Suarez), first triumphed through the Independents, but Lilburne, the boldest thinker among English democrats, said it would be better for liberty to bring back Charles Stuart than to live under the sword of the Protector. Lilburne was one of the first to understand the necessary

[1] *Rambler*, May 1861, p. 17.   [2] *H.F.*, p. 59.   [3] *Ibid.*, p. 35.

conditions of democracy and to realize that in England it was economic inequality which prevented its success. The revolution of 1688 confined power to the landed aristocracy—in Defoe's phrase the divine right of the freeholders, and the second revival of democracy was due to America:

> The Stuarts had been willing that the colonies should serve as a refuge from their system of Church and State, and of all their colonies the one most favoured was the territory granted to William Penn. By the principle of the Society to which he belonged, it was necessary that the new State should be founded on liberty and equality. But Penn was further noted among Quakers as a follower of the new doctrine of Toleration. Thus it came to pass that Pennsylvania enjoyed the most democratic constitution in the world, and held up to the admiration of the eighteenth century an almost solitary example of freedom.[1]

According to Acton the American Revolution established a pure democracy—"democracy in its highest perfection, armed and vigilant, less against aristocracy and monarchy than against its own weakness and excess. Whilst England was admired for the safeguards with which, in the course of many centuries, it had fortified liberty against the power of the Crown, America appeared still more worthy of admiration for the safeguards which, in the deliberations of a single year, it had set up against the power of its own sovereign people." Acton continues: "It resembled no other known democracy, for it respected freedom, authority, and law. It resembled no other constitution, for it was contained in half-a-dozen intelligible articles. Ancient Europe opened its mind to two new ideas—that Revolution with very little provocation may be just; and that democracy in very large dimensions may be safe."[2]

---

[1] *H.F.*, p. 84 (1878; *aetat.* 44).
[2] *Ibid.*, pp. 84–85. Cf. the later passages: "It was to enjoy freedom, liberty of conscience, and the right to tax themselves, that they [the American colonists] went into the desert. There were points on which these men anticipated the doctrines of a more unrestrained democracy, for they established their government not on conventions, but on divine right, and they claimed to be infallible" (*F.R.*, p. 21).... "A commentator adds that this notion of the infallible perception by the people of their true interest,

The American Revolution was the spark which turned French revolutionary thought into action. But the French did not realize that democracy must limit itself and avoid the errors of absolute power which the revolution inherited from the old régime, and the Paris mob behaved as irresponsibly as, though not more cruelly than the Bourbon monarchs:

> The deepest cause which made the French Revolution so disastrous to liberty was the theory of equality. Liberty was the watchword of the middle class, equality of the lower. It was the lower class that won the battles of the third estate; that took the Bastille, and made France a constitutional monarchy; that took the Tuileries, and made France a republic. They claimed their reward. The middle class, having cast down the upper orders with the aid of the lower, instituted a new inequality and a privilege for itself. By means of a tax-paying qualification it deprived its confederates of their vote. To those, therefore, who had accomplished the Revolution, its promise was not fulfilled. Equality did nothing for them. The opinion, at that time, was almost universal, that society is founded on an agreement which is voluntary and conditional, and that the links which bind men to it are terminable for sufficient reason, like those which subject them to authority. From these popular premises the logic of Marat drew his sanguinary conclusions. He told the famished people that the conditions on which they had consented to bear their evil lot, and had refrained from violence, had not been kept with them. It was suicide, it was murder, to submit to starve and to see one's children starving, by the fault of the rich. The bonds of society dissolved by the wrong it inflicted. The state of nature had come back, in which every man had a right to what he could take. The time had come for the rich to make way for the poor. With this theory of equality, liberty was quenched in blood, and Frenchmen became ready to sacrifice all other things to save life and fortune.[1]

The following passages further illustrate Acton's view of the French Revolution:

> At the Revolution there were many Frenchmen who saw in federalism the only way to reconcile liberty and demo-

and their unerring pursuit of it, was very prevalent in the provinces, and for a time in the States after the establishment of American independence" (*F.R.*, p. 22).   [1] *H.F.*, pp. 88–89.

cracy, to establish government on contract, and to rescue the country from the crushing preponderance of Paris and the Parisian populace. . . . Mirabeau . . . planned to save the throne by detaching the provinces from the frenzy of the capital, and he declared that the federal system is alone capable of preserving freedom in any great empire.[1]

The French were accustomed to irresponsible power. They were not likely to consent that the power in their hands should be inferior to that which had been exercised over them, or to admit that an entire people is not above the law which it obeys.[2]

The constitutional experiment, first tried on the Continent under Lewis XVI, failed mainly through distrust of the executive and a mechanical misconstruction of the division of power. Government had been incapable, the finances were disordered, the army was disorganized; the monarchy had brought on an invasion which it was now the mission of the Republic to repel. The instinct of freedom made way for the instinct of force, the Liberal movement was definitely reversed, and the change which followed the shock of the First European Coalition was more significant, the angle more acute, than the mere transition from royal to republican forms. Unity of power was the evident need of the moment, and as it could not be bestowed upon a king who was in league with the enemy, it had to be sought in a democracy which should have concentration and vigour for its dominant note. Therefore supremacy was assured to that political party which was most alert in laying its grasp on all the resources of the State, and most resolute in crushing resistance. More than public interests were at stake. Great armies were approaching, guided by vindictive *émigrés*, and they had announced the horrors they were prepared to inflict on the population of Paris.[3]

The Revolution had begun with a Liberalism which was a passion more than a philosophy, and the first Assembly endeavoured to realize it by diminishing authority, weakening the executive, and decentralizing power. In the hour of peril under the Girondins the policy failed, and the Jacobins governed on the principle that power, coming from the people, ought to be concentrated in the fewest possible hands and made absolutely irresistible. Equality became the substitute of liberty, and the danger arose that the most welcome

[1] *F.R.*, p. 37.   [2] *Ibid.*, p. 113.   [3] *Ibid.*, p. 240.

form of equality would be the equal distribution of property. The Jacobin statesmen, the thinkers of the party, undertook to abolish poverty without falling into Socialism. They had the Church property, which served as the basis of the public credit. They had the royal domain, the confiscated estates of emigrants and malignants, the common lands, the forest lands. And in time of war there was the pillage of opulent neighbours. By these operations the income of the peasantry was doubled, and it was deemed possible to relieve the masses from taxation, until, by the immense transfer of property, there should be no poor in the Republic. These schemes were at an end, and the Constitution of the year III closes the revolutionary period.[1]

To understand the development of Acton's philosophy of democracy it will be necessary also to follow in some detail his analysis of nineteenth-century democracy. This is what he says: "The democratic revival after Napoleon came from Spain.[2] The Spaniards had fought against the French for a king who was a prisoner in France. They gave themselves a constitution, and placed his name at the head of it. They had a monarchy without a king. It required to be so contrived that it would work in the absence, possibly the permanent absence, of the monarch. It became, therefore, a monarchy only in name, composed, in fact, of democratic forces. The notion was of a king who should flourish only in name and, as Acton puts it, "should not even discharge the humble function which Hegel assigns to royalty, of dotting 'i's' for the people."[3]

The Cadiz constitution of 1812 was overthrown by the restored monarchy of France in 1823. When, five years later, under Martignac the restored monarchy in France was turning in a constitutional direction, French Liberals were distrustful. Martignac failed. The extreme Royalists came in:

> In labouring to transfer power from the class which the Revolution had enfranchised [i.e. the middle class] to those which it had overthrown [i.e. the aristocracy] Polignac and

---

[1] *F.R.*, pp. 342–343.
[2] *H.F.*, p. 89. The word liberal is also Spanish. (Croce also notices the significance of this.)
[3] *Ibid.*, p. 89.

THE STATE, GOVERNMENT, AND DEMOCRACY

La Bourdonnaie would gladly have made terms with the working man. To break the influence of intellect and capital by means of universal suffrage, was an idea long and zealously advocated by some of their supporters. They had not foresight or ability to divide their adversaries, and they were vanquished by the united democracy.

Later, Acton continues—and this brings him to the heart of his analysis:

> The ministers of Louis Philippe, able and enlightened men, believed that they would make the people prosper if they could have their own way, and could shut out public opinion. They acted as if the intelligent middle class was destined by heaven to govern. The upper class had proved its unfitness before 1789; the lower class, since 1789. Government by professional men, by manufacturers and scholars, was sure to be safe, and almost sure to be reasonable and practical. Money became the object of a political superstition, such as had formerly attached to land, and afterwards to labour. The masses of the people, who had fought against Marmont, became aware that they had not fought for their own benefit. They were still governed by their employers.
>
> When the king parted with Lafayette, and it was found that he would not only reign but govern, the indignation of the republicans found a vent in street fighting. In 1836, when the horrors of the infernal machine had armed the crown with ampler powers, and had silenced the republican party, the term Socialism made its appearance in literature. Tocqueville, who was writing the philosophical chapters that conclude his work, failed to discover the power which the new system was destined to exercise on democracy. Until then, democrats and communists had stood apart. Although the socialist doctrines were defended by the best intellects of France, by Thierry, Comte, Chevalier, and Georges Sand, they excited more attention as a literary curiosity than as the cause of future revolutions. Towards 1840, in the recesses of secret societies, republicans and socialists coalesced. Whilst the Liberal leaders, Lamartine and Barrot, discoursed on the surface concerning reform, Ledru-Rollin and Louis Blanc were quietly digging a grave for the monarchy, the Liberal party, and the reign of wealth. They worked so well, and the vanquished republicans recovered so thoroughly, by this coalition, the influence they had lost by a long series of

crimes and follies, that, in 1848, they were able to conquer without fighting. The fruit of their victory was universal suffrage.[1]

From that time the promises of Socialism have supplied the best energy of democracy. Their coalition has been the ruling fact in French politics.[2]

Acton goes on to say that this coalition created "the saviour of society," and the Commune, and that it still (i.e. in 1878) entangled the footsteps of the Republic. "It is the only shape in which democracy has found an entrance into Germany. Liberty has lost its spell; and democracy maintains itself by the promise of substantial gifts to the masses of the people."

It is in the light of his historical analysis that Acton's judgment on democracy, to which the above leads up, must be taken. He points out that the ablest political writers of his own generation—Tocqueville, Calhoun, Mill, and Laboulaye—have drawn, in the name of freedom, a formidable indictment against it. "They have shown democracy without respect for the past or care for the future, regardless of public faith and of national honour, extravagant and inconstant, jealous of talent and of knowledge, indifferent to justice but servile towards opinion, incapable of organization, impatient of authority, averse from obedience, hostile to religion and to established law." Acton continues: "Evidence indeed abounds even if the true cause be not proved ... As much might be made good against monarchy, and an unsympathizing reasoner might in the same way argue that religion is intolerant, that conscience makes cowards, that piety rejoices in fraud."

But between 1878, when these words were written, and the end of his life, 1902, Acton's view of democracy was modified in the light of English, French, and American experience. The most prosperous nations in the world, he wrote, France and America, are governed by the masses. His last lecture at Cambridge concluded, as we have seen, with a reference to the United States in the words "a community more powerful, more prosperous, more intelligent, and more free than any other which the world has seen."[3] Shortly before he had referred to "that force which makes the law and is above the law, the

[1] *H.F.*, pp. 91–92.   [2] *Ibid.*   [3] *L.M.H.*, p. 314.

logic of facts and the opinion of the nation."[1] As he put it in a letter in 1881: "There is no constructive power among the Whigs. There is some among the Democrats, because their principles have been thought out, and provide legislation for generations."[2]

There was always a note of reserve in Acton's view of democracy. He believed that there was a strong temptation in a democracy for men to be swayed by the mass, and not to face up to their moral responsibility,[3] and that there was often an affinity between democracy and conservatism, though he once wrote (1877) that socialism (i.e. complete socialism) was "the infirmity that attends mature democracies."[4] The extension of the franchise in 1884 he thought marked a crisis in the British constitution. As late as the date of the *Inaugural* (1895) he confessed that he foresaw no certainty of the triumph of what is ethically right. He believed that it was due to the genius of one man, Gladstone, that in England democracy had not led to class war or mob rule. Under Gladstone, he wrote, democracy has set bounds to its power, and this was Gladstone's work.[5] In his manuscripts he wrote that there was just a very little Aristotle in the nineteenth-century version of the doctrine of the "golden mean," and just a very little Plato in modern socialism.[6] America was unique in having deliberately contrived effective constitutional checks to prevent abuse of the power of the majority. Yet he also copied in his notes the following passage from Harrington: "God who has given his law to the soul of that man who shall voluntarily receive it is the only interpreter of his law to that soul: such at least is the judgment of Democracy."[7]

Democracy means conscience; but to be effective there must be constitutional safeguards to secure the supremacy of those tested convictions which rest on experience and certain knowledge. Or, as Acton put it in another manuscript, "Not what each man chooses—But what all men believe, is law."[8] In another manuscript (Add. 4939) Acton writes: "The essence of Democracy to esteem the rights of others as one's own was

[1] *L.M.H.*, p. 264 (1899).
[2] *L.M.G.*, p. 117.
[3] Add. 4916.
[4] *H.F.*, p. 63.
[5] *Corr.*, p. 235.
[6] Add. 4916.
[7] "System of Politics," *Works*, 509.
[8] Add. 4901.

not only Stoic. It received a glorious sanction from Christ"; and in Add. 4945: "Why Democracy? It means, Liberty given to the mass. Where there is no powerful democracy, freedom does not reign."[1]

[1] Add. 4870. (Under heading "Is law obj[ective] or subj[ective]. See Usteri, Ihering, Schmidt, Hahn, Rödet, Walter.")
Cf. Add 4945: "Conservatism. There is no answer to their case, apart from religion. If happiness is the end of Society, then liberty is superfluous. It does not make men happy.... It is the sphere of duty—not of rights." Cf. also Add. 4944: "Not prosperity or material progress, not happiness or civilisation, not science or religion, not democracy or nationality, all these things have been its [liberty's] tributaries and servants—but they have, in turn, been rivals and obstacles"; and Add. 4950: "Distinction between liberal and democratic contained in that between conscience, opinion."

V

SOCIALISM

REVIEWING the works of Molinari, the Belgian economist, in 1864, Acton, then aged thirty, expressed his disagreement with what he referred to as the socialist system of universal administration.[1] Six years earlier he had been trying to arrange for the review of Robert Owen's autobiography immediately it appeared.[2] In 1873 he tried hard to persuade Gladstone to read Marx's *Capital*, expressed surprise that Gladstone had not yet had time to read it, and indicated the book's importance as the *Koran* of the new socialists.[3] In the famous essay on nationality Acton said that the theory of nationalism was more criminal and absurd than the theory of socialism,[4] and in a number of passages in his study of democracy Acton's disagreement at that date (1878) with socialism is distinctly marked.

Acton traces the use of the term Socialism to 1836, though he notices earlier writers such as Mably, Morelly and Fourier, and he regards the last as the real originator of modern socialism.[5] Tocqueville, at that time, failed to notice the influence of socialism on democracy. Till then democrats and socialists had stood apart. Socialist doctrines were defended by the best intellects of France, by Thierry, Comte, Chevalier, and Georges Sand.[6] Republicans and socialists combined towards 1840. This co-operation was so effective that they easily overturned the July Monarchy in 1848 and the result was universal suffrage. Since then socialism has been the inspiration of democracy. The violent and revolutionary condition of France was primarily due to the antagonism of rich and poor, of property

---

[1] *H.F.R.*, Jan. 1864, pp. 310–312.

[2] *Gasquet*, p. 35. There are a number of quotations from Owen, and from Marx in the Acton MSS., the latter mainly from the *Critique of Political Economy*.

[3] *Corr.*, p. 169. [4] *H.F.*, pp. 299–300.

[5] *Hawarden Letters*. More's *Utopia* he terms the origin of modern communism. [6] *H.F.*, pp. 91–92 (1878).

and labour, and this was the cause of the socialist character of the revolution of 1848.[1] Universal suffrage led to Napoleon III, and the combination of republicans and socialists produced the Commune of 1871 and was the most important element under the Third Republic. Socialism was the only form in which democracy made any headway in Germany.

In 1878 Acton believed that economics was destined to achieve the kind of certainty that belongs to natural science. He therefore expected at that date that the controversy between economists and socialists would reach a final decision. But he emphasized that a new phase of the struggle had emerged through the rise of a middle party, the academic socialists, represented by such economists as Roscher and Wagner. Acton regarded this movement as the most serious attempt that had ever been made to disprove the weighty judgment of Rousseau, that democracy is a government for gods, but unfit for man.[2]

The academic socialists, or socialists of the chair, captured most of the more important economic professorships in Germany, and had their counterparts in France (Laveleye) and England (Ingram and Cliffe Leslie). The most eminent of these men was Roscher. And when Acton first read Henry George he wrote that he was less impressed than he otherwise would have been because he had previously met most of Henry George's ideas in the writings of the academic socialists.[3] He added that he believed that Henry George had in large measure the ideas of the age to come.[4] Acton regarded Gladstone as a practical exponent of the main ideas of the academic socialist school. He said he agreed with Chamberlain that there was latent socialism in the Gladstonian philosophy.[5] He regarded socialism, as we have seen, as the chief inspiration of democracy, and as early as 1881 he foresaw that its programme would be the work of generations.[6] In one of his letters Acton spoke rather drily of economists who are not made sleepless by thinking of the sufferings of the poor, and in another of "working children to death in factories." As early as the sixties, discussing the poor law, he wrote that those in want through no fault of

[1] *Rambler*, Oct. 1862, p. 551.
[2] *H.F.*, pp. 94–99.
[3] *L.M.G.*, p. 170 (1883).
[4] *Ibid.*, p. 175 (1884).
[5] *Ibid.*, p. 212 (1885).
[6] *L.M.G.*, p. 117.

their own, have a claim on the State.[1] But at that time he was suspicious of public works to relieve unemployment as likely to increase the power and possible tyranny of the State (he was thinking more particularly of Napoleon III).

Acton's estimate of Roscher gives one clue to his maturer views on these questions. He regarded Roscher and Tocqueville as the two most important writers of the nineteenth century, and he noted that Roscher regarded the *Réforme Sociale* of Le Play as the most important book on social science.[2] Roscher's starting point was that the ancients understood distribution better than we do.[3] He began his work at the time when some of the generalizations of the classical economists were being severely criticized in the light of comparative statistics.[4] Acton noticed the judgment of Dunoyer, that socialism is merely the present system logically carried out. But, he adds, on the other side, if it is right that the State should do so much, the reign of the log was usurpation, and the ancient ways were wrong. Then the indictment brought by Considérant and Engels against the society of 1840 is just, and the order of things which produced so much sorrow was criminal.[5] Here it has to be remembered that Acton regarded economics as being as much an ethical as a material science.[6] And a warmer note can also be detected in the reference in 1888 to the question why some socialists are liberal.[7]

The foregoing passages can be supplemented by the notes he made on socialism, which are in the Acton MSS. in the Cambridge University Library. These are contained in a folder (Add. MSS., 5487) in which are 167 pages or slips. These are of the greatest interest as showing the steps by which Acton reached his conclusions, and his method, which was not to rest content till he had succeeded in putting together a stronger case for the view he rejected than its supporters themselves could furnish. This makes his conclusions all the more impressive when they are reached. It should, however, be emphasized

---

[1] *Gasquet*, p. 246.
[2] *H.E.*, p. 386 (1886). Acton puts Le Play in the category "Partial Socialism" (Add. 5487).
[3] *Ibid.*, p. 389. [4] *Ibid.*
[5] *Ibid.*, pp. 390–391. [6] *Ibid.*, p. 176 (1861).
[7] *Ibid.*, pp. 488–489.

that, as it is not possible to date these notes exactly, and as they are almost certainly prior to the *Letters to Mary Gladstone* quoted above, and to the article in the *Historical Review* in 1886, they do not modify, but only amplify what is stated earlier, and where there is a conflict, the printed material is in general a better guide to Acton's final conclusions. The salient passages, which are in note form, are given below:

Acton begins his notes (page 1): "Observe—Conservatives said that Communism is the consequence of Liberalism. The Communists easily believed it. And the influence of religion, though in favour of patience, was not in favour of confidence." Acton proceeds to put down all that he can find to say in favour of socialism[1] before giving his own judgment. These notes run as follows:

> Socialism. Sanctioned by Religion, by philosophy, by the experience of great nations—Revelation. Catholic and Protestant authorities supported it. How respectable it appeared. . . . Communism could not seem a crime to anyone. The Fathers. Berthold. The Franciscans. Humanists. The law of association and property in common. . . . In France Socialism attacked economy—and the Socialists were beaten by the economists. Proudhon by Bastiat. But Bastiat made matters worse by his Harmony. Instead of conciliation he hardened the antagonism. In Germany it began late. From Fichte down, it only repeated foreign theories. At last Rodbertus Marx Lassalle. Pol. economy could not stand this attack. Some points gave way. (Pages 9–12.)

Acton then turns to note the direction of social change:

> The whole progress of society is towards the elevation of masses. Centuries have been at work upon it. The theory of progress, of liberty, of equality, are preached and praised alike by science and by religion. And then, new masses of men find themselves unbenefited by this general law. Brentano's new book shows this best. . . . Socialism arises from equality. Also from state of nature. [It says] Renounce effects of conquest and violence in the State, also in society. Return to primitive liberty, before class divisions, also as to

---

[1] *Acton MSS.*, Add. 5487, pp. 9, 11, 12, 14, 15, 16, 18, 19, 23–25, 30, 31, 34, 37, 38. It seems probable that some, possibly all of the notes, are prior to 1878, when the essay on democracy was first published.

property. It belonged to the community. This should be restored. All this failed in the Fr. Rev. S. Simon and Fourier failed. It rose again by the alliance 1836 [i.e. of socialists and republicans].[1]

Acton then notes the relation of socialism to religion:

> Idea not repugnant to Canon Law, of administering the wealth of the rich for the good of the poor. . . . Socialism common wherever there is intense religious zeal. . . . Essenes, Early Christians, Anabaptists, Monasticism, Camisards . . . In early Xty. [Socialism] believed by the Fathers. But not exactly a law—only a tendency. It failed. It remained a thing to strive for. Besides the actual friends of Socialism—Fathers, Canon Law, mendicant orders, O[ld] T[estament] . . . Many gave indirect encouragement: Locke . . ., Smith, Malthus, Montesquieu? Rousseau? . . . Communism already in XIV century. Wicliffe's position towards it—Arnold of Brescia, Paschalis II, The Franciscans, The Waldenses, The Lollards, The Taborites, The Brethren, The Mystics. It came with a great momentum. Especially where there were Sects. Here was a new Sect, a new departure. . . . Cousin. The purest and most desirable happiness comes from the happiness of others. How the monks did it, especially the mendicants. Thus it came down to the moderns with a great prestige.[2]

Meanwhile Acton had considered other arguments:

> France 1750—Socialism was sporadic until then, in literature. Then it began to tell—and was a fixed product of French thought. So also the idea of progress. . . . [Comparative statistics quoted] proves the weakness of economic laws by which men are made to suffer. . . . Condition of Europe after 1830, when industry grew so strong. Laws made by a class, in its own interest. Emigration discouraged, to keep down the price of labour. . . . Nothing done for education—even discouraged. Association of labour forbidden by law. No factory laws. Slavery under England, France, Spain, Portugal, Holland. Serfdom in Russia. Servitude in

---

[1] *Acton MSS.*, Add. 5487, pp. 14, 15. Cf. the statement of one socialist argument in a later MS. which reads: "Socialism: Holmbury, Aug. 26 1893. Power dependent on property. When power is declared equal, property should be equal." (Add. 4952).

[2] Add. 5487, pp. 16, 18, 23, 24, 30, 38.

Germany, Austria. . . . Confiscations of the Rev[olution] confirmed by the Restoration . . . By the Charte . . . If they could confiscate what they chose for the public good—that is socialism. If it could be done for the safety of the Govt. it could be done for the poor. . . . Lilburne wished properties to be equal.[1]

After noting these arguments Acton writes (p. 39): "Socialism the worst of all enemies of freedom because, if it could fulfil what it promises, it would render such a service to the world that the interests of freedom would pale, and mankind would carry over its allegiance to the benefactor who had a higher claim on its gratitude."[2] Acton adds (pp.41–42): "Socialism is not a product of our age, though only now terrible . . . Only the French Rev[olution] made it formidable." He continues (p. 42): "Liberty essential to full energy of labour. Private property to economy—security of the future. Development of the proletariate by the French Revolution. Labour is the whole of society. . . . The established order overturned—questioned—exposed. In nothing so absurd as in the promotion of poverty."

Acton adds the following reflections (pp. 47, 55, 58):

This century has seen the growth of the worst enemy freedom has ever had to encounter—Socialism. Strong, because it solves a problem pol[itical] economy has, until now, failed to solve. How to provide that the increase of wealth shall not be at the expense of its distribution. Truth, that what the speechless masses of the poor need is not political privileges which they cannot enjoy, but comfort—without which political influence is a mockery or a snare. It has made the common movement of politics contemptible. Can only be realised by a tremendous despotism.[3] Christianity needs hostile to the accumulation of wealth. . . . Promotes the comfort of the poor. Favours equitable distribution. Therefore some form of Socialism is clearly Christian. . . . The Incas had an exact Census, a thing unknown to the Spaniards. It was a system of communistic distribution of land. And the most terrible despotism on earth.

[1] *Ibid.*, pp. 19, 25, 31, 34, 37.
[2] Acton's definition of freedom is the security of the weaker groups and freedom of conscience, and its necessary securities, i.e. self-government.
[3] I take this to refer to socialism not "comfort."

The remainder of the notes (pp. 60–167) give Acton's final conclusion:

> Com[munism] Admitted that the existing economy of society condemned—irrevocable doom, misery, depravity, untimely death—In the terrible language of one of the greatest economists: Malthus III admits A. S[mith] did not attend sufficiently to the poor and thought that the funds used for labour increased with national wealth—which is wrong. . . . Justin says: *Erant omnia communia* . . . Thus there was participation in power from the first, but not liberty—for there was no personal property. Property is collective until there is security. Where there is security, then there is personal property, and then there may be liberty. . . . Socialism . . . not without success in Paraguay . . . On the old ground, Socialism cannot be beaten.[1] . . . Scientific Socialism the greatest recent event in the history of Dem[ocracy]. Attempt to obtain the legitimate reforms, without the dangerous change threatened. This is part of the Remedy.[2]

It seems clear that it is against complete, that is, totalitarian socialism that Acton's strictures are directed, and that it is to liberal socialism that his views ultimately incline—as much socialism, that is, as the disinterested study of economics warrants. This really follows directly from his initial assumptions: (1) private enterprise had failed to solve the problem of distribution; (2) what the poor needed before they could make their political power effective was comfort and security; (3)

---

[1] That is, at the level of abstraction of the classical economists.

[2] The most probable interpretation of Acton's meaning in this context is the socialism of the academic socialists. Roscher differed from them by his international point of view. Wagner, whom Acton specially commended, favoured the nationalization of some industries. (See Rae, *Contemporary Socialism*, Chapter XI—"State Socialism." Rae regards Wagner's position as substantially identical with that of Rodbertus.) The academic socialists were pioneers in the economic interpretation of history. Acton studied all the economists of the historical school—Roscher, Wagner, Hildebrand, Knies, Schmoller, Brentano and many others. Max Weber is, of course, the best known member of the historical school today. He has to be studied in the light of Professor Tawney's criticisms, especially for his neglect of Machiavelli. One of the best known appreciations of the historical school as a whole is by Schumpeter. Here too the most important idea is the idea of development.

division of power is the condition of liberty; (4) the right of self-government is inherent in all corporations and associations.

For these reasons the State must not control the whole of economic life. And Acton was greatly interested in the ideas of Marlo, which in some respects resembled those of the English Guild Socialists. I think Acton would have sympathized with their ideals. The best example of the successful working of the principle is in the government of the ancient Universities, which practise the old mediaeval principle of self-government, subject to occasional guidance at long intervals by a Royal Commission and an Act of Parliament.

This conclusion is confirmed by a passage in the *History of Freedom*: "The political produce of the Middle Ages was a system of States in which authority was restricted by the representation of powerful classes, by privileged associations and by the acknowledgment of duties superior to those which are imposed by man. As regards the realization in practice of what was seen to be good, there was almost everything to do. But the great problems of principle had been solved."[1] Among the privileged associations referred to were the mediaeval guilds.

No one can be sure what view Acton would have adopted on contemporary economic issues. What is certain is the principles and tests he would have employed. Of every proposal he would have asked, Is it just? Is it in accordance with the permanent will of the community? Is it practicable? Will it be efficient? Will it increase or diminish real freedom?

His overriding judgment is that liberal progress aims at a point where the public is subject to no restrictions but those of which it feels the advantage.[2] This judgment may be supplemented from a later manuscript where, after enumerating the social and political gains since the end of the seventeenth century, he wrote a list under the heading, How much to come? The first three items on the list are Peace, Socialism, Education.[3]

It has not been generally recognized how thoroughly Acton studied economics and socialism. The reference to the second edition of the first volume of *Das Kapital* in the letter to Gladstone in 1873 as a new book, implies that Acton had compared the second edition with the first, issued six years earlier, and

[1] H.F., p. 39 (1877). [2] Ibid., p. 23 (1877). [3] Add. 4870.

had recognized it for what it has since been realized to be, namely, virtually a new book. Acton had previously read Marx's much earlier *Critique of Political Economy*, and the copy with his own annotations is in the Acton Library at Cambridge. He quoted from the *Anti-Dühring* in one of the notes to his *Inaugural*. In one of his manuscripts he lists under the heading Partial Socialism the following names: Le Play, Wagner, Schäffle, Schmoller, Held, Cherbuliez, Brentano.[1] Another page of the same manuscript lists eighteen writers on Communism. He read the economists of many schools, Marshall, Marlo, Cournot, to name only a few. He notes the circulation figures for socialist newspapers in Germany, and the growth of social democracy in Zurich. Acton is the only nineteenth-century writer who was completely master of the philosophy, politics, and economics of both his own age and of earlier ages also.

The intensity of Acton's feeling about the social question may be judged from the following passage written in 1878:

> The old notions of civil liberty and of social order did not benefit the masses of the people. Wealth increased, without relieving their wants. The progress of knowledge left them in abject ignorance. Religion flourished, but failed to reach them. Society, whose laws were made by the upper class alone, announced that the best thing for the poor is not to be born, and the next best, to die in childhood, and suffered them to live in misery and crime and pain. As surely as the long reign of the rich has been employed in promoting the accumulation of wealth, the advent of the poor to power will be followed by schemes for diffusing it.[2]

Acton was a true prophet. He was in favour of as much socialism as is compatible with real freedom and a sense of economic responsibility. He believed that the diffusion of wealth was one of the ways in which the State could give real, though indirect help to the individual.

[1] Add. 5487.   [2] *H.F.*, p. 94.

VI

NATIONALITY AND POWER

ACTON'S essay on nationality, published in 1862, and written when he was only 28, has been more widely studied and discussed than any of his writings.[1] In the inter-war period it was frequently referred to, notably in the writings of Mr. C. A. Macartney, Professor E. H. Carr, and in the study group report on nationalism published by the Royal Institute of International Affairs. This is the more remarkable in that it can be estimated with reasonable confidence that little in the essay would have been left unmodified if Acton had revised it in later life. It remains none the less an extremely illuminating study, and is one of the many examples of Acton's almost uncanny prophetic insight. Its value has also been noticed in the United States and it is extensively quoted in the volume in Professor Langer's series by Professor R. C. Binkley on *Realism and Nationalism*.[2]

The argument of the essay is as follows. Before the French Revolution the rights of nationalities were neither recognized by governments nor asserted by the people.[3] The interest of the reigning families, not those of the nations, determined the frontiers. "The eighteenth century acquiesced in this oblivion of corporate rights on the Continent, for the absolutists cared only for the State, and the Liberals only for the individual."[4] In war-time, as there was no national cause at stake, there was no attempt to rouse national feeling. "The courtesy of the rulers towards each other was proportionate to the contempt for the lower orders."[5] The art of war became a slow and learned game.

The modern problem of nationality began with the partition of Poland. There the monarchy was elective; and the ruler was outside the charmed circle of dynastic relationships. "A

[1] Reprinted in *History of Freedom and Other Essays* (London, 1907).
[2] New York, 1935. [3] *H.F.*, p. 273.
[4] *Ibid.* [5] *Ibid.*, p. 274.

monarch without royal blood, a crown bestowed by the nation, were an anomaly and an outrage in that age of dynastic absolutism. The country was excluded from the European system by the nature of its institutions. It excited a cupidity which could not be satisfied. It gave the reigning families of Europe no hope of permanently strengthening themselves by intermarriage with its rulers, or of obtaining it by bequest or inheritance."[1] The partition of Poland was an act of wanton violence, committed in open defiance of popular feeling and public law. For the first time in modern history a great State was suppressed, and a whole nation divided among its enemies.

The partition of Poland, the most revolutionary act of the age of absolutism, awakened the theory of nationality, converting a dormant right into an aspiration, and a sentiment into a political claim. "No wise or honest man," wrote Burke, "can approve of that partition, or can contemplate it without prognosticating great mischief from it to all countries at some future time."[2] Acton comments: "Thenceforward there was a nation demanding to be united in a State—a soul, as it were, wandering in search of a body in which to begin life over again."[3] The cry was raised that a whole people was deprived of its right to constitute an independent community. Before the claim could be effectively asserted, the Europe of the old régime had been laid in ruins by the revolutionary and Napoleonic wars.

The modern theory of nationality arose partly as a consequence of, partly as a reaction against, the French Revolution. As the system which overlooked nationality was opposed by Liberalism in two forms, the English and the French, so the supporters of nationality proceed on the very different principles of the English Revolution of 1688 and of the French Revolution of 1789. When the France of history fell and the old sovereignty was destroyed, a new principle of unity was needed. The state of nature was made the basis of the nation, and descent was put in the place of tradition. The French people was regarded as a physical product, not a historic unit. "It was assumed that a unity existed separate from the representation and the government, wholly independent of the

---

[1] *H.F.*, p. 275.
[2] "Observations on the Conduct of the Ministry," *Works*, v, 112, quoted by Acton, *op. cit.*, p. 275.   [3] *H.F.*, p. 376.

past, and capable at any moment of expressing or of changing its mind. In the words of Sieyès, it was no longer France, but some unknown country to which the nation was transported."[1] The central power possessed an authority derived from the whole people. Its power and its will were personified in the Republic One and Indivisible. "The title signified that a part could not speak or act for the whole—that there was a power supreme over the State, distinct from, and independent of, its members; and it expressed, for the first time in history, the notion of an abstract nationality."[2] In this way, the idea of the sovereignty of the people gave birth to the idea of nationality.[3]

Later Napoleon called a new power into existence by attacking nationality in Russia, delivering it in Italy, and by governing in defiance of it in Germany and in Spain:

> The sovereigns of these countries were deposed or degraded; and a system of administration was introduced which was French in its origin, its spirit, and its instruments. The people resisted the change. The movement against it was popular and spontaneous, because the rulers were absent or helpless; and it was national, because it was directed against foreign institutions. In Tyrol, in Spain, and afterwards in Prussia, the people did not receive the impulse from the government, but undertook of their own accord to cast out the armies and the ideas of revolutionized France. Men were made conscious of the national element of the revolution by its conquests, not in its rise. The three things which the Empire most openly oppressed—religion, national independence, and political liberty—united in a short-lived league to animate the great uprising by which Napoleon fell. Under the influence of that memorable alliance a political spirit was called forth on the Continent, which clung to freedom and abhorred revolution, and sought to restore, to develop, and to reform the decayed national institutions.[4]

The principle of nationality, which the first partition of Poland had generated, to which the French Revolution had given a basis of theory, which had been stimulated by reaction against Napoleon, received its hardest blow at the Congress of

---

[1] H.F., p. 277. [2] Ibid.
[3] Ibid. [4] Ibid., pp. 281–282.

Vienna and was, writes Acton, "matured by the long error of the Restoration into a consistent doctrine."[1] The absolute monarchs of Eastern Europe "devoted themselves to suppress with equal care the revolutionary spirit by which they had been threatened, and the national spirit by which they had been restored."[2] Austria took the lead in repressing it. In the period that ensued, the idea that national claims are above all other rights gradually came to predominate. Finally it became the complete and consistent theory, that the State and the nation must be co-extensive. "It is," says Mill, "in general a necessary condition of free institutions, that the boundaries of governments should coincide in the main with those of nationalities."[3]

Mazzini was the chief prophet of nationalism, which developed chiefly in opposition to Austria.[4]

The real cause of the energy which the national theory has acquired was, however, the triumph of the democratic principle in France, and its recognition by the European Powers.[5]

"The theory of nationality," writes Acton, "is involved in the democratic theory of the sovereignty of the general will."[6] To have a collective will, unity is necessary, and independence is required in order to assert it. Unity and nationality are more essential to the notion of the sovereignty of the people than the dismissal of monarchs, or the revocation of laws. The absolutism against which nationality revolts denies equally that absolute right of national unity which is a product of democracy, and the claim of national liberty which belongs to the theory of freedom. "These two views of nationality, corresponding to the French and to the English systems, are connected in name only, and are in reality the opposite extremes of political thought."[7] In the one case nationality is founded on the perpetual supremacy of the collective will, in the other nationality is an essential but not a supreme element in determining the

---

[1] *H.F.*, p. 283. [2] *Ibid.*
[3] *Considerations on Representative Government*, quoted by Acton, *H.F.*, p. 298. Cf. Woodrow Wilson's similar ideas, which underlay the settlement of 1919.
[4] Compare the following passage written in 1877: "The singular co-operation of the purest Conservative intellect with red-handed revolution, of Niebuhr with Mazzini, was made to yield the idea of nationality, which, far more than the idea of liberty, has governed the movement of the present age." *H.F.*, p. 59.
[5] *Ibid.*, p. 287.   [6] *Ibid.*   [7] *Ibid.*, p. 288.

forms of the State. "Whenever," writes Acton, "a single definite object [other than liberty] is made the supreme end of the State, be it the advantage of a class, the safety or the power of the country, the greatest happiness of the greatest number, or the support of any speculative idea, the State becomes for the time inevitably absolute."[1] While the theory of unity makes the nation a source of despotism and revolution, the theory of liberty regards it as the bulwark of self-government, and the foremost limit to the excessive power of the State. The combination of different nations in one State is as necessary a condition of civilized life as the combination of men in society. Christianity rejoices at the mixture of races as paganism identifies itself with their differences. In the ancient world idolatry and nationality went together, and the same term is applied in Scripture to both. Christianity imposed a new principle of self-government, and a nation became a moral and political being developed in the course of history by the action of the State.[2] The difference between nationality and the State is that our connection with the race is merely natural or physical, our duties to the political nation are ethical.[3]

The denial of nationality implies the denial of political liberty.[4]

"The greatest adversary of the rights of nationality is the modern theory of nationality."[5] By making the State and the nation commensurate with each other in theory, it reduces practically to a subject condition all other nationalities within the frontiers.

Acton concludes as follows:

> If we take the establishment of liberty for the realization of moral duties to be the end of civil society, we must conclude that those States are substantially the most perfect which . . . include various distinct nationalities without oppressing them. The theory of nationality is a retrograde step in history. First, it is a chimera. The settlement at which it aims is impossible. Secondly, the national theory marks the end of the revolutionary doctrine and its logical exhaustion. In proclaiming the supremacy of the rights of nationality,

[1] *H.F.*, p. 288.
[2] *Ibid.*, pp. 291–292.
[3] *Ibid.*, p. 292.
[4] *Ibid.*, p. 297.
[5] *Ibid.*

the system of democratic equality goes beyond its own extreme boundary, and falls into contradiction with itself by setting up a principle above democracy itself. Its course will be marked with material as well as moral ruin.

The experience of Europe between 1862, when these words were written, and 1950, only serves to underline the significance and the accuracy of Acton's predictions.

Later Acton appears to have modified his view, and to have thought it not unreasonable that men should wish the State to take its limits from the nation,[1] and his vision widens from the multi-national State to a world of federal democracies.[2]

But as late as 1888 Acton wrote to Gladstone: "Nationality is the great carrier of custom, of unreflecting habit and transmitted ideas that quench individuality. Nationality has to be dealt with discriminatingly. It is not always liberal or constructive."[3] A late manuscript in Add. 4940 reads: "N.B. Reasons for nationality. Rémusat. Mill. Proceeds from Democracy. Uniform opinion, on a foundation not educated."

The Master of Trinity writes in his Autobiography:

"Dons of all subjects crowded to his [Acton's] oracular lectures, which were sometimes puzzling but always impressive. He had the brow of Plato, and the bearing of a sage who was also a man of the great world. . . . What he said was always interesting, but sometimes strange. I remember, for instance, his saying to me that States based on the unity of a single race, like modern Italy and Germany, would prove a danger to liberty; I did not see what he meant at the time, but I do now!"[4]

In the documents on Hitler's foreign policy published by the United States State Department on 17 July 1949 there is one, known as the Hossbach Memorandum, which expounded clearly to a meeting of military chiefs held on 10 November 1937 the nature of Hitler's policy. One sentence reads: "The aim of German policy was to make secure and to preserve the racial community and to enlarge it. It was therefore a question of space."[5]

---

[1] *H.E.*, p. 348 (1886).   [2] *Ibid.*, p. 587 (1889).
[3] *Corr.*, p. 182. The best clue to Acton's mature views on nationality is his support of Home Rule for Ireland.
[4] G. M. Trevelyan, *An Autobiography and Other Essays* (1949), p. 18.
[5] *The Times*, 18 July 1949.

Acton's maturer views on German nationalism appear in his manuscripts. This is what he writes:[1]

"For generations European politics turned on the impotence of Germany. Prussia made it potent."

Treitschke maintains that what may be "a true ideal" of politics "in the Atlantic" is not such "in a state which is not isolated."

Treitschke is instructive for us, because he is an "example of the aversion for England that has arisen in the new Germany."[2]

What we have to do is "to judge [and] try the cause of history, and politics, which is living history, not by a physical or [a] metaphysical, but by a moral standard."

"[Treitschke] rather admires Canning. [In the pages of Treitschke] Canning appears as a great statesman guided by no purpose but the interests of commercial England, but disguising this, his true and legitimate policy, by clever pretences of humanity, liberality, sympathy with the oppressed, respect for the sacred rights of nations."

"[Treitschke] generally attacks the Tories. [For him] they are men who flinch from the trouble of thinking."

In the light of the doctrine of continuity, which goes back from Sybel and Ranke to Burke and Leibniz, Treitschke has on his hands the problem of explaining the innovating policy of Prussia.

One German writer [Rotteck] has pointed out the "poverty of German Liberalism," and this is specially true if it is compared with, say, French Liberalism as represented by Constant. The same writer argues that "German Liberalism [is] merely theoretical." It is "not founded on class interests," and is "not an expression of force." In this it is "unlike [German] socialism."

Treitschke is "indignant about" the British occupation of the Transvaal and "angry at the Jingoes for bringing on the Turkish War."

The Frankfort Parliament of 1848 was called the "professors' parliament." "The professors who there failed to create an empire by votes, proceeded to do it by creating opinion. They

[1] This section is based on Add. 4956.
[2] This part of the manuscript probably dates from about 1890—or possibly earlier.

worked for the first time for a cause. History began to be written for a purpose. That purpose was to repress sympathy with Austria, with the smaller States, with Catholicism, with Democracy, and to make men feel the need of shelter and concentration under the most vigorous and the most intelligent of monarchical governments."

"In a famous and characteristic passage Mommsen declares that [ancient] Rome reigned over the barbarous West by virtue of superior culture, and over the cultured East, by superior organization. [This is] the same title by which England rules over the splendour of Delhi[1] and the desolation of Saskatchewan."

"The new creation—[the new German Empire]—demanded a new theory. Authority was repudiated by the war of 1866, Nationality by the possession of Posen."

There remained "Liberalism."

"All established theories [were either] insuff[icient] or perilous in application.

"Nationality gives a short shrift to the holders of Poland, Conservatism [was] condemned by the war of 1866." "Liberalism" [so called] was the result.

Treitschke "would admit even this." "The real thing [in his eyes] is the higher organization and culture"—the plea by which Mommsen defended Rome.

For Treitschke "the future depended on emancipation from Austria. The Zollverein, the Universities—[these] were the first step." Prussia he calls "the land of social freedom."

"But [in fact] here is conservative authority in a new form. [In reality] they oppose liberality all along the line. Other antagonisms are reconciled; they will make terms with Austria, [with] Socialism, [with] the Pope, [with] the Jews, never with the party doctrine that would sacrifice the [German] empire to preserve a principle."

"They may ally themselves with Austria, with the proletariat, with the Pope, with the Jews—but not with Liberals."

Treitschke "thinks that a minister must ultimately yield to parliament. [He] vaguely thinks [that] a sort of practical Liberalism lies before Bismarck."

[1] In another place Acton referred to "the saying of the philosopher, that Liberalism will lose India."

He is "suspicious of confessionalism," and he calls "divines the born worshippers of power."

Acton warned England of the German danger in an article published in 1886, exposing the Prussian doctrine that whatever is, is right.[1] He reiterated the warning in his Cambridge lectures a dozen years later.

Acton's remark about power has become proverbial: "Power tends to corrupt, and absolute power corrupts absolutely."[2] In his *Ethical and Political Thinking*[3] Mr. Carritt observes that the thought is Greek. In his *Inaugural* Acton said, "suspect power more than vice."[4] In the notes he quoted two passages which illustrate the same idea. One is from Leibniz: "those who have more power are liable to sin more; no theorem in geometry is more certain than this."[5] The other is from Wordsworth: "There is, in fact, an unconquerable tendency in all power, save that of knowledge, acting by and through knowledge, to injure the mind of him by whom that power is exercised."[6] Acton quoted the dictum of Fénelon, "power is poison." And we have already noticed Acton's alternative form of the same judgment, "the possession of unlimited power corrodes the conscience, hardens the heart, and confounds the understanding."[7] But Mary Gladstone records that at the very end of his life Acton regretted the severity of some of his judgments.[8]

The prophet of power is Machiavelli: "Knowledge, civilization, and morality have increased; but three centuries have borne enduring witness to his political veracity."[9] The authentic interpreter of Machiavelli, "the *Commentarius Perpetuus* of the *Discorsi* and *The Prince*, is the whole of later history."[10] By plausible and dangerous paths men are drawn to the doctrine of the justice of History, of judgment by results, "the nursling of the nineteenth century, from which a sharp incline leads to *The Prince*."[11]

[1] *H.E.*, p. 382. For the relation of nationality to the idea of development cf. Acton's manuscript notes on Burke quoted in Chapter II *ante*.
[2] Letter to Creighton, 1887. *H.E.*, p. 504.
[3] Oxford, 1947. [4] *L.M.H.*, p. 24.
[5] *Ibid.*, p. 339. [6] *Ibid.*
[7] *H.F.*, p. 11 (1877). [8] *Acton, Gladstone and Others.*
[9] *H.F.*, p. 212 (1891). [10] *Ibid.*
[11] *Ibid.*, p. 219.

When we say that public life is not an affair of morality, that there is no available rule of right and wrong, that men must be judged by their age, that the code shifts with the longitude, that the wisdom which governs the event is superior to our own, "we carry obscurely tribute to the system which bears so odious a name."[1] Morley maintains that the equity of history requires that we shall judge men of action by the standards of men of action. Retz thinks that the vices of an archbishop may be the virtues of a party leader. Many successful public men deprecate what Sir Henry Taylor calls much weak sensibility of conscience. Lord Grey said to Princess Lieven, "I am a great lover of morality, public and private; but the intercourse of nations cannot be strictly regulated by that rule." While Burke was denouncing the French Revolution, Walpole wrote: "No great country was ever saved by good men, because good men will not go to the lengths that may be necessary." The main principle of Machiavelli is asserted by Bacon, his most eminent English disciple: "It is the solecism of power to think to command the end, and yet not to endure the means." Acton adds that Bacon leads up to the familiar Jesuit: The end justifies the means.

The austere Pascal said that justice changed its quality in changing its climate. "Locke, according to Mr. Bain, holds that we shall scarcely find any rule of morality, excepting such as are necessary to hold society together, and these too with great limitations, but what is somewhere or other set aside, and an opposite established by whole societies of men."[2] A critic of Montesquieu extracts from him the conclusion that nothing is absolute in religion, ethics, reason or politics. Turgot discovered in the mercantile economists the doctrine of Helvetius that there is no place for probity in the relations of States.

With the Germans *"Die Weltgeschichte ist das Weltgericht"* became a popular epigram. The same identification of history with justice is shown in the indecisive Providentialism which French have shared with English divines. Thirlwall hesitates to say that whatever is, is best, but, he writes, "I have a strong faith that it is for the best."

An optimism ranging to the bounds of fatalism is the philosophy of many, especially of historians. Scherer describes

[1] *H.F.*, p. 219.   [2] *Ibid.*, p. 220.

progress as objective logic, Ranke calls Time the best touchstone, and Sybel regards the judgment as a profound generalization. The doctrine of success is common to Richelieu and Napoleon. Darwin, having met Carlyle, noted that "in his eyes might was right," and added that he had a narrow, unscientific mind. Goldwin Smith professed to discover the same lesson: "History, of itself, if observed as science observes the facts of the physical world, can scarcely give man any principle or any object of allegiance, unless it be success." Martineau attributed the same doctrine to Mill: "Do we ask what determines the moral quality of actions? We are referred, not to their spring, but to their consequences." Bentham used to relate how he found the greatest happiness principle in 1768, and gave a shilling for it, at the corner of Queen's College, Oxford. He found it in Priestley. He might have gone on finding it in Beccaria and Hutcheson, all of whom trace their pedigree to the *Mandragola*. It is the centre of unity in all Machiavelli, and "gives him touch, not with unconscious imitators only, but with the most conspicuous race of reasoners in the century."[1]

What, in England, has been the occasional aphorism of a masterful mind, has been supported abroad in accredited systems and successful political movements. "When Hegel was dominant to the Rhine, and [his disciple] Cousin beyond it," circumstances favoured the reputation of Machiavelli. For Hegel taught that the course of history stood beyond and outside virtue, vice, and justice. Cousin taught that the apology of an age consisted in its existence. Renan concluded that honesty is the worst policy.

The national movement which united Italy and Germany opened a new era for Machiavelli. Italians and Germans constructed, not securities, but forces. "Machiavelli's time had come."[2] Men said that he was simply a faithful observer of facts, that he discovered the true line of progress and the law of future society. It was said that he was a patriot, a republican, a Liberal, and, above all, a man sagacious enough to know that politics is an inductive science.

The Italian Revolution, passing from the Liberal to the national stage, adopted his name and placed itself under his

[1] *H.F.*, p. 223.   [2] *Ibid.*, p. 225.

invocation. The first act of the provisional government of Tuscany in 1859 was to issue a decree for the publication of a complete edition of Machiavelli at the public expense.

Laurent observed that Machiavelli's posterity had vowed his name to infamy while practising his doctrine. Baudrillart recognized his universality, saying he was the politician of every century. In Kuno Fischer's progress through the systems of metaphysics, "Machiavelli appears at almost every step."[1] His influence is visible to Dr. Abbott throughout the whole of Bacon's political writings. "Hobbes followed up his theory to the conclusions which he abstained from."[2] Fichte set himself to rehabilitate him, declaring that it would be absurd to robe a prince in the cowl of a monk. Ranke said that Machiavelli was a meritorious writer maligned by people who could not understand him. Freeman complained that Mommsen seemed unable to understand that a small State can have any rights.[3] Acton concludes:

> He [Machiavelli] is the earliest conscious and articulate exponent of certain living forces in the present world. Religion, progressive enlightenment, the perpetual vigilance of public opinion, have not reduced his empire, or disproved the justice of his conception of mankind. He obtains a new lease of life from causes that are still prevailing, and from doctrines that are apparent in politics, philosophy, and science. Without sparing censure, or employing for comparison the grosser symptoms of the age, we find him near our common level, and perceive that he is not a vanishing type, but a constant and contemporary influence. Where it is impossible to praise, to defend or excuse, the burden of blame may yet be lightened by adjustment and distribution, and he is more rationally intelligible when illustrated by lights falling not only from the century he wrote in, but from our own, which has seen the course of its history twenty-five times diverted by actual or attempted crime.[4]

Twice elsewhere Acton gave his judgment on Machiavelli:

> Machiavelli was an acute politician, sincerely anxious that the obstacles to the intelligent government of Italy should be swept away. It appeared to him that the most

[1] *H.F.*, p. 228.   [2] *Ibid.*
[3] *Ibid.*, p. 222.   [4] *Ibid.*, p. 231.

vexatious obstacle to intellect is conscience, and that the vigorous use of statecraft necessary for the success of difficult schemes would never be made if governments allowed themselves to be hampered by the precepts of the copy-book. Machiavelli's teaching would hardly have stood the test of Parliamentary government, for public discussion demands at least the profession of good faith. It gave an immense impulse to absolutism by a studied philosophy of crime.[1]

As there is no such thing as right, politics are an affair of might, a mere struggle for power. Such was the doctrine which Venice practised . . . and which two illustrious writers, Machiavelli and Guicciardini, made the law of modern societies.[2]

Venice "was a republic not of landowners but of shipowners." It was the first to revert to the ancient notion of the State acting for its own purposes.[3]

In the sixteenth century, with the triumph of Charles V, the motive of domination became a reigning force in Europe . . . It was the supreme manifestation of the modern State according to the image which Machiavelli had set up, the State that suffers neither limit nor equality, and is bound by no duty to nations or to men, that thrives on destruction, and sanctifies whatever things contributed to increase of power.

This law of the modern world, that power tends to expand indefinitely, and will transcend all barriers, abroad and at home, until met by superior forces, produces the rhythmic movement of History. Neither race, nor religion, nor political theory has been in the same degree an incentive to the perpetuation of universal enmity and national strife. The threatened interests were compelled to unite for the self-government of nations, the toleration of religions, and the rights of man. And it is by the combined efforts of the weak, made under compulsion, to resist the reign of force and constant wrong, that, in the rapid change but slow progress of four hundred years, liberty has been preserved, and secured, and extended, and finally understood.[4]

Those who remember with honour men like Hampden and Washington, regard with a corresponding aversion Peter the

---

[1] *H.F.*, pp. 40–41 (1877).   [2] *L.M.H.*, p. 81 (1899).
[3] *L.M.H.*, p. 172.   [4] *L.M.H.*, p. 289 (1899).

Great and Frederick William I. "But without the first, Europe might be French, and without the other, it might be Russian."[1]

The common element in Richelieu, Peter the Great, Frederick the Great, Napoleon, Bismarck, is that their idol was the absolute State, the State regarded as power released from duty.

"The true theory of freedom excludes all absolute power."[2] This principle was recognized by the end of the Middle Ages, when "absolute power was deemed more intolerable and more criminal than slavery."[3] The mediaeval theory of politics "restrained the State in the interest of the moral law, of the Church, and of the individual."[4] That is part of the true philosophy of politics.

[1] *L.M.H.*, p. 172.
[2] *H.F.*, p. 153.
[3] *Ibid.*, p. 39.
[4] *L.M.H.*, p. 80.

VII

THE IMPORTANCE OF IDEAS

THE importance of ideas was one of Acton's favourite themes. In his *Inaugural* he spoke of ideas "which are not the effect but the cause of public events."[1] Ideas are "the spiritual property that gives dignity and grace and intellectual value to history."[2] "Ideas which, in religion and in politics, are truths, in history are forces. They must be respected; they must not be affirmed."[3] From the scientists we may learn the development of ideas which "are the charter of progress and the vital spark in history."[4]

Elsewhere Acton speaks of the eighteen or twenty systems of ideas which had made the age he lived in—most of them religions or substitutes for religion. Towards the end of his review of Bright's *History of England* (1837–1880) Acton writes:

> The question would remain whether it is best ... to make history with individual character, class interests, and the fortuitous changes of opinion, or with the ceaseless conflict of defined forms of thought ... It would be a luminous moment if, for the perpetual round of violence and weakness, folly and crime, somebody would display the operation of the original materials that supplied the French Revolution, the distinct systems that divided the three assemblies and

---

[1] *L.M.H.*, p. 3. Cf. Add. 4946: "Germinal events—ideas; and Add. 4949: "The Whig governed by compromise. The Liberal begins the reign of ideas." Cf. also: "Ideas mainly govern the world. That is the reason of progress. If they alone governed, progress would be constant. Because demonstration is irresistible. But it is partly governed by habit, conditions, interests, passions. All this retards. Laplace against steamboats, Arago against railways. It is a law. Not founded on dullness" (Add. 4941); and Add. 4943: "Study of history better than writing of history. The writer sacrifices so much for effect. This to fix images on men's minds. And the image conceals the reality. History deals with ideas—facts alone useless."

[2] *L.M.H.*, p. 3.

[3] *Ibid.*, p. 17. This is rather the view of the scientific historians whose philosophy Acton was stating than of Acton himself.

[4] *Ibid.*, p. 21.

THE IMPORTANCE OF IDEAS

governed the several constitutions; the eighteenth-century law of nature, the American rights of man, English parliamentary institutions, the abstract constitutionalism of Montesquieu, Voltaire's humanitarian code, Protestant toleration, Jansenist theories of Church and State, the perfectibility of the encyclopaedists, the Whiggism of Holbach, the Helvetian doctrine of equality, Rousseau's democracy, the socialism of Mably, Turgot's political economy, the unguarded sentence in the *Wealth of Nations* which gave to the Provençal priest the fulcrum to overturn the monarchy of Louis XIV, the conditional contract which Marat transmuted into a theory of massacre.[1]

Similarly in a letter to Mary Gladstone (15 March 1880) he refers to "the impersonal forces which rule the world, such as predestination, equality, divine right, secularism, congregationalism, nationality, and whatever other ruling ideas have grouped and propelled associations of men."[2]

And again, to the same correspondent:

> We all know some twenty or thirty predominant currents of thought or attitudes of mind or system-bearing principles, which jointly or severally weave the web of human history and constitute the civilized opinion of the age. All these, I imagine, a serious man ought to understand, in whatever strength or weakness they possess, in their causes and effects, and in their relations to each other. The majority of them are either religions or substitutes for religion. For instance, Lutheran, Puritan, Anglican, Ultramontane, Socinian, Congregational, Mystic, Rationalist, Utilitarian, Pantheist, Positivist, Pessimist, Materialist, and so on.[3]

Twenty years earlier Acton entertained a similar view, but with a shorter list of "systems of thought." Writing to Simpson, he says:

> There are half-a-dozen systems prevailing in the country, one worse than the other, and if each of them received such elucidatory treatment as you have bestowed upon this Positivist [Buckle], the result would be a complete diagnosis of the state of English intellect. The utilitarian school has much sympathy with the regular Positivists, though distinct from them. . . . Then there would be the "Apostles of the

---

[1] *H.E.*, p. 488.   [2] *L.M.G.*, p. 8.   [3] *Ibid.*, p. 167 (1883).

Flesh," "the muscular Christians," more popular in their action, but with a kind of speculative foundation—Kingsley, Maurice, etc.[1]

In another letter printed by Gasquet, Acton wrote: "I venerate that villainous adventurer [Raleigh] for his ideas on political economy[2] and universal history."

Referring to the Commonwealth period, Acton says: "Seen from a distance the value of that epoch is not in that which it created, for it left not creations but ruins, but in the prodigious wealth of ideas which it sent into the world. It supplied the English Revolution, the one that succeeded, the American, the French, with its material. And its ideas became efficacious and masterful by denying their origin. For at first they were religious, not political theories. When they renounced their theological parentage, and were translated into the scientific terms of politics, they conquered and spread over the nations as general truths, not as British exports."[3]

Acton adds:

> Our topic is, how absolute monarchy, which just then succeeded so brilliantly over the Channel, was attempted in England, under conditions of no apparent danger, failed and failed at a great cost. And how, in the course of the struggle, ideas were developed which proved ultimately strong enough, as well as sufficiently lasting, to carry out an entirely new structure of constitutional government. It is the point where the history of nations turned into its modern bed. It is the point where the Englishman became the leader of the world.[4]

Acton's "philosophy of philosophy" is given in the following passages:

> Those ... who believe that the world is governed ultimately by ideas, and that some analysis of these ideas is necessary if we are to think at all, are neither surprised nor disturbed by the fact that no philosophy is able to establish itself as a final solution of the difficulties involved in the

---

[1] *Gasquet*, p. 21 (1858).

[2] P. 353 (1869). Raleigh's economic ideas are discussed in Dr. Bonar's book on early theories of population.

[3] *L.M.H.*, p. 205. Also quoted *ante*, Chapter III.

[4] *Ibid.*, p. 205.

existing world. To them it is no condemnation of a philosophy that it makes way for another, or is followed by a temporary lull in philosophical interest. The test by which they would judge a philosophical thinker is not whether his conclusions are accepted at the present hour, but whether he gave any real impulse to thought, whether his influence proved an abiding one, whether his ideas, changed it may be in form and modified by further knowledge, have passed into the ordinary thoughts and language of men. And it is because they regard this as the true criterion, because they refuse to believe that any great philosophy, however much its conclusions may be modified, can really pass away—that they regard the isolation which has characterized English philosophy during the last century [i.e. since Hume] as a subject of regret.[1]

Philosophical discussion must remain barren and profitless as long as the terms in dispute are considered without reference to the history of their origin. It is only when we become acquainted with history that we are able to appreciate them at their worth. We are saved from a rough and ready rejection of metaphysical abstractions when we find that the physical sciences themselves are based on metaphysical abstractions derived from the early philosophy of Greece.[2]

To amuse Mary Gladstone Acton wrote in her Diary the intellectual history of the world in a hundred names (1884).[3] Here are some selections, which illustrate as nothing else could the importance Acton attached to ideas, and which even at the cost of some monotony it is worth while to quote:

> Confucius "limited and guided the thought of a quarter of mankind." The Avesta "taught the purest unrevealed religion." Buddha "made the most tolerant religion the most numerous." Herodotus invented history. Hippocrates

---

[1] *Chronicle*, 30 Nov. 1867, p. 859.   [2] *Ibid.*
[3] *Hawarden Letters*, pp. 187-191. To be precise, a list of the hundred books which "had most moved the world" (omitting the Bible)—with a list of brief reasons for the choice. Mountstuart Grant Duff congratulated Mary Gladstone, adding "Acton the Great." The names and the reasons for the choice were written on different pages. I have put them together. Occasionally I have adapted a phrase to make the sentence run more easily, or to turn a comment into a sentence, e.g. for "Herodotus. Invention of history" I have put "Herodotus invented history."

"founded medicine." Plato's is "the strongest and most lasting philosophy."[1] Aristotle "instituted the art of discerning truths." Zeno "led men to the Gate of Christianity." Archimedes discovered mechanics. The Almagest [of Ptolemy] gave "an explanation of the universe which for 1600 years satisfied everybody except Alphonso of Castile." Pliny "governed men's ideas of Nature till yesterday." Cyprian discusses the organization of ecclesiastical unity. Origen was responsible for the "conception of religious science." Eusebius "preserves the knowledge of Early Christianity." Athanasius "predominated over Arianism." Augustine was "the deepest influence of one mind in the Church." Pelagius "gave religious form to the most powerful of errors." St. Vincent of Lérins "exposed the theory of tradition." Pseudo-Dionysius introduced Pagan ideas into Christianity. The Salic Law was "the victorious formula of Teutonic Society." Tribonian "twice ruled the world with 1,000 years between." Plutarch's *Moralia* provided "the Charter of the Ascetic Life." The Koran—"stronger than the Gospel for half of Christendom." Anselm devised "a mercantile system of religion." Abelard illustrates the "use of religion apart from faith." Gratian "propounded persecution as an ecclesiastical law." Peter Lombard provided the "framework of mediaeval theology." Maimonides "influenced alike Christian,[2] Moslem and Jew." St. Francis originated "the strongest religious idea since the Apostles." Aquinas "devised Whiggism to prop religious absolutism." Roger Bacon in his *Opus Majus* suggested the discovery of America. Dante's *Divine Comedy* exhibits "imagination and faith without reasoning faculty." In Gerson Imperialism blossomed into Gallicanism. The *Imitatio Christi* "touched the largest number of Christian Souls." Lorenzo Valla tested ecclesiastical question by scientific methods. Raymond Lully "established the theory of Witchcraft." Machiavelli "released Power from Duty." Erasmus "revealed antiquity." Luther ascribed divine right to the "civil power in Church and State." Calvin "wrought Protestant principles into a system." Socinus, the teacher of toleration, founded Unitarianism. The *De Revolutionibus* [of Copernicus] [marked] "the emancipation of science." Loyola "organized arbitrary

---

[1] Cf. *H.F.*, p. 18. "The most splendid intellect ever bestowed on man."
[2] e.g. Aquinas and Albertus Magnus. Dr. Leon Roth has published a study of Maimonides and Descartes (O.U.P.).

power in religion." Montaigne is the "earliest classic of scepticism." Hooker's *Ecclesiastical Polity* gives the "Anglican philosophy of Church and State." Baronius "first held a mirror to Catholicism." Francis Bacon "subjected Philosophy to experiment." Kepler "discovered the laws of the universe." Galileo originated "inductive science." In Grotius "International Law gave birth to the Rights of Man." Descartes "gave new tests of certainty." Harvey was the "starting point of scientific medicine." Jansen (by his *Augustinus*) "produced that division in the French Church which led to its fall, spoilt the Revolution and inaugurated Imperialism." Robinson [famous for his Farewell to the Pilgrim Fathers] propounded "The Atomic Theory in Church and State." Spinoza provided "Ethics without Dogma." Bayle (by his *Dictionary*) "founded rationalism." Richard Simon was the "first [to embark on] Biblical criticism." Newton's *Principia* gives the "Laws of Nature." Fénelon's Télémaque "dissevered religion from dogma." Locke "founded rights and duties on sense." Leibniz expounded the "notion of continuity." Thomasius placed "human sense above divine law." Voltaire "made Deism popular." Montesquieu defined the theory of Constitutionalism.[1] Hume's Essays constituted a "philosophy of negation." Helvetius made "materialism a basis of morals, politics, and education." Rousseau "built up democracy on the natural equality and innocence of man." Beccaria "introduced reason into criminal law." The *Encyclopédie* shows "reason and humanity without spiritual faith." Turgot "inspired the legislators of the Revolution." Tom Paine's Commonsense was the "signal of American independence" [see F. S. Oliver's *Hamilton*]. Adam Smith's *Wealth of Nations* gave a "scientific backbone to liberal sentiment." Herder was the "source of specific German unbelief." Kant's *Critique of Practical Reason*—"Infallible reign of Conscience a substitute for God." Hamilton's *Federalist* is the "textbook of Conservative Democracy." The most famous pamphlet of Sieyès (*Qu'est-ce que le tiers état*) provides "the design of the Revolution." Burke's *Appeal from the New to the Old Whigs* "differentiated Whig from Liberal." Condorcet's *Tableau des Progrès* is the work of "the dogmatist of Perfectibility and Progress." Lavoisier was "the making of chemistry." Laplace propounded the "mechanical scheme of the Universe." Fourier [in 1808, by his *Théorie des Quatre*

---

[1] "The Constitutional theory defined."

Mouvements] "originated modern socialism." De Maistre's *Du Pape* forged the "alliance of Religion with absolute Monarchy." Bentham "opposed Utility to Authority and Revolution." Savigny showed "Evolution in History." Niebuhr was the pioneer of method in historical research. Hegel argued for "continuous development in Institutions and Doctrine." Strauss is the critical investigator of the Origin of Christianity. [Grimm's] *Comparative Grammatik* originated "comparative method in Language," and Cuvier in Physiology. Fénelon's *Lettre à M. Dacier* showed the way to the discovery of the East. Comte put "scientific observation in place of God." Quetelet made Statistics a guide to Government; Oersted ("Electricity"), Charles Darwin ("Evolution in Nature"), and Vinet ("Conscience and Liberty a law in Church and State") conclude the list.

This list should be rounded off by three other names to which Acton attached great importance: Marx ("the *Koran* of the New Socialists"—Letter to Gladstone, 1873), Roscher (Historical Economics), and Cournot, the mathematical economist, whom Acton was "urgently recommending" in 1895.

Acton regarded French revolutionary ideas as the cause of the war with England in 1793, and particularly the Decrees of 19th November and 15th December 1792, the former calling upon all peoples to rise against their governments, the latter threatening with war any people which did not revolt:

> The successful convulsion in France led to a convulsion in Europe; and the Convention which, in the first illusions of victory, promised brotherhood to populations striking for freedom, was impolitic, but was not illogical. . . . Nobody imagined that the new system of international relations could be carried into effect without resistance or sacrifice, but the enthusiasts of liberty, true or false, might well account it worth all that it must cost, even if the price was to be twenty years of war. This new dogma is the real cause of the breach with England.[1]

What Acton said in 1862 (*aetat.* 28) about governments founded on religion also well illustrates the importance of ideas, and is curiously relevant to Russia (and its foundation, the communist religion) and to Eastern Europe in 1949:

[1] *F.R.*, pp. 317–318.

A religious government depends for its existence on the belief of the people. Preservation of the faith is *ratio summa status*, to which everything else must yield. Therefore, not only the civil power enforces the religious law, but the transgressions of the religious must be watched and denounced—therefore espionage and religious detectives, and the use of the peculiar means of information religion provides to give warning to police. The domain of conscience not distinct, therefore, from the domain of the State—sins, crimes, and sins against faith, even when private, without proselytism, are acts of treason. Seclusion from the rest of the world necessarily follows, if the rest of the world has not the same religion, or even if it is not governed on the same principle. Therefore travel and commerce, facilities of communication, etc., necessarily proscribed, for they would be solvents of a State founded on religion only. But all these prohibitions restrain material as well as intellectual well-being. Poverty and stationary cultivation, that is to say, in comparison to the rest of the world, retrogression, the price of such a government. Two things put an end to this. The economical dependence on other countries which needs ensure, ultimately breaks down the seclusion, as the determination of capital to exploit undeveloped resources is resistless in the long run. And the increase of communication gradually destroys barriers and brings the forbidden knowledge and desires into the sequestered community. All this is perfectly applicable to Tibet or Merv.[1]

It is unnecessary to give further examples of the supreme importance Acton attached to ethical ideas and the idea and analysis of conscience. In the history of political doctrine he believed nearly every chapter had still to be written[2] and he regarded the revolution of 1688 ("the greatest thing done by the English nation") as establishing the doctrine that the State is founded on contract. In his letter to Creighton he writes that Christianity is not a mere system of metaphysics which borrowed some ethics from elsewhere. "It is rather a system of ethics which borrowed its metaphysics elsewhere."[3] Acton's

---

[1] *Gasquet*, pp. 253–256, 5 Jan. 1862.

[2] *F.R.*, p. 164. "In the history of political doctrine, where almost every chapter has yet to be written, none will be more valuable than the one that will show what is permanent and progressive in the ideas he [Sieyès] originated."

[3] *H.E.*, p. 504.

quotations in his *Inaugural* from Cournot's *Marche des Idées* and the same writer's *Enchaînement des Idées Fondamentales* further illustrate the general point. "The idea of freedom," Acton wrote, "has two hundred definitions."

The lecture on the heralds of the French Revolution[1] is full of illustrations of the importance Acton attached to ideas, and especially those of Montesquieu, Voltaire, Turgot, Rousseau and Diderot. The American Revolution was the spark which turned thought into action. And the ideas of Adam Smith are the real source of socialism.[2] "Ideas are the justifying cause of party."[3]

> The danger which menaces the continuance of our constitution proceeds simply from the oblivion of those Christian ideas by which it was originally inspired.[4]

Acton's place in the history of thought is shown by the fact that he had a sharper sense of interpendences than any of his contemporaries, e.g. he notes that Liberalism flourished when the idea of conscience flourished, and he adopts the view of Cuvier of the conjunction between the course of inductive science and the progress of civilization.

Acton did not think ideas the only progressive forces in history. He thought that advance was "along diagonals," that is, compromises between ideas and ideals on the one hand, and on the other, class interests, prejudice, and custom.[5]

NOTE ON HUME

The place of Hume in the history of thought is so special that there is a defining power in the relation to him of any other thinker. For this reason it is worth noting the evidence for Acton's view of him. The decisive one is the compendious summary of Hume's *Essays* in one line already quoted (written in Mary Gladstone's Diary): "Philosophy of Negation."[6] Acton regarded Hume as, in one sense, derived from Locke. He notices Hume's writings on the influence of climate[7] and the doctrine "sequence is cause."[8] Acton has an amusing com-

---

[1] *F.R.*, Chapter I. [2] *L.M.G.*, p. 92. [3] *Ibid.*, p. 200.
[4] *H.F.*, p. 209 (1858; *aetat.* 24). [5] *H.E.*, pp. 488–489.
[6] *Hawarden Letters*, pp. 188–189.
[7] *H.E.*, p. 332. [8] *Ibid.*, p. 336.

ment on Hume's view of Machiavelli: "Hume spoils a serious remark by a glaring eighteenth-century comment: 'There is scarcely any maxim in *The Prince* which subsequent experience has not entirely refuted. The errors of this politician proceeded, in a great measure, from his having lived in too early an age of the world to be a good judge of political truth.' "

VIII

THE ADVANCEMENT OF LEARNING[1]

SINCE the French Revolution historiography and sociology have shown the influence of the contrasted conservative and liberal schools. German conservative historiography was a reaction against the French Revolution and was inspired by Burke. When the French revolutionary armies conquered Germany they left no institution standing but the monarchy of Frederick the Great. The Germans fortified themselves against French revolutionary ideas by studying the past, attempting to subject the will and conscience of the living to the will and conscience of the dead.[2] They never realized that the Revolution itself was historic, having roots that could be traced far back in the ages. But they doubled the horizon of Europe, studied India as well as Greece, mediaeval as well as classical Rome. Mythology and philology also felt their influence. Creuzer's *Mythology*, Bopp's *Conjugations*, Grimm's enthusiasm for ancestral Germany and Otfried Müller's zeal for the factor of race were among its products.

The Conservative line of writers, under the name of the romantic or historical school, had its seat in Germany, looked upon the revolution as an alien episode, the error of an age, a disease to be treated by the investigation of its origin, and strove to unite the broken threads, and to restore the normal conditions of organic evolution. The Liberal school, whose home was France, explained and justified the Revolution as a true development, and the ripened fruit of all history. These are the two main arguments of the generation to which we

---

[1] This chapter is condensed from essays, lectures and manuscripts. In Acton the development of knowledge is an integral part of the philosophy of freedom. Cf. *H.F.*, p. 2: "Its [liberty's] advance is recorded in the increase of knowledge, as much as in the improvement of laws." Cf. also Add. 4944: "Those great and comprehensive thinkers, who are the lawgivers and founders of knowledge. Buckle's *Hist. of Civilization*, II, 388."

[2] *H.E.*, p. 346 (1886).

owe the notion and the scientific methods of history.[1] These constitute a deeper movement in the human mind than the Renaissance itself.

The conservative writers were inspired by Burke's maxim that wisdom and religion dictate that we should follow events, not lead or force them. When their ideas were taken up by reasoners they were found to involve a system of scientific definitions charged with interminable consequences.[2] Their philosopher was Schelling, who taught that the State does not exist for human purposes and is not governed by human laws but by the cosmic force alone.

On this basis Savigny developed the school of historical jurisprudence. According to Savigny the sovereign legislator is not the government but the nation. Law, like language, proceeds from its primitive nature and its experience and is part of its identity. The deliberations of lawgiving consist in ascertaining, not what is best, but what is consistent with usage. Laws are found, not made, for the treatment adapted to successive emergencies is already latent in the public conscience, and must be evolved from precedent. Laws and constitutions expand by sustenance drawn from the constant and original spring. The force preparing the future is the same that made the past, and the function of the jurist is to trace and to obey it faithfully, without attempting to explain it away.[3]

This doctrine predominated for half a century and yielded only slowly to the keener dialectics and deeper philosophy of Ihering. It is the strongest of all the agencies that have directed German effort in historiography viewed as a remedy for the eighteenth century and the malady of vain speculation.

In the mind of Savigny and his followers their doctrine made for progress and independence, but not for liberty. The notion that each generation of men is powerless over its own fortunes, and receives them subject to inherited conditions, combined well with the rooted conservatism of the country. But it possessed that property of the works of genius, that it could be applied in opposite directions. If the nation is the source of law, it is reasonable to infer that national consent is a normal element in legislation, and that the State ought legitimately to

[1] *L.M.H.*, p. 14. [2] *H.E.*, p. 347.
[3] *Ibid.*

take its limits from the nation. Niebuhr, in unguarded moments, drew one of these inferences, and Dahlmann the other.[1]

Niebuhr's *Roman History* began the evolution of historic science. He argued that the processes of history are so well defined that it is possible to work back from the known to the unknown. This was the doctrine of fixed lines, invariable laws, and overruled action of men. When he filled the meagre outline of Manlius by transferring to him the character of Mirabeau, he gave the example which Stanley followed when he put Lord Shaftesbury into the Reformation, and Mr. Golightly into the Jewish monarchy.[2]

The historical school penetrated everywhere and remodelled every branch of legal study except ecclesiastical and comparative law, which resisted the national principle.

The same influence spread to the writing of Greek history and its results were made known in England by Thirlwall and Grote.

The critical epoch which is the transition to scientific history lies between 1824 and 1828—Ranke, Müller, Gieseler, Neander, Menzel, Niebuhr's second edition, and Stenzel.

Ranke was profoundly influenced by Niebuhr, whose sad example persuaded him that science and practical life should be kept separate. Ranke's dogma is impartiality. Ranke speaks of transactions and occurrences when it would be safe to speak of turpitude and crime. For the infallible conscience, the universal and unwritten law, the principles of eternal justice are the eighteenth-century phantoms against which the romantic and historical school rose in defiance.[3]

At the university Ranke was outshone by Gans, the mouthpiece of Hegel, and afterwards by Droysen, the mouthpiece of Imperialism. Ranke outlived all rivalry and nearly all antagonism. But in his own home the dissent of militant patriotism was expressed in the words of Dove, that pure history cannot satisfy the need of a struggling and travailing nation.

The tendency of the nineteenth-century German to subject all things to the government of intelligible law, and to prefer the simplicity of resistless cause to the confused conflict of free

---

[1] *H.E.*, p. 348. This passage constitutes a crucial judgment. In Add. 4938 Acton writes: "Niebuhr—Half an eagle and half a sheep."

[2] *H.E.*, p. 349.   [3] *Ibid.*, p. 355.

wills, was completed in his own way by Hegel. He displayed all history by the light of scientific unity, as the manifestation of a single force, whose works are all wise, and whose latest work is best. Even the *Volksgeist* of historical jurisprudence was less dazzling than Hegel's *Weltgeist*, which made the smallest allowance of hypothesis for the largest quantity of phenomena. Science was propitiated by visions of unity and continuity, religion by the assurance of incessant progress, politics by the ratification of the past. Liberty and morality were less well provided.

Hegel's influence on historical studies has endured—the idea of continuous progression which was first discovered by Leibniz, the point in common between his anticipation of Hegel and his anticipation of Darwin. Hegel's success was not in explaining events, but in explaining the action and succession of ideas.

The idea of development was also applied to Christianity. As Acton puts it: The generation of 1830, which in a variety of converging ways assigned the property of growth undetermined by will or wit of man, of development without forfeiture of identity, to the civil law, the academic philosophy, and the Aryan grammar, was not tempted to deny an analogous prerogative to Christianity.[1]

The man who grafted Hegel on Ranke was Baur. According to Baur the business of history is not so much with facts as with ideas, and the idea, not the fact, of the Resurrection is the basis of the Christian faith. Doctrines are developed out of notions, not out of events. Whether or no the belief is true, he refuses to inquire. In the most characteristic passage ever written by a German historian, he declares that it is a question beyond the scope of history.[2] Baur's mastery in tracing the march of ideas through the ages, over the heads of men, was a thing new in literature. He maintained that the formation and growth of doctrine is consistent and normal, not accidental or arbitrary. To this school is due the term the Formation of truth. (Elsewhere Acton noticed the theory of Comte, who maintained that the day would come when positivist philosophers would manufacture doctrines and compel mankind to accept them. Huxley said that Positivism was Catholicism minus Christianity.)

[1] *H.E.*, p. 368. [2] *Ibid.*, p. 369.

Baur's greatest adversary was Humboldt, whose mind was often shaped by some favourite classic, as were Böck by Plato, Creuzer by Plotinus, Trendelenburg by Aristotle, and Roscher by Thucydides.

The dogma of the scientific historians was that the truth is worth living for, and honesty, in fact, the best policy. This yields to nobody now the fresh emotion of discovery. Lanfrey wrote that the only patriotism of the historian was love of truth, and the best of the French reviews has said the same— The only cause we serve is that of science. A clever fellow assured Lasker that he lied no more, having observed that it is less profitable than it used to be, and that truth, on the whole, answers better. In the second quarter of the nineteenth century these principles were enjoying the short span which Schopenhauer assigns to truth, between the paradox of yesterday and the commonplace of tomorrow.

Thiers thought Napoleon a criminal and a madman, and concealed his opinion in twenty volumes. Ranke was indifferent to the issues he discussed and concealed his opinion in seventy volumes. Stubbs claimed that a man might read his books and mistake him for a radical. Acton adds: By what secret channels error filters into the mind, most people have read in Bacon, and may read much better in Spencer.[1] The ideal historian adumbrated by Rothe, Kampschulte, Roscher, Dümmler, Löning, Gierke, Gass, is a man armed at all these points, and the discipline that makes him opens further visions of penetrating ethics, not obvious on the beaten track.[2]

Lessing, however, said that in reality no writer—no historian —could ever describe any age but his own.

The revolution of 1848 compelled attention to the problems of the day. Gervinus prophesied a democratic, not a Prussian future. He personated the average German, the average middle-class German from the smaller towns of the smaller States, crowded with information, sceptical and doctrinaire, more robust than elastic or alert, instructive but not persuasive, with a taste for broad paths and the judicious forcing of open locks. He began his history of the nineteenth century at the

---

[1] But in Add. 4943 Acton writes: "Hereditary for innate—that is all H. Spencer."
[2] *H.E.*, pp. 373-374.

lowest ebb of national sentiment, and he left it, a fragment in eight volumes, when reviving nationality discarded his dogmas. Gervinus died disowning the results of 1870.

Gervinus and Sybel exhibit the contrast between north and south, and between the time before and after 1848. Sybel deplored the French Revolution as a catastrophe that threw back intelligent progress for half a century. He began his studies with two essays on Burke, and both in his history and in his review he adopted the dogmatic terms of Burke and Savigny.

The year 1848, which sent more than one hundred professors to Frankfort, had been detrimental to the British and Baconian maxim that knowledge is power. In Sybel they were united. He was learned in the wisdom of universities and eminently conversant with the working of political forces, a man of life and action, and an expert. He became the first classic of German imperialism, and helped to form that garrison of distinguished historians that prepared the Prussian supremacy together with their own, and came to hold Berlin like a fortress. Things were different when the writing of history had not been woven into the web of national greatness and was carried on by private enterprise. Men living in a small way were not often practical, but they were generally disinterested. Göttingen, Tübingen, and Heidelberg had some advantages for historical study over Berlin, where *William Tell* was a forbidden play. Among their leisurely professors were men who found, like Dahlmann, that Frederick the Great stuck in their throats, and men like Gervinus and Ewald who repudiated the precept that what their country wanted was force before freedom. The disconcerting verdict of events ruined their credit as readers of the signs of the times. It seemed that the past had not revealed to them its inmost secret, and they were disparaged in consequence. The men who took betimes the side of the big battalions, showed, it was thought, superior penetration into the things beneath the sun. They brought history into touch with the nation's life, and gave it an influence it had never possessed out of France. They won for themselves the making of opinions, mightier than laws. The most clear-sighted of those who resolved, after the failure of the Revolution of 1848, that the future of Germany belonged to Prussia, was Droysen.

Droysen affirmed that unity could never come from liberty and the votes of parliaments, and that it required a power strong enough to crush resistance at home and abroad. The rest of his life was devoted to Prussian politics and the imperial arts, and he was one of that central band of writers and statesmen and soldiers who turned the tide that had run in Germany for six hundred years, and conquered the centrifugal forces that had reigned in Germany longer than the commons have sat at Westminster. Droysen's long *History of Prussian Policy* brought him popularity and power. Being asked by what subtle charm he had changed Frederick from a plain soldier into a mighty conqueror, Droysen replied that it was nothing but the stern sense of duty.[1] To those who do not require convincing Droysen is as persuasive as the avowed defenders of other causes.

More brilliant and powerful than Droysen was Treitschke. He attacked the notion of a separate science of society, as the sphere of religion, morality, economy and knowledge, as a vast community organically distinct from the State and able to control it.[2] The idea has been made by Lorenz von Stein the key to the French Revolution, in a work exposing the economic cause of political science. Treitschke marshalled his forces on a broader front than any other man, and he accounts for the motives that stir the nation, as well as for the councils that govern it.

Bernhardi combined long and intimate initiation in secrets of state with military science and the knowledge of an original and profound economist. He represses the inclination to think that what is explained is excused, that all ideas are reasonable and all events opportune. Bernhardi was the ablest of the German writers on Napoleon, and the affinity that may be discovered between the first consul in the plenitude of his own ideas, and much that is peculiarly Prussian, does not disarm this admirer of Frederick and friend of Moltke.

There is no considerable group less in harmony with English sentiments than that which is mainly represented by Sybel, Droysen and Treitschke, with Mommsen and Gneist, Bernhardi and Duncker on the flank.[3] As there is no symptom of declining favour and authority, it is important to understand

[1] *H.E.*, p. 379.   [2] *Ibid.*, p. 380.   [3] *Ibid.*, p. 382 (1886).

along what lines of reasoning men so eminent, so quick to inquire into every new thing, have adhered to maxims which it has cost the world much effort to reverse. Their theory is distinct from the plea of the partisan. They say that the historian displays the laws governing human life. It is not his duty to expound a private view, or to explain, like the wise Castilian, how much better the universe would be contrived if he had been consulted in time. He attends to the ship's course, not to the passengers. The forces to be reckoned are those, which, in the long run, prevail. The historian, in their view, justifies only that which is just by the judgment of experience. For them it is heresy to choose a side that seems good in our eyes, to reject the appointed course and the dominion of law, and degrade the life of nations under the anarchy of casual and disconnected causes. In their philosophy consistency in the powers that direct the world is the supreme acquisition of all German thought. It is, they say, not partiality but renunciation of party to hold that the world works well, that what lives permanently in the light and strife of civilization lives rightfully, that whatever perishes has earned its fate. It is the philosophy of Emerson proclaiming "the skill with which the great All maketh clean work as it goes along, leaves no rag, consumes its smoke." Or as an English classic wrote: "Somehow or other it is always the Eternal's wisdom which at last carries the day."

The Germans argue that history is the conscience of mankind. They are inheritors of the line that comes down from Burke. They set up what they regard as imperishable moral forces for an intermittent Providence, the play of passion, and the blind will of man. Their doctrine proceeds from the scientific as well as from the political experience of their country. And it is held even by those who do not stand with both feet within the charmed circle that binds the writing of history to the making of politics. It is held by Mommsen, who scouts the idea of explaining Roman conquests by Roman perfidy, by Waitz, who said that a man had no right to pit himself against the judgment of the nation, and by Kurtz, who equally adopts the doctrine of success.

When the euthanasia of metaphysic anticipated by Carlyle was setting in about 1850 physical science came forward as its rival, and history as its heir. The philosophers themselves turned into historians, and beat their speculations into facts. Kuno Fischer opened his great work on modern metaphysics by defining philosophy as the self-knowledge of history. Schaarschmidt called philosophy and history the same thing. Comte began the third volume of the *Politique Positive* with the words that the preponderance of history over philosophy was the characteristic of the time he lived in.[1] One philosophical review declared that the history of systems was a substitute for the systems themselves. Metaphysicians were won by the assurance that the philosophical idea is the substance of all history. The historic mind had always glowed beneath the metaphysical ice cap. Goethe described it as one of his last steps in mental progress to have the unseen past always present.

The scientific era had its own lesson for historians. The world proceeded on its new path with increasing velocity. The law of material progress became a manifest reality. A new conception of history arose of which Du Bois Reymond was the prophet. In this view the future depends on truths and forces being, and to be, discovered. The past survives only by supplying available material that may be a guide for science and an equivalent of power. The function of the writing of history is to reveal the futility of the past and to display the conquest of uncertainty and probability by natural science. On this hypothesis, we live under a dynasty that begins with Copernicus and that will never pass away. All else is ballast to be discharged. As mere denial of history the new conception is an old one. But it promoted the neglected history of scientific ideas and promises greatly to enrich both historians and philosophers.

The idea that the fine arts are a result of all that is at work in nations led to an attempt to focus their entire life, and the design of a history of civilization grew out of the history of art. Burckhardt's *Renaissance* and Friedländer's *Sittengeschichte* are the only works in the German language in which the intellectual view of the subject has been adequately studied. But Riehl, a scholar quickened by journalism, a student of art, an original political writer and teacher of the social sciences, revealed in his lectures new views of history deeper than any existing in literature.

Students of the French Revolution have not ceased to dispute

[1] *L.M.H.*, p. 22.

the real nature of the event. The pride of nobles, the intolerance of priests, philosophy, the levity and violence of the national character, the result of that struggle between classes that constitutes the unity of the history of France are among the suggested causes.[1]

The first historian who wrote with authority was Droz. He was a man of sense and experience, with a true if not a powerful mind. He shows the turning point (September 1789) with an absolute sureness of judgment. He meant to write a treatise on the natural history of revolutions. It became a history of rejected opportunities by a constitutional royalist of the English school. He shows how disorder and crime grew out of unreadiness, want of energy, want of clear thought, and definite design.

Lamartine was one of those legitimists who believed that the revolution of 1830 had killed monarchy, who considered the Orleans dynasty a sham, and set themselves at once to look ahead towards the inevitable Republic. With the intuition of genius he saw sooner than most men, more accurately than any man, the signs of what was to come. In six years, he said, we shall be masters. He was mistaken only by a few weeks.[2] He laid his plans so that, when the time came, he should be the accepted leader. He therefore wrote the *History of the Girondins*, to idealize the Revolution and to prepare a Republic that should not be a terror to mankind, but should submit easily to the fascination of melodious and sympathetic eloquence. Lamartine gained his purpose. He contributed to institute a Republic that was pacific and humane, responsive to the charm of phrase and obedient to his own master hand which had written of the glories of the Gironde. He believed that without his book the reign of terror would have been repeated.

Louis Blanc was a socialist politician who helped, after 1840, to cement that union of socialists and republicans which overthrew the monarchy, and went to pieces on the barricades in June 1848. He settled in London and spent several years at work in the British Museum on the pamphlets of the French Revolution, a collection exceeding anything in Paris. He is the expounder of the Revolution in its compulsory and illiberal aspect. He argues that the masses have more to suffer from

[1] *F.R.*, p. 346. [2] *Ibid.*, p. 347.

abuse of wealth than from abuse of power, and need protection by the State, not against it. Louis Blanc is the admirer and advocate of Robespierre. When he comes to the September massacres he bids us remember the massacre of St. Bartholomew.

Michelet, as an archivist, had unique advantages. For him the Revolution is the advent of justice, and the central fact in the experience of mankind. There is no forgiveness for those who resist the people in the consciousness of their might. What is good proceeds from the mass, what is bad from individuals. Mankind is a righteous judge of the affairs of man. The light which comes to the learned from reflection comes to the unlearned more surely by natural inspiration. Power is due to the mass by reason of instinct, not by reason of numbers. They are right by dispensation of Heaven. Michelet is the most illuminating of the democratic historians. "We often," comments Acton, "read of men whose lives have been changed because a particular book has fallen into their hands, or, one might say, because they have fallen into the hands of a particular book."[1] Of such books there are two on the revolutionary shelf. One is Taine, and the other Michelet.

The fourth book of the revolutionary party is that of Villiaumé. Lamartine esteemed Vergniaud. Louis Blanc esteemed Robespierre, and Michelet, Danton. Villiaumé went a step farther, and admired Marat.

While the revolutionary historians, aided by public events, were predominating in France, the conservatives competed obscurely, and at first without success. Genoude was for many years editor of the leading royalist journal. When the Bourbons were expelled for the second time, in 1830, the legitimists found themselves identified with a grudging liberality and a restricted suffrage. In the *Gazette de France* Genoude adopted the opposite policy, and overtrumped the liberal Orleanists. He insisted on the sovereignty of the people, on the widest extension of the franchise. When his friend Courmenin drew up the Constitution of 1848, Genoude induced him to adopt universal suffrage. The notion of a legitimate throne, restored by democracy, was borrowed from Bolingbroke, and it nearly prevailed in 1873. It gives some relief and originality to Genoude's book on the Revolution.

[1] *F.R.*, p. 352.

A better book is by Amédée Gabourd. He says, with reason, that no writer has sought truth and justice with more perfect good faith, or has been more careful to keep aloof from party spirit and accepted judgments. Gabourd was a constitutionalist, and the revolution of February 1848 was the ruin of a system which he had expected to last for ever. But he remained true to his principles.

The Doctrinaires were the men in the best position to understand the Revolution and to judge it rightly. They accepted the results rather than the motives. They rejoiced in the reign of reason, but they required the monarchy to be duly limited and the Church as established by the Concordat, in order to resume the chain of history and the reposing influence of custom. They were leaders without followers, and it was said of them that they were only four, but pretended to be five in order to strike terror by their number. Their greatest writer was Guizot. His discourses on the Revolution give approximately and in the shape of tales of a grandfather his views in old age, and we do not possess them in completely authentic form.

The Doctrinaire historian is Barante. He had the distinction and the dignity of his friends, their book learning and their experience of public affairs. After 1848 he published nine volumes on the Convention and the Directory. Like the rest of his party Barante always acknowledged the original spirit of the Revolution as the root of French institutions. But the movement of 1848, directed as it was against the Doctrinaires, against their monarchy and their ministry, had much developed the conservative element which was always strong within them. Barante composed his work in the spirit of opposition to the revival of Jacobin ideas and the rehabilitation of Jacobin character. But coming from such a man, the book is a disappointment.

A more powerful conservative writer on the Revolution was Sybel. He was the first to prove, if not to discover, that the Revolution was not simply a break or a reversal but in part a development of tendencies at work in the old monarchy.

In France the deeper studies began with Tocqueville. He was a Liberal of the purest breed, a Liberal and nothing else, deeply suspicious of democracy, equality, centralization, utilitarianism. Of all writers he is the most widely acceptable, and the hardest to find fault with. He is always wise, always right, and as just as Aristides. His intellect is without flaw, but it is limited and constrained. He knows political literature and history less well than political life. His originality is not creative, and he does not stimulate with gleams of new light or unfathomed suggestiveness.

Two years later, in 1858, a work began to appear which is still more instructive. Duvergier de Hauranne had long experience of public life. Having quarrelled with the Doctrinaires, he led the attack which overthrew Guizot, and was one of three on whom Thiers was relying to save the throne, when the king went away in a cab and carried the dynasty with him. He devoted the evening of his life to a history of parliamentary government in France, which extends in ten volumes to 1830. It contains more profound ideas than any other work in literature. During the Restoration, the great controversy of all ages, the conflict between reason and custom was fought out on the higher level. The question at that time was not which of the two should prevail, but how they should be reconciled, and whether rational thought and national life could be made to harmonize.

Laboulaye was a man of like calibre. Like Tocqueville he had saturated himself with American ideas, and like him he was persuaded that the revolutionary legacy of concentrated power was the chief obstacle to free institutions. His lectures on the Revolution were published in a review. Laboulaye was a scholar and a statesman, and always knew his subject well. As a guide we can have none more helpful.

No man feels the grandeur of the Revolution till he reads Michelet, or the horror of it without reading Taine.

Emancipation from dependence on memoir writers is represented by Sybel, Taine, and Sorel.

Sybel said of himself that he was three parts politician, so that only the miserable remnant composed the professor. He stood firmly by the doctrine that men are governed by descent, that the historic nation prevails invincibly over the actual nation, that we cannot cast off our pedigree. Therefore the growth of things in Prussia seemed to him to be almost normal, and acceptable in contrast with the condition of a people which attempted to constitute itself according to its own ideas. Political theory as well as national antagonism allowed him no sympathy with the French. In diplomatic matters he is far ahead of other writers, except Sorel. Having been an opposition leader, and what in Prussia is called a Liberal, he went over to Bismarck, and wrote the history of the new German Empire under his inspiration. Sybel criticized Thiers for comparing the Constitution of 1799 to the British Constitution. Thiers did nothing of the kind. In the page alluded to Thiers tried to display the superiority of a government which is the product of much experiment and incessant adaptation to the artificial outcome of political logic.[1]

Sybel's view is that the Revolution went wrong quite naturally, that the new order was no better than the old, because it proceeded from the old, rose from an exhausted soil, and was worked by men nurtured in the corruption of the old régime. He uses the Revolution to exhibit the superiority of conservative and enlightened Germany. As there is little to say in favour of Prussia, which crowned an inglorious war by an inglorious peace, he produced his effect by piling up to the utmost the mass of French folly and iniquity. With all its defects it is an instructive work. Sybel lived to see himself overtaken and surpassed, for internal history by Taine, for foreign affairs by Sorel.

Taine was trained in the systems of Hegel and Comte. His fundamental dogma was the denial of free will and the absolute dominion of physical causes over the life of mankind. A violent effort to shape the future by intention and design seemed to him the height of folly. To him the idea of starting afresh, of emancipating the individual from the mass, the living from the dead, was a defiance of the laws of nature. Man is civilized, in his view, and trained, by his surroundings, his ancestry, his nationality, and must be adapted to them. The natural man, whom the Revolution discovered and brought to the surface, is, according to Taine, a vicious and destructive brute, not to be tolerated unless caught young, and perseveringly disciplined and controlled.[2]

---

[1] The wording of this reference to the British Constitution is one of the most revealing indications of Acton's standpoint to be found in the entire range of his published writings.   [2] *F.R.*, p. 370.

Taine is a pathologist. His work is the most scientific we possess and in part the most exhaustive. His indictment is the weightiest ever drawn up. His cruel judgments are not dictated by party. But he is incompetent as to the literature and general affairs of Europe. Where Taine failed, Sorel succeeded. He was secretary to the Senate, and not an abstract philosopher but a politician. He writes, as it were, from the point of view of the French Foreign Office. He is more friendly to the principles of the Revolution than Sybel, without being an apologist.

The greatest living authority, said Acton in 1895, is Aulard. He is the characteristic product of 1889 and the centenary of the Revolution. Then its history began to be studied in a new spirit.

The best we have by English writers on the French Revolution is the three chapters in the second volume of Buckle, and the two chapters in the fifth volume of Lecky.

"Don't let us utter too much evil of party writers, for we owe them much. If not honest, they are helpful, as the advocates aid the judge; and they would not have done so well from the mere inspiration of disinterested veracity. We might wait long if we watched for the man who knows the whole truth and has the courage to speak it."

Acton's ideal was the writer who would deal evenly with friend and foe—assuming it would be possible for an honest writer to have a friend.[1]

Acton's dogma was not impartiality but sincerity, which he defined as stating a stronger case for the view we reject than its supporters can do.

[1] *F.R.*, p. 373.

IX

THE HISTORY OF FREEDOM[1]

FREEDOM must be seen in the light of its development. The appeal to national tradition and the higher law, that is, to the conscience of mankind and to the universal reason, to individual and collective moral responsibility, has marked the parallel lines of all human advance. The triumphs of freedom have been due to minorities. The greatest obstacle to freedom has been uncertainty and confusion about its nature. False ideas have been more damaging than hostile interests. Increase of insight and knowledge has been as important as political or constitutional change. Institutions may be illusory, for their merit depends on the ideas that produce and the spirit that sustains them. Liberty means security that everyone shall be protected in doing what he believes to be his duty. The most certain test of freedom is the amount of security enjoyed by minorities.

As early as the Israelites there was government based on federation, contract, and the principle of self-government. The principle was recognized that a constitution grows from a root by a process of development. The most profound political genius of antiquity was Solon. The essence of Democracy, he said, is to obey no master but the law. Pericles was the first to grasp the idea of political equality. Under Pericles everything was to be decided by argument in open discussion. The object of his constitution was to prevent the predominance of any single interest. All history has been occupied with the endeavour to upset the balance of power by giving the advantage to money, land, or numbers. Class conflict followed. The possession of unlimited power demoralized the democracy of Athens. Its quick decline was due to the absence of an effective fixed standard of right and wrong. The main point in the method

---

[1] This slight sketch is intended only to indicate Acton's point of view. It is condensed from essays and lectures.

of Socrates was essentially democratic, judgment by the reason and conscience of the individual.

The *Laws* of Plato and the *Politics* of Aristotle are the books from which we can learn most about politics, that is to say, constitutional government and the division of sovereignty from Plato, and from Aristotle mixed and partly democratic government, and the idea of the supremacy of law.

The Socratic philosophers vindicated conscience against authority, and the Stoics taught that the unity of mankind implies the existence of rights and duties common to all men which legislation neither gives nor takes away. Their conception of freedom as the birthright of mankind survived in the law of nations. Through the Roman jurists the ideas of the Stoics entered Roman law.

The vice of the ancient State was that, to use an expressive anachronism, it was Church and State in one. Under the Roman empire began the dogma that by the hypothesis of a popular origin absolute power may be as legitimate as constitutional freedom. And the code of Justinian became the greatest obstacle, next to feudalism, with which liberty had to contend. Ancient liberty was bound up with slavery.

The Stoic law of nature prepared the way for Christian teaching. The injunction Render unto Caesar was the repudiation of absolutism and the inauguration of freedom. But beyond reflection and experience there was needed a faculty of self-government and self-control, developed like its language in the fibre of a nation and growing with its growth. This vital element was provided by the great migrations.

In the Middle Ages the feudal hierarchy was resisted by the ecclesiastical hierarchy. To that conflict of four centuries we owe the rise of civil liberty. Liberty was not the aim of either party; but it was the means by which the temporal and spiritual power called the nations to their support. The doctrine that prevailed was the divine right of the people to raise up and bring down princes. Both sides appealed to the sovereignty of the people, as is shown in the writings of Aquinas and Marsilius. The Crusades stimulated urban development, and the townspeople tried to obtain for their own class and interest the command of the State. The upheaval of the middle class disclosed the needs and aspirations of the suffering poor.

In principle, though not in practice, the Middle Ages solved the great problems of politics. Representative government was almost universal. Taxation was inseparably united with representation. Slavery was almost extinguished. Absolute power was deemed more intolerable and more criminal than slavery. The right of insurrection was defined as a duty. Authority was restricted by the representation of powerful classes, privileged associations, and by the acknowledgement of duties superior to those imposed by man—the law of nature, which is the law of reason, and of God.

The most profound of the causes that have transformed modern society can be regarded as a mediaeval inheritance—the idea of conscience. Its action was to limit power by causing the sovereign voice within to be heard above expressed will and settled custom. By that hypothesis the soul became more sacred than the State. That is the root from which liberty of conscience was developed and all other liberty needed to confine the sphere of power, in order that it may not challenge the supremacy of what is highest and best in man. The securities by which this purpose has been attempted constitute the central problem of all subsequent history. But the passion for power over others can never cease to threaten mankind.

The method of modern progress has been revolution—due rather to the attraction of ideal right than to provocation by actual wrong. The claims inspiring these revolutions have been universal. Over long periods there has been a slow advance of moral over material influence, the triumph of general ideas. Hence the Dutch, English, American, and French Revolutions.

Progress imposes increasing sacrifices on society—on behalf of the cripple and the victim of accident, the idiot and the madman, the pauper and the culprit, the old and infirm, the curable and the incurable.[1] The growing dominion of disinterested motive, this liberality towards the weak, in social life, corresponds to that respect for the minority, in political life, which is the essence of freedom. It is an application of the same principle of self-denial, and of the higher law.[2]

On the whole the line of development has been from force and cruelty to consent, humanity, and rational persuasion.

It was towards the year 1500 that European nations reached

[1] *L.M.H.*, p. 33. [2] *Ibid.*

full measure of differentiation, while the idea of an international code, overriding the will of peoples and the authority of sovereigns, had not yet dawned.

The modern world begins with the Turkish invasion. Spain became a great Power. France had acquired vast areas by the expulsion of the English. England achieved peace under the Tudors. Italy was inexhaustibly rich in the luxuries of civilization. The first chapter of the history of the modern State is the contest of France and Spain for the control of Italy. The Italian wars laid down the conditions of modern politics, codified and reduced to a system by Machiavelli. The motive of domination became a reigning force in Europe.

Slavery was fast disappearing in Europe when it was revived as a consequence of the geographical discoveries of the Portuguese. Half a century after the death of its founder, negro slavery began to control the destinies of America.[1] The geographical discoveries transformed the conditions of freedom by moving the political centre of gravity from land to sea, by altering the relation of classes in Europe, by making portable property predominate over landed property, and by profoundly affecting European finance. Increase of wealth involving increase of power depended thenceforward on the control of distant regions.[2]

The modern type of individual man took shape under the influence of the Renaissance. The humanists had an independent judgment. The invention of printing meant the work of the Renaissance would last.

Luther rebelled against the Renaissance Papacy, and broke the chain of authority at its strongest link. He gave independence to the individual conscience.[3] But Luther's political teaching was conservative, and Lutheran writers constantly condemned the democratic literature that arose in the second age of the Reformation.[4] Sarasa was the first to proclaim the infallibility of conscience.[5] The greater part of the political ideas of Milton, Locke, and Rousseau can be found in Lessius,

---

[1] *L.M.H.*, p. 53.

[2] *Ibid.*, p. 70. Cf. Add. 4937: "Cabot sent the English to North America thereby doing a greater deed than all the Conquistadores." And: "The trade of Eastern Asia is the secret of wealth and power in Europe." (*Ibid.*)

[3] *H.F.*, p. 271.   [4] *Ibid.*, p. 42.   [5] *L.M.H.*, p. 116.

Molina Mariana, and Suarez.[1] Calvin believed in self-government, the control of the State by the Church, and wanted to remodel society as well as religion. Calvin's influence checked the reigning idea that nothing limits the power of the State.[2]

The party of liberty—Castellio, Socinus, Coornhert in the sixteenth century, like Williams and Penn, Locke and Bayle in the seventeenth—were not Protestants on the original foundation. They were Sectaries, and the charge of human freedom was transferred from the Churches to the Sects, to Socinians and Arminians and Independents and the Society of Friends.[3]

In England, under Henry VIII, what prevailed was not a theological but a political view. The sovereignty of the modern State, uncontrolled by the opinions of men, commanded the minds both of Thomas Cromwell and of Gardiner. Thomas Cromwell is the first public man known to have studied Machiavelli. It was the advent of a new polity.[4]

The fundamental change, the transformation of reformation into revolution was made in the Netherlands, and was the result of the violence of Philip II. His endeavour to substitute his will for self-government led first to an aristocratic and then to a democratic movement. It was in the Netherlands that the sects were raised which ultimately made England free.

In France the religious wars ended in the triumph of the Crown over the nation and of the State over the Church.[5]

In almost every case the rulers of the sixteenth century used religious zeal and passion as instruments for the increase of power.[6] The work of a thousand years in keeping Church and State apart was thrown away.[7] Calvin preached, and Bellarmine lectured, but Machiavelli reigned.[8]

The Edict of Nantes, which closed the French religious wars, marks an epoch in the progress of toleration, that is, in the history of liberty, which is the marrow of all modern history.[9] But it was power rather than conscience that was recognized. Socinians in the sixteenth century and Independents in the seventeenth went much deeper.[10]

[1] *H.F.*, p. 82. [2] *L.M.H.*, p. 136. [3] *Ibid.*
[4] *Ibid.*, p. 142. [5] *Ibid.*, p. 155. [6] *H.F.*, p. 43.
[7] *Ibid.* [8] *Ibid.*, p. 44. [9] *L.M.H.*, p. 171.
[10] *Ibid.*

The Thirty Years' War ended with the admission of Calvinists to equal rights with other religions. Concerning liberty of conscience not a word was said. The power of the interfering State was not shorn, but the idea that the divisions of Christendom might be healed by force passed away from the minds of men.[1]

The English evolution in politics was distinctive. The peculiar note of the seventeenth century was the combination and alternation of appeals to precedent and principle.[2] When James I united the Crowns of Scotland and England the country obtained the benefit of being an island, protected by the sea. There was no longer a hostile and warlike neighbour, compelling military preparation and the concentration of power, which made foreign governments absolute. The Stuarts adopted from Machiavelli the idea of the State pursuing purposes of its own, and from Luther the idea of divine right.

The Independents cherished the ideal of local self-government and of democracy. When the direct effects of their victory passed away, their ideas survived. At first these ideas were religious, not political. When they renounced their theological parentage and were translated into the scientific terms of politics, they conquered and spread as general truths, not as British exports.[3]

In the course of the struggle which ended in the Revolution of 1688 ideas were developed which ultimately proved strong enough, as well as sufficiently lasting, to carry out an entirely new structure of constitutional government. It is the point where the history of nations turned into its modern bed. It is the point where the Englishman became the leader of the world.[4]

The discovery of the seventeenth century was that religious liberty is the generating principle of civil, and that civil liberty is the necessary condition of religious. Some of the Independents grasped the principle that it is only by abridging the authority of States that the liberty of Churches and individuals can be assured.[5] Lilburne and Harrington understood that equality of power could not be preserved together with an extreme inequality of property.[6]

The victorious Whigs of 1688 made compromise the soul of

[1] *L.M.H.*, p. 194. [2] *Ibid.*, p. 195. [3] *Ibid.*, p. 205.
[4] *Ibid.* [5] *H.F.*, p. 52. [6] *Ibid.*, p. 83.

their party. They became associated with the great interests of trade, banking, and the city. It was not until the American Revolution that Whig principles became universalized.

The English Revolution was the supreme achievement of Englishmen, and their bequest to the nations. Forty years of agitation had produced the leaven which has leavened the world.[1] It is the greatest thing done by the English nation.[2] It established the State upon a contract. It substituted the Whig theory of government for the Tory theory on the fundamental points of political science.[3] The king became a servant during good behaviour. Authority was limited, regulated and controlled. The great achievement is that this was done without bloodshed, without vengeance, without exclusion of entire parties, with so little definiteness in point of doctrine that it could be accepted, and the consequences could be left to work themselves out. But the settlement was perfectly compatible with the oppression of class by class, and of the country by the State, as the agent of a class.[4]

At the same time in France, the Revocation of the Edict of Nantes had marked the highest point of absolutism. The theory of government triumphed which Bossuet borrowed from Hobbes, and Charles II and James II had failed to establish in England. This is the theory that refuses to admit that the subject should have a will, a conviction, a conscience of his own, but expects that the spiritual side of him shall be sacrificed to the sovereign, like his blood and treasure.[5]

The crisis of English freedom coincided with the crisis of European freedom. The idea of a predominant Power in Europe was part of absolutism.[6] It proceeded from the same love of authority, the same pride of greatness, the same disregard for the equal rights of man, the same pretension to superiority and prerogative, international as well as national.

The issue for England was decided in the wars of the English and Spanish Successions. In the latter England's commercial existence also was at stake.[7] It was due to Marlborough that England became one of the great Powers. By the peace England acquired the slave trade and the commerce of the world,[8]

[1] *L.M.H.*, pp. 217–218.   [2] *Ibid.*, p. 231.   [3] *Ibid.*
[4] *Ibid.*, p. 232.   [5] *Ibid.*, p. 245.   [6] *Ibid.*, p. 249.
[7] *Ibid.*, p. 255.   [8] *Ibid.*, p. 263.

and the revolution settlement received the sanction of the public law of Europe.

The essential innovations in England, Cabinet, Premier, government by party, were not effected by statute, but by that force which makes the law and is above the law, the logic of facts and the opinion of the nation.[1] Walpole did more than any other man to establish the new system of government. He was a good administrator. His chief object was to divert the country from speculation to the profits of industry and trade.[2] The South Sea affair had shown that much capital was seeking investment. The two great openings for trade were with the Mediterranean and with Spanish America. The South American trade presented infinite possibilities, and it was considered worth a war.[3] This was no part of Walpole's policy, but it was part of his policy to let the nation, in the last instance, decide. Walpole was quite content to preserve government by the rich, in the interest of their own class. He did nothing to check the slave trade. The criminal Code became annually more severe. The treatment of prisoners and of the poor hardly bears description.

Bolingbroke appealed to the Crown to abolish class government. The elevation of the State over the dominant classes had been the part of intelligent Monarchy in every age. It is the spell by which Bolingbroke transformed Toryism, and introduced the party called the King's Friends, which became a power in the middle of the century, and which was put an end to by the younger Pitt, after they had lost America.

One essential change, the freedom of the Press and publication of parliamentary debates, was not achieved till 1774.

While England was establishing constitutional government an opposite movement was proceeding in Russia and Prussia. The Muscovite empire, by the action of one man, Peter the Great, passed from lethargy and obscurity to a dominant position among the nations.[4] For Peter civilization was material, not moral. The absolute State was his idol.

Frederick the Great's father was the Peter the Great of Prussia.

Military monarchy, represented by Prussia and Russia, is

[1] *L.M.H.*, p. 264.   [2] *Ibid.*, p. 273.
[3] *Ibid.*, p. 274.   [4] *Ibid.*, p. 277.

the greatest danger that remains to be encountered by the Anglo-Saxon race.[1]

The victory in the Seven Years' War gave England resources which, if they had been husbanded and developed, would have made her mistress of the world.

On the Continent there followed the age of the Repentance of Monarchy. The competent expert, inspired by the great writers, became supreme. There was increased provision for popular education, relief of poverty, public works, a tendency to abolish torture, to doubt the morality of the slave trade.

The rational and humanitarian movement did much for welfare but little to promote the securities for freedom.

The Seven Years' War renewed the interrupted march by involving America in the concerns of Europe. That consequence followed the conquest of Canada. Montcalm had foretold that if the English conquered Canada they would lose America. The purpose of taxing the colonies was to obtain unequivocal recognition of British sovereignty.[2] There were some among the Whigs who knew the policy by which since then the empire has been reared, Adam Smith, Dean Tucker, and Edmund Burke. But the great mass went with the times, and held that the object of politics is power.[3]

The colonies had been growing richer, and were the heirs of unbounded wealth. The real foundation of discontent was the British attack on the growth of manufacture, the second cause was the attempt to enforce the navigation laws. The attempt to tax without representation was the last straw.

The founder of the revolutionary doctrine was Otis, who appealed to the higher law. The American dispute involved a principle, the right of controlling government. The Americans gave up everything, not to escape oppression, but to honour a precept of unwritten law. That was the transatlantic discovery in the theory of political duty.[4] Marshall, the greatest of constitutional lawyers, and Daniel Webster, the great expounder of the American constitution, who stands, in politics, next to Burke, both agree in saying that the amount of the proposed taxation was trivial and of no interest.[5] Acton writes, the object of these men was liberty, not independence.[6]

[1] *L.M.H.*, p. 289 (1899).   [2] *Ibid.*, p. 306.   [3] *Ibid.*
[4] *F.R.*, pp. 24–25.   [5] *Ibid.*, p. 25.   [6] *Ibid.*

American principles profoundly influenced France, and determined the course of the French Revolution.[1] The French heralds of the Revolution were Domat, Jurieu, Maultrot, Fénelon, Voltaire, Montesquieu, D'Argenson, Turgot, Rousseau, Diderot.

American example and French theory produced the spark which ignited the French Revolution. The occasion was the deficit, the record of bad government. Half the property of France was not taxed in its proportion. Privilege was a relic of feudalism, which meant power given to land and denied to capital and industry. Feudalism meant class government.[2] Louis XVI was sincere in taking the first step to concert with the French people a permanent constitution. But he abdicated before the States-General and the rival classes were abandoned to the fatal issue of a trial of strength.[3] Behind political reform there was social revolution.

The assault on the restricted distribution of power involved an assault on the concentration of wealth. The connection of the two ideas is the secret motive of the Revolution.[4]

The Third Estate carried to an end in seven weeks the greatest constitutional struggle that has ever been fought out by speech alone.[5] The French people had been called to the enjoyment of freedom by every voice they heard: by the King, the notables, the supreme judiciary, the clergy, the aristocracy, the British example, the American example, and by the national classics, who declared, with a thousand tongues, that all authority must be controlled, that the masses must be rescued from degradation, and the individual from constraint.[6] The cleavage between the political, and the social democrat, which has become so great a fact in modern society, was scarcely perceived.[7]

The battle was between people doomed to poverty by the operation of law, and people who were prosperous at their expense.[8] When the nobles insisted on the veto of their own

---

[1] *F.R.*, p. 32. France was affected by the American Revolution, not by the American Constitution. It underwent the disturbing influence, not the conservative (*Ibid.*, p. 35).

[2] *Ibid.*, p. 41. [3] *Ibid.*, p. 45. [4] *Ibid.*, p. 54.
[5] *Ibid.*, p. 56. [6] *Ibid.*, p. 57. [7] *Ibid.*, p. 58.
[8] *Ibid.*

Estate, only a breach with legality could fulfil the national will.[1] The broad principle on which the Commons acted was that the Third Estate was really the nation.[2]

The King's attempt to overawe the Assembly at Versailles with foreign troops led the Assembly to rely on the people of Paris. Their friends had the support of the capitalists, who looked to them to prevent the national bankruptcy which the Court and the nobles were bringing on.[3] The action began the imperishable effects of which will be felt by everyone to the last day of his life.[4] Power began to pass from the Assembly to the people of Paris.

The most decisive date in the Revolution is 4 August, the fall of the social system of historic France, and the substitution of the Rights of Man.[5] The essence of the French ideal was, as in America, liberty founded on equality, as contrasted with the English system, which was liberty founded on inequality. The France of history vanished on August 4. The transfer of property was considerable, and the peasants' income was increased by 60 per cent.[6] The people were resolved not to be oppressed by monarchy or aristocracy, but they had no experience or warning of oppression by democracy. It was not realized that the plebiscite might be a tyranny.

The final text of the Declaration of Rights was meagre and ill-composed, but it is the triumphant proclamation of the doctrine that human obligations are not all assignable to contract, interest, or force.[7] The Preamble implies that our duties to God constitute our rights towards mankind.[8] The universal rights laid down are four: Liberty, Property, Security, Self-defence. The system of guarantees is as sacred as the rights it protects—representation, toleration, freedom of the Press, equality and security of rights, eligibility for office, proportionate taxation. The agent who exercises power is responsible to the sovereign people. Education, poverty, and constitutional revision are left to future legislation. This is the perpetual heritage of the Revolution. It is the beginning of a new era.[9]

Acton comments: This single page of print outweighs libraries, and is stronger than all the armies of Napoleon.

[1] *F.R.*, p. 66.
[2] *Ibid.*, p. 67.
[3] *Ibid.*, p. 81.
[4] *Ibid.*, p. 82.
[5] *Ibid.*, p. 94.
[6] *Ibid.*, p. 100.
[7] *Ibid.*, p. 106.
[8] *Ibid.*
[9] *Ibid.*, p. 107.

The stamp of Cartesian clearness is upon it, but without the logic, the precision, the thoroughness of French thought. There is no indication that Liberty is the goal, and not the starting point, that it is a faculty to be acquired, not a capital to invest, or that it depends on innumerable conditions, which embrace the entire life of man.[1] The country could not learn without teaching that popular power may be tainted with the same poison as personal power.[2] The Liberals, like Mounier and Malouet, hoped by the division of powers and the multiplication of checks to make their country as free as England or America. They desired to control the representatives by a Second Chamber, the royal veto, and the right of dissolution. For them the Constitution was a means of regulating and restraining the national will. For their rivals it was an instrument for accomplishing the popular will. The democrats refused to resist the people. There was, as yet, little concentration of the workers in towns, for the industrial age had hardly dawned, and it was hard to understand that the Third Estate itself contained divergent interests and the material of a coming conflict.[3]

In the following eighty-six years France had fourteen Constitutions, an average of one every six years. The failure of the first was due to want of management.

In addition to the democrats there were the jurists and the economists. The jurists were eager for legal reform and became the lawgivers of successive Assemblies and completed their code under Napoleon. The economists were as systematic and definite as the lawyers, and through Dupont de Nemours their theories obtained enduring influence.[4]

Robespierre regarded representation as treason to true democracy, and believed that Parliamentary votes ought to be brought into harmony with the wishes of the constituency by the Press, the galleries and the mob. The population of Paris, being the largest single portion of sovereign power, expressed the will of the people, in Robespierre's judgment, more certainly than deputies. Acton writes: Robespierre stands at the end of the scale, and the idea of Liberty, as it runs through the various sets of thought, is transformed into the idea of force. From Sieyès to Barnave, from Barnave to Camus, from Camus

[1] *F.R.*, p. 107. [2] *Ibid.*, pp. 107–108.
[3] *Ibid.*, p. 109. [4] *Ibid.*, p. 116.

to Buzot, and from Buzot the Girondin to Robespierre the Jacobin who killed the Girondins, we traverse the long line of possible politics; but the transitions are finely shaded, and the logic is continuous.[1]

The constitutional scheme was mainly due to Sieyès. He substituted eighty departments, besides Paris, for the historic Provinces. It is the measure which has mainly made the France of today. Power was not really divided between the legislative and the executive, there was no Senate, no initiative, no dissolution, no effective veto, no reliance on the judicial or the Federal element. Taken together these defects subverted the principle of division which is essential for liberty. The Conservatives refused a Second Chamber because they did not wish the Constitution to succeed. It was on this account that Royer-Collard said that all parties in the Revolution were honest except the Conservatives. The National Assembly swept away every security against unchecked democracy. Its reign lasted only from 16 July to 6 October.

The compulsory removal of the Government to Paris made the democracy preponderant. The constitutional cause, opposed by the Conservatives, was deserted by the Liberals. The Left were enabled to carry out their interpretation of the rights of man. They distrusted the King, and they were persuaded that securities for individual freedom are unnecessary in a popular community. These two views tended to the same practical result, to strengthen the legislative power, and to weaken the executive power. Mirabeau's statesmanlike idea was that the supreme need of the moment was vigorous administration, because all the assistance which order derives from habit and tradition had been lost. But the democratic monarch desired by Mirabeau might have become as dangerous as an arbitrary ruler, and his administration might have proved as great an obstacle to parliamentary government as French administration has always been since Napoleon.[2] The decision on 7 November forbidding deputies to take office ruined the Constitutional Monarchy.[3]

The best of the political legacy of the Revolution was the work of Sieyès. But in one department of public life the Revolution made a bad beginning. The bulk of the clergy were democratic.

[1] *F.R.*, p. 117. [2] *Ibid.*, p. 144. [3] *Ibid.*

The Assembly, by a series of hostile measures, turned them into enemies, and thereby made the Revolution hateful to a large part of the French people. This was the cause of the conflict which brought the movement to ruin. One powerful factor was the memory of religious persecution. There was also the financial question. Abolition of tithe made the clergy financially dependent on the State, which had therefore a specially powerful motive to appropriate what remained of Church property, which was put at the service of the nation. The Civil Constitution of the Clergy attempted to regulate the relations of Church and State, and the Assembly attempted to enforce it, while refusing a formal declaration that it meant no interference with the exclusive domain of religion. Two-thirds of the clergy refused to give the required oath.

The Civil Constitution injured the Revolution by creating a strong current of hostile feeling, and by inducing Louis to seek protection from Europe against his own people. The negotiation which led to the general war began in the middle of the religious crisis. The National Assembly did not see that its ecclesiastical policy violated the first principles of the Revolution. Toleration was disregarded. The Revolution went to ruin by its failure in dealing with the problem. It is also the best example of the harm which resulted from distrust of the executive.

Barnave attempted to save property and to secure middle-class rule. In this way the masses were given over to the Jacobins.

The Queen adopted the policy of coercing the French people by foreign arms, either by a demonstration of power or by invasion. The Revolution was confronted by Europe.

The errors of the National Assembly can be reduced to one. Having put the nation in the place of the Crown they gave it the same unlimited power, believing that a government representing the people could do no wrong. But they were not responsible for the European war. Between French principles and European practice there could be neither conciliation nor confidence.[1] The French Conservatives deliberately abandoned the constitutional King to his fate. In the new Assembly the dispute was not for doctrines but for power.

[1] *F.R.*, p. 198.

The ultimate cause of the war was the determination of Marie Antoinette not to submit to the new constitution. The Emperor told the Russian Minister that the cause of intervention against France was "the common cause of all crowned heads."[1] Austria refused to renounce the policy of coercing France, and the Revolution itself became aggressive. Burke had already proclaimed the doctrine of frightfulness,[2] and the European monarchs issued threats intended to inspire terror at a distance of 300 miles. This suggested the use of terror by the French. The weapon of terror, forged by the Royalists, served the cause it was intended to destroy.[3]

The French successfully withstood the onslaught of monarchical Europe, and discovered that the Continent was at their mercy. The King of Prussia abandoned Louis to his fate, having contributed to his dethronement by entering France, and to his execution by leaving it.[4]

The conquest of Europe by the French began, and the French doctrine of universal insurrection alienated England which entered the war on the execution of Louis. It was Danton who overthrew the monarchy and made the Republic. The King refused to revoke his veto on the banishment of the non-jurors. The Queen refused to be saved by Lafayette on constitutional terms, and preferred to rely on foreign armies. The revolutionary town-councillors who now came to the front, creatures of Danton, were responsible for the atrocities which followed.

The constitutional experiment, begun under Louis XVI, failed mainly through distrust of the executive and a mechanical misconstruction of the division of power.[5] The instinct of freedom gave way to the instinct of force, and the Liberal movement was reversed. Unity of power against the enemy became the order of the day. The threat of terror from abroad was met by terror at home. The new municipality provided a dictatorship, and the most conspicuous figures were Marat and Robespierre. About thirteen or fourteen hundred perished in the massacres. These crimes, and others equally great in the history of other countries, are still defended by historians.[6] The abolition of Monarchy was carried in the Convention

---

[1] *F.R.*, p. 208.   [2] *Ibid.*, p. 213.   [3] *Ibid.*, p. 214.
[4] *Ibid.*, pp. 219–220.   [5] *Ibid.*, p. 240.   [6] *Ibid.*, p. 248 (1895).

without discussion, and the Republic was proclaimed on receipt of the news of Valmy.

Pitt received information that Danton would save the King for £40,000. Pitt hesitated just too long. He explained that his reason for hesitation was that the execution of Louis would raise such a storm in England that the Whigs would be submerged.[1]

The Constitution of 1791 failed because it carried the division of powers and the reaction against monarchical centralization so far as to paralyse the executive.[2] The Convention proceeded to govern by revolutionary measures, arbitrary representatives were sent to the departments, and the revolutionary tribunal and the Secret Committee of Public Safety were set up.

The aim of the Jacobins was dictatorship, exercised in the name of the whole people. War against continental absolutism was the price of revolution.[3] The Jacobins triumphed by the help of the insurrectionary committee. The extinction of the Girondins removed the last obstacle to the Reign of Terror. Its purpose was to save France by the concentration of power. A new Republican Constitution was adopted which attempted to combine direct democracy with representative government. Robespierre, who had shown socialist inclinations in April, now revoked his earlier language, and insisted on security of property and proportionate, not progressive, taxation. Happiness, not Liberty, was declared the supreme end of civil society. The Constitution of 1793, says Acton, is superior to its reputation, and it rescinded the offer of support to insurgent nations, and renounced intervention and aggression. In regard to property, as in other things, it was marked by a pronounced Conservatism.[4] It was never carried out, and France was governed under extraordinary powers, and the *levée en masse* turned France into a nation of soldiers. The Committee of Legislation presented the first draft of a Code of Civil Law, which was the basis of the Code of Napoleon. The days of Robespierre's established reign were from 25 September 1793 to 26 July 1794. In March Hébert was financed by foreign bankers to finish the tyranny of Robespierre. The attempt

[1] *F.R.*, p. 254. [2] *Ibid.*, p. 256.
[3] *Ibid.*, p. 259. [4] *Ibid.*, pp. 271-272.

failed, and by a large expenditure of money Robespierre had Paris on his side. From April Robespierre was absolute. He perished by the monstrous imposture of associating divine sanction with the crimes of his sanguinary rule.[1] The Feast of the Supreme Being was held on 8 June. It raised fears that it was intended to be a starting point for divine right. The law of Prairial suppressed the formalities of law in political trials. Executions rose from an average of 32 to 196 a week. After the great French victory at Fleurus the Terror came to an end. It had been endured while the danger lasted, and with the danger, it came to an end. Robespierre's enemies made terms with the Plain, he was outlawed and sentenced to death. Robespierre's ultimate objects are not known.[2]

The French Revolution was an attempt to establish in the public law of Europe maxims which had triumphed by the aid of France in America.[3] The case for the French Revolution was even stronger than the case for the American Revolution.

In the war on land France achieved preponderance in 1795. Carnot, the organizer, owed his success to arbitrary control over promotion, and the cheapness of French lives. He could sacrifice as many men as he required.

A new Constitution, the Directory, was adopted by a languid vote. It offered securities for order and liberty such as France had never enjoyed.[4] It marks the close of the Revolutionary period.

When tension developed between Royalists and supporters of the Convention, Bonaparte hurried to headquarters and was appointed second in command. The Royalists were defeated, and Paris felt, for the first time, the grasp of the master.[5]

In the following year, October 1796, Napoleon first expressed the ambition, subsequently realized in the Concordat, to make terms with the Church.[6] Napoleon's mission was to destroy the inorganic Europe of the old régime.[7] Napoleon provoked national feeling by attacking nationality in Russia, delivering it in Italy, by governing in defiance of it in Germany and Spain.[8] But nationality received its severest blow at the Congress of Vienna. The liberal, or, rather, the democratic

---

[1] *F.R.*, p. 285.
[2] *Ibid.*, p. 300.
[3] *Ibid.*, p. 317.
[4] *Ibid.*, p. 342.
[5] *Ibid.*, p. 344.
[6] *H.E.*, p. 449.
[7] *Ibid.*, p. 443.
[8] *H.F.*, p. 281.

revival came from Spain,[1] but the Constitution of 1812 was overthrown by the French in 1823, the supreme triumph of the restored French monarchy. But the extreme Royalists ruined that monarchy, which was overthrown by the united democracy in 1830. The shock of the July revolution was felt in Poland, Belgium, Switzerland, and England.

The Reform Bill was carried in the streets of Paris.[2]

Till 1827 England had been governed by Lord Liverpool, chosen, not by the nation, but by the owners of the land. The English gentry were well content, and valued the safe sterility of Lord Liverpool's mind. His mediocrity was his merit. His career exemplifies the natural affinity between the love of conservatism and the fear of ideas.[3]

In America, in the Presidency of Monroe, there was the "era of good feeling," when most of the incongruities which had come down from the Stuarts had been reformed, and the motives of later divisions were not yet active. The causes of old-world trouble, ignorance, pauperism, the glaring contrast between rich and poor, religious strife, public debts, standing armies and war, were almost unknown. No other age or country had solved so successfully the problems of free societies.[4]

In France, Talleyrand, at the height of his authority and fame in 1830, defied the wrath of the Government, and compelled Louis Philippe to refuse the offer to his son of the Crown of Belgium.[5] Early in life he had accepted the essential philosophy of Liberalism as interpreted by Montesquieu, Turgot, Adam Smith and Bentham.[6] In 1786 he had defended the Commercial Treaty as based on the true natural laws that could put an end to the rivalry of nations. He believed that France and England ought to be inseparable in the cause of reason and justice against the world of divine right.

In Switzerland after 1815 democracy was in abeyance. The national will had no organ. A new federal constitution was adopted in 1847 ostensibly charged with the duty of carrying out democracy. By 1874 the railways, and the vast interests they had created, made the position of the cantonal governments untenable. The new Constitution of 1874 is one of the most significant works of modern democracy. A Swiss jurist

[1] *H.F.*, p. 89.   [2] *H.E.*, p. 489.   [3] *H.F.*, p. xii.
[4] *Ibid.*, p. 56.   [5] *H.E.*, p. 400.   [6] *Ibid.*

has expressed its spirit by saying that the State is the appointed conscience of the nation.[1]

Under the bourgeois monarchy in France, the ministers believed that they could make the people prosper if they could have their own way. They supposed that the intelligent middle class was destined by Heaven to rule.[2] They believed that government by professional men, by manufacturers and scholars was sure to be safe, and almost certain to be reasonable and practical. Money became the object of a political superstition, such as formerly attached to land, and afterwards attached to labour. The masses became aware that they were still governed by their employers. Republicans and socialists coalesced, and were victorious in 1848. The fruit of the victory was universal suffrage.[3]

Since then the promises of socialism have supplied the best energy of democracy. The coalition of democracy and socialism has been the ruling fact in French politics. It was responsible for Napoleon III, the Commune of 1871, and was a powerful factor under the Third Republic. It is the only shape in which democracy has found an entrance into Germany. Liberty has lost its spell, and democracy maintains itself by the promise of substantial gifts to the masses of the people.[4]

The great danger of democracy is the tyranny of the majority, or rather of the party, not always the majority, that succeeds in carrying elections. The remedy is proportional representation. It is profoundly democratic.[5] The best check on democracy is federalism.[6]

The fall of Guizot discredited the maxim that reason is sovereign. Comte's influence told in the same direction, for he said that Positivist philosophers would manufacture political ideas, which no one would be permitted to dispute.

Economics seems destined to achieve scientific certainty. The argument between economists and socialists has entered a new phase by the rise of a middle party.[7]

In England, till 1832, the upper class enjoyed undivided sway, and used it for their own advantage. Almost all that has been done for the good of the people has been done since the rich

[1] *H.F.*, p. 91.   [2] *Ibid.*, p. 92.   [3] *Ibid.*
[4] *Ibid.*, p. 93 (1878).   [5] *Ibid.*, p. 97 (1878).   [6] *Ibid.*, p. 98.
[7] *Ibid.*, pp. 98–99 (1878).

lost the monopoly of power. The masses had to keep their sense of responsibility, of their danger, of the condition from which they had been rescued, of the objects still before them, and the ancient enemy behind.[1]

The supreme merit of Gladstone is that under his leadership democracy set bounds to its power.[2] In England democracy did not degenerate into class war or mob-rule, or dictatorship.

English history in the nineteenth century should be written not only in terms of class interests, but also of the ceaseless conflict of defined forms of thought. The historian should explain wherein a Conservative differs from Whig and Tory, where a Liberal draws the line against Whig and Radical, how you distinguish a philosophic from an economic Radical, or Manchester from Birmingham, at what point democracy begins, how it combines with socialism, why some socialists are Liberal, and some democrats Tory.[3]

The most characteristic Liberal invention of the nineteenth century was open competitive examination for the Civil Service.[4] Compulsory education is the greatest revolution since the sixteenth century.[5]

It is the poor who have the greatest stake in the country, because for them misgovernment means, not restricted luxury, but pain, and want, and degradation, and risk to their own lives and to their children's souls.[6]

The world owes religious liberty to the Dutch Revolution, constitutional government to the English, federal republicanism to the American, political equality to the French Revolution and its successors.[7]

The freest country in the world as well as the richest and most powerful is America.[8] Liberal Americans look forward to the spread of federal democracies all over the world.[9] The three principal items on the world's agenda are Peace, Socialism, and Education.[10]

---

[1] *L.M.G.*, p. 94 (1881). [2] *Corr.*, p. 235. [3] *H.E.*, pp. 488–489.
[4] *Acton MSS*. I did not take a note of this reference.
[5] *Gasquet*, p. 329. [6] *L.M.G.*, pp. 49–50.
[7] *L.M.H.*, pp. 13–14 (1895). [8] *Ibid.*, p. 314 (1901).
[9] *H.F.*, p. 587. [10] Add. 4870.

X

ACTON'S RELATION TO OTHER THINKERS

Acton himself defined his relation to the most important thinkers. Of Heraclitus he writes:

> Between the rigid didactics of the early Pythagoreans and the dissolving theories of Protagoras, a philosopher arose who stood aloof from both extremes, and whose difficult sayings were never really understood until our time. Heraclitus, of Ephesus, deposited his book in the temple of Diana. The book has perished, like the temple and the worship, but its fragments have been collected and interpreted with incredible ardour, by the scholars, the divines, the philosophers, and politicians who have engaged the most intensely in the toil and stress of this century. The most renowned logician of the last century adopted every one of his propositions; and the most brilliant agitator among Continental Socialists composed a work of eight hundred and forty pages to celebrate his memory.[1]

After these references to Hegel and Louis Blanc, Acton continues:

> The only thing fixed and certain in the midst of change is the universal and sovereign reason, which all men may not perceive, but which is common to all. Laws are sustained by no human authority, but by virtue of their derivation from the one law that is divine. These sayings, which recall the grand outlines of political truth which we have found in the Sacred Books, and carry us forward to the latest teaching of our most enlightened contemporaries, would bear a good deal of elucidation and comment.[2]

But in the history of political science the highest place belongs to Plato and Aristotle: "The *Laws* of the one, the

[1] *H.F.*, p. 21.
[2] *Ibid.*, p. 22. Cf. Add. 4870: "Heraclitus . . . the deepest of early philosophers . . . anticipated subsequent development."

Politics of the other, are, if I may trust my own experience, the books from which we may learn the most about the principles of politics. The penetration with which those great masters of thought analyzed the institutions of Greece, and exposed their vices, is not surpassed by anything in later literature; by Burke, or Hamilton, the best political writers of the last century; by Tocqueville or Roscher, the most eminent of our own."[1]

In his manuscripts[2] Acton writes, "The [Greek] teachers are still our teachers, and except Xty. still the most powerful influence existing on the intellect of the world." "Sophocles, Aristophanes, Thucydides, Plato, Aristotle, Demosthenes—The whole world since then has produced but one man equal to any one of them—and that man was Shakespeare." "What was the matter at Athens? Poverty." "Those nations are happy which do not resent the complexity of life. The Athenians had the unhappy prerogative that they were the cleverest of mankind." "How they all detest Athenian democracy—Thucydides, Euripides, Sophocles, Aristophanes, Isocrates, Lysias, Socrates, Plato, Aristotle, Xenophon, Andocides, Demosthenes. Hence its immense value. It produced all that was in it—made the principles develop all their results. Showed what the perils of Democracy, even the most gifted are." "Their incomparable writers and orators still teach the great lesson of freedom." "Socrates taught ἀγαθοὶ νομοι—a law independent of the State, and superior to it. So not positive law is divine—but that law by which it is to be judged." "The idea of preventing the prevalence of one party is at the bottom of the Politics of Aristotle, Polybius, Cicero, the Stoics." "Danger of a class of society getting the control of the State. The object is to prevent that."

It was the Stoics who led the way to freedom: "Their test of good government is its conformity to principles that can be traced to a higher legislator. . . . The great question is to discover, not what governments prescribe, but what they ought to prescribe; for no prescription is valid against the conscience of mankind."[3] Zeno led men to the very Gate of Christianity.

---

[1] *H.F.*, p. 22. But cf. Add. 4945: "Freewill denied by Socrates and Plato. Affirmed by Aristotle. Till then, no real liberty."
[2] Add. 4870.   [3] *H.F.*, p. 24.

Their doctrines were adopted by the Roman jurists, and they find their highest development in Cicero, Seneca, and Philo. St. Augustine, after quoting Seneca, exclaimed: "What more could a Christian say than this Pagan has said?" The answer is, Render under Caesar. The only lesson of early Christianity was freedom of conscience.[1]

Augustine Acton characterized as the deepest influence of one mind on the Church.[2] He quotes Augustine's philosophy of historiography: "No one would discover, for no one would discuss unless roused by the blows of misrepresentation. Truth would not be sought so industriously, if it had no enemies to tell lies of it."[3] Augustine's rebuke of the superstitious is also quoted: "If the State of which we are secular children passes away, that of which we are spiritual children passes not."[4] And a passage from the *City of God*: "The fratricide was the first founder of the secular State."[5] In his manuscripts Acton wrote that when Pelagius appealed to conscience Augustine went against him. Augustine removed the criterion from within to outside. In his eyes an external authority alone is safe. The inner man is corrupted by original sin. The passage in *Romans* (xiv. 23) which Aquinas made the basis of a theory of conscience Augustine misinterpreted (see Meyer's *Commentary*).[6] Augustinianism was an impediment to the idea of conscience.[7]

Acton notices, without comment, that Alcuin of York, in the eighth century, was the first in Christian times to propound *Vox populi vox dei*, and John of Salisbury, in the twelfth, the first Christian advocate of tyrannicide. "Aquinas devised Whiggism to prop religious absolutism."[8] Before him Anselm is equated with "a mercantile system of religion," Abelard with "the use of religion apart from faith," Gratian with natural law.[9] Peter Lombard provided the framework of mediaeval theology, Maimonides influenced alike Christian, Moslem and Jew, and especially Aquinas and Albertus Magnus. Aquinas

[1] Add. 4870. [2] *Hawarden Letters*, p. 187.
[3] *H.E.*, p. 342. [4] *Sermo* cv.
[5] *H.F.*, p. 191. [6] Add. 4901.
[7] Add. 5395.
[8] *Hawarden Letters*, p. 187. Cf. Add. 4940: "A very liberal modern might be composed of St. Thomas and his antipode Marsilius, taken in equal quantities, just proportion."
[9] Add. 4870.

was the first Whig. Marsilius founded government on consent. In Gerson Ghibellinism blossomed into Gallicanism.[1] Lorenzo Valla applied scientific methods to ecclesiastical claims.[2] He is the founder of freedom of speech in history.[3] He is the first in the line of discoverers, which includes Sigonius, Mabillon, Borghesi and Morgan, who have made history a science.[4]

Machiavelli released power from duty.[5] Hobbes followed up Machiavelli's arguments to the conclusions Machiavelli abstained from.[6] Marx's *Kapital* is a Koran.[7]

In his manuscripts Acton wrote, "Hobbes, like Locke, denies its [conscience's] existence." Adam Smith, in his *Theory of Moral Sentiments* (II, 287), "says that the notion of Conscience was first analyzed in reply to Hobbes." "Hobbes rejects Conscience, for the sake of arbitrary monarchy—The two went together. So that Butler's restoration of Conscience is a preliminary to the establishment of freedom." "After Hobbes, all liberty resided in the restoration of Conscience."[8]

The point of universal agreement, the point which gives an element of truth to Hobbes, and which Hobbes identifies as utility, the point which Lord Lindsay describes as "an agreed method of settling differences," in Acton is represented by the common ethical presuppositions which, experience shows, entail constitutional government. In Add. 4954 Acton writes: "Hobbes first built politics on the state of nature. Supreme power can be delegated, but not divided—Rousseau said it cannot be delegated."

The French moralists separated ethics from religion—Charron, Pibrac, Duvair, and others.[9] Hooker and Grotius separated politics from religion. Grotius is the founder of real political science because he based it on the law of nature and on a series of real and hypothetical contracts.[10]

Acton's indebtedness to seventeenth-century thinkers has already been abundantly illustrated. The most important are Harrington, Lilburne, Williams, Penn, Bayle, Locke, Leibniz.

[1] *Hawarden Letters*, p. 187.　　[2] *Ibid.*
[3] *L.M.H.*　　[4] *H.E.*, p. 460.
[5] *Hawarden Letters*, p. 188.　　[6] *H.F.*, p. 228.
[7] *Corr.*, p. 169.　　[8] Add. 4901, pp. 255, 259, 358, 362.
[9] *N.B.R.*, July 1870, p. 540. Cf. Add. 4939: "Charron, Sagesse, 11.3,4. Law of nature eternal, perpetual, ineffaceable by time or sin."
[10] *H.F.*, p. 46. See also Appendix IX.

It is Acton's debt to William Penn that needs special emphasis here. Acton adopted the theory of the inner light in a passage of great interest on a solemn occasion;[1] "A man of ordinary proportion or inferior metal knows not how to think out the rounded circle of his thought, how to divest his will of its surroundings and to rise above the pressure of time and race and circumstance, to choose the star that guides his course, to correct, and test, and assay his convictions by the light within, and, with a resolute conscience and ideal courage, to remodel and reconstitute the character which birth and education gave him." More generally, in the same place: "the equal claim of every man to be unhindered by man in the fulfilment of duty to God—a doctrine laden with storm and havoc, which is the secret essence of the Rights of Man, and the indestructible soul of Revolution."

Fénelon is twice given a sympathetic portrait: "It is the vision of a higher world to be intimate with the character of Fénelon, the cherished model of politicians, ecclesiastics, and men of letters, the witness against one century and precursor of another, the advocate of the poor against oppression, of liberty in an age of arbitrary power, of tolerance in an age of persecution, of the humane virtues among men accustomed to sacrifice them to authority, the man of whom one enemy says that his cleverness was enough to strike terror, and another, that genius poured in torrents from his eyes."[2] A larger sketch is given in Acton's second lecture at Cambridge (Heralds of the French Revolution):

> The revolt of conscience began with him before the glory of the monarchy was clouded over. His views grew from an extraordinary perspicacity and refinement in the estimate of men. He learnt to refer the problem of government, like the conduct of private life, to the mere standard of morals, and extended further than any one the plain but hazardous practice of deciding all things by the exclusive precepts of enlightened virtue.... In the judgment of Fénelon, power is poison.... Nothing but a constitution can avert arbitrary power.... He would transfer the duties of government to local and central assemblies; and he demands entire freedom of trade, and education provided by law, because

[1] *Inaugural.*   [2] *Ibid.*

children belong to the State first and to the family afterwards. He does not resign the hope of making men good by act of parliament, and his belief in public institutions as a means of moulding individual character brings him nearly into touch with a distant future.

He is the Platonic founder of revolutionary thinking . . . Fénelon treated Louis XIV in all his grandeur more severely than the disciples of Voltaire treated Louis XV in all his degradation.

Acton's relation to Hume needs emphasis because of Hume's special place in the history of thought. The *Essays* Acton characterized as a "philosophy of negation."[1] He notices Hume's doctrine that sequence is cause, and his fatuous comment on Machiavelli that he lived at too early a period of the world's history to be a good judge of political truth.[2]

Acton found the classical English philosophy of history in Adam Smith.[3] He gave a scientific backbone to liberal sentiment.[4] But Adam Smith cares for morality, not for truth.[5] He founds society on self-interest and/or sympathy, he knows not which.[6] His logical effect is the French Revolution and socialism.[7] He has to be traced back, Acton wrote, to his sources, Steuart, Cantillon, Hume, Turgot, Mercier de la Rivière,[8] and, of course, Locke.[9]

Burke has a unique importance in Acton's thought which has always been recognized.[10] But there are two Burkes, and it was the liberal Burke that Acton venerated as a philosopher. At the age of twenty-four Acton regarded the *Appeal from the New to the Old Whigs* as "the law and the prophets." In 1888, at the age of fifty-four, Acton said that he would have hanged Burke on the same gallows as Robespierre.[11] This was said half in jest; but only half. In the closing passage of the *Inaugural* he

[1] *Hawarden Letters*, p. 188.   [2] *H.F.*, p. 218.
[3] *Ibid.*, p. 591.   [4] *Hawarden Letters*, p. 188.
[5] Add. 5393.   [6] Add. 4965.
[7] *L.M.G.*, p. 92.   [8] Add. 5481.
[9] *Corr.*, p. 230.
[10] See also Acton's manuscripts on Burke, cited Chapter II *ante*, and cf. Add. 4939: "Discoveries in Politics since Montesquieu. Burke, Turgot, Smith, Rousseau, Sieyès, Savigny, Bentham, Hamilton, Calhoun, Constant, Kant, Hare, Rodbertus."
[11] *L.M.G.*, 2nd ed., p. 187.

said that Burke "when true to himself"[1] was our greatest teacher. What Acton meant he explained by a quotation from Burke:

> My principles enable me to form my judgment upon men and actions in history, just as they do in common life; and are not formed out of events and characters either present or past. History is a preceptor of prudence, not of principles.
> The principles of true politics are those of morality enlarged; and I neither now do, nor ever will admit of any other.

That was Acton's creed.

Between 1858, the date of the uncritical praise of the conservative Burke, and 1895, the date of the passage just quoted, there are several places where Acton clearly indicates what can be said against as well as in favour of Burke. To Gladstone Acton wrote: "One day I shall say to a pupil: 'Read Burke, read him night and day, he is our best political writer.' And the pupil will answer: 'Dear me, I thought he broke up the Whig party and trained no end of men to conservatism.' I shall have to answer: 'Yes; both sayings are true.' "[2]

Similarly in his letters to Mary Gladstone Acton gives both sides of the case:

> You can hardly imagine what Burke is for all of us who think about politics, and are not wrapped in the blaze and whirlwind of Rousseau. Systems of scientific thought have been built up by famous scholars on the fragments that fell from his table. Great literary fortunes have been made by men who traded on the hundredth part of him.[3]

On the other hand Goldsmith's cruel line "And to party gave up what was meant for mankind" is "literally true."[4] "Burke," wrote Acton, "loved to evade the arbitration of principle. He was prolific of arguments that were admirable but not decisive. He dreaded two-edged weapons and maxims that faced both ways. Through his inconsistencies we can perceive that his mind stood in a brighter light than his language; but he refused to employ in America reasons which might be

---

[1] *L.M.H.*, p. 28.   [2] *Corr.*, p. 227.
[3] *L.M.G.*, pp. 56–57. This refers to German historiography, and to Macaulay, Brougham, and Mackintosh (see Chapters II and VIII *ante*).
[4] *Ibid.*, p. 49.

fitted to Ireland, lest he should become odious to the great families and impossible with the King. Half of his genius was spent in masking the secret that hampered it."¹

Burke's appeal to expediency Acton specially condemned, and notably in Morley who got it, said Acton, from Burke.

With these serious qualifications it is not easy to overestimate the influence of Burke on Acton. Out of the elements of the American crisis Burke built "the noblest political philosophy in the world." "Burke at his best is England at its best. Through him and through American influence upon him, the sordid policy of the Walpolean Whigs became a philosophy, and a combination of expedients was changed into a system of general principles."² And again: "In the American speeches of Chatham and Camden, in Burke's writings from 1778 to 1783, in the *Wealth of Nations*, and the tracts of Sir William Jones, there is an immense development. The natural bounds are overcome. . . . Burke's address to the colonists is the logical outcome of the principles of liberty and the notion of a higher law above municipal codes and constitutions, with which Whiggism began."³

In Acton's study of the influence of America on the French Revolution there are many references to Burke:

> The most significant instance of the action of America on Europe is Edmund Burke. We think of him as a man who, in early life, rejected all generalities and abstract propositions, and who became the most strenuous and violent of conservatives. But there is an interval when, as the quarrel with the Colonies went on, Burke was as revolutionary as Washington. The inconsistency is not as flagrant as it seems. He had been brought forward by the party of measured propriety and imperative moderation, of compromise and unfinished thought, who claimed the right of taxing, but refused to employ it. When he urged the differences in every situation and every problem, and shrank from the common denominator and the underlying principle, he fell into step with his friends. As an Irishman, who had married into an Irish Catholic family, it was desirable that he should adopt no theories in America which would unsettle Ireland. He had learnt to teach government by party as an almost sacred dogma, and party forbids revolt as a breach of the laws of

¹ *L.M.G.*, p. 49.   ² *L.M.H.*, p. 276.   ³ *Ibid.*, pp. 217-218.

the game. His scruples and his protests, and his defiance of theory, were the policy and the precaution of a man conscious of restraints, and not entirely free in the exertion of powers that lifted him far above his tamer surroundings. As the strife sharpened and the Americans made way, Burke was carried along, and developed views which he never utterly abandoned, but which are difficult to reconcile with much that he wrote when the Revolution had spread to France.[1]

Acton continues:

In his address to the Colonists he says: "We do not know how to qualify millions of our countrymen, contending with one heart for an admission to privileges which we have ever thought our own happiness and honour, by odious and unworthy names. On the contrary, we highly revere the principles on which you act. We had much rather see you independent of this crown and kingdom, than joined to it by so unnatural a conjunction as that of freedom and servitude. We view the establishment of the English Colonies on principles of liberty, as that which is to render this kingdom venerable to future ages. In comparison of this, we regard all the victories and conquests of our warlike ancestors, or of our own times, as barbarous, vulgar distinctions, in which many nations, whom we look upon with little respect or value, have equalled, if not far exceeded us. Those who have and who hold to that foundation of common liberty, whether on this or on your side of the ocean, we consider as the true and the only true Englishmen. Those who depart from it, whether there or here, are attainted, corrupted in blood, and wholly fallen from their original rank and value. They are the real rebels to the fair constitution and just supremacy of England. A long course of war with the administration of this country may be but a prelude to a series of wars and contentions among yourselves, to end at length (as such scenes have too often ended) in a species of humiliating repose, which nothing but the preceding calamities could reconcile to the dispirited few who survived them. We allow that even this evil is worth the risk to men of honour when rational liberty is at stake, as in the present case we confess and lament that it is."[2]

Acton goes on to note that at other times Burke spoke as

[1] *F.R.*, p. 27. [2] *Ibid.*, pp. 27–28.

follows: "Nothing less than a convulsion that will shake the globe to its centre can ever restore the European nations to that liberty by which they were once so much distinguished. . . . Christ appeared in sympathy with the lowest of the people, and thereby made it a firm and ruling principle that their welfare was the object of all government. In all forms of government the people is the true legislator. The remote and efficient cause is the consent of the people, either actual or implied, and such consent is absolutely essential to its validity. . . . Privilege of the crown and privilege of Parliament are only privilege so long as they are exercised for the benefit of the people. The voice of the people is a voice that is to be heard, and not the votes and resolutions of the House of Commons. . . . It would be a strange thing if two hundred peers should have it in their power to defeat by their negative what had been done by the people of England. . . . All human laws are, properly speaking, only declaratory; they may alter the mode and application, but have no power over the substance of original justice. A conservation and secure enjoyment of our natural rights is the great and ultimate purpose of civil society. . . . It is the law of nature, which is the law of God."[1]

Acton comments: "I cannot resist the inference from these passages that Burke, after 1770, underwent other influences than those of his reputed masters, the Whigs of 1688. And if we find that strain of unwonted thought in a man who afterwards gilded the old order of things and wavered as to toleration and the slave trade, we may expect that the same causes would operate in France."[2]

The conservative Burke Acton sees as the ancestor of the German historians whose limitations he exposed in the first number of the *English Historical Review*. The German historians failed to see that the Revolution itself was historic, having roots that could profitably be traced far back. Where German historians failed French historians succeeded. Here we may recall Acton's treatment of French and German historiography in the nineteenth century, bearing in mind that Acton believed

[1] *F.R.*, pp. 28–31.
[2] *Ibid.*, p. 31. The lectures from which these extracts are taken were delivered in 1895 to 1899 (*aetat.* 61 to 65). Acton's MS. notes on Burke have already been quoted (Chapter II above).

that where both Germans and Frenchmen failed, Englishmen and Americans had succeeded, that is in the practical solution of the problem of combining continuity and liberal progress, for which Acton's formula was the sovereignty of the developed conscience, the conscience developed by experience and knowledge. The problem Burke posed to Acton was: Is politics to be treated philosophically or historically? Acton firmly answers, Both. But it is conscience that is supreme, conscience founded on experience and permanent and tested convictions resting on absolutely certain knowledge.

Summarizing, we may say, Acton's indebtedness to earlier writers lies on the surface, but his most important principles he took from the Bible, especially the fundamental formula of all his thought, tradition and the higher law.[1] From the Old Testament he took the ideas of contract, federation, and development, from the New Testament the most important of all his principles, Render to Caesar.

From Heraclitus Acton takes the idea of the sovereign and immutable reason, the one thing fixed in a universe of change, from Plato constitutional government, division of sovereignty, and the notion of an ideal standard.[2] Aristotle gives him the best formulation of the ideal of mixed government or polity, Aquinas the best expression of the mediaeval form of Whiggism. Grotius founded international law on natural law. In his manuscripts, under the heading Grotius, Acton wrote: "If a principle is set up, shall you not sacrifice your country to it? Shall you not prefer your party, which represents your principle to your country which represents none?" But in the same

[1] The number of what are approximately synonyms for "tradition and the higher law" and analogous distinctions in Acton's writings is rather large, e.g. precedent and principle, empiricism and rationalism, continuity and revolution, continuity and progress, national and universal, custom and reason, Caesar and God, the lower and the higher series, fact and opinion, this world and the next, economics and religion (cf. MSS.: "Religion and political economy rule the world—that is, what men think best for themselves in this world and the next"). In Acton's view it is the development of conscience which is the heart of the matter. "Christianity and the British Constitution" is really in part another analogue for conscience and development. Acton's method consists in giving the greatest possible weight to both factors and combining them. But it is conscience that is supreme. In short, Acton combined the historical and natural rights schools.

[2] Cf. Introduction to A. E. Taylor's translation of the *Laws*.

manuscript there is an entry: "Edinburgh [Review], Oct. 1876, p. 500. Passage from Ruskin showing the need of continuous growth in politics." Here, as always, the opposed points of view are present to Acton's mind. The thinkers of the Puritan revolution saw as far in many directions as we do now.[1] These are the ideas of religious freedom, separation of Church and State, self-government, diminution of inequalities of wealth, the economic interpretation of history. Williams and Penn give the finest exposition of the doctrine of toleration, Leibniz, in the *lex continui*, anticipates Hegel and Darwin. Locke, said Acton, is always reasonable and sensible, but diluted, pedestrian, and poor. But he looms tremendously, filling an immense space, the master of Hume, Adam Smith, and Rousseau, and on toleration nearly the principal classic. He is, says Acton, the largest of all Englishmen. Montesquieu is described as being "clever and pretentious."[2] Hume's Essays are a philosophy of negation.[3] Rousseau Acton pronounces a "true theorist," but chiefly on account of his later writings, which, he said, were "loaded with political wisdom." Rousseau's essay on the Constitution of Poland showed that he realized that the social contract theory was not universally applicable.[4] As a theorist of democracy Acton preferred Sieyès, above all for the argument that the national will is discovered by discussion. Adam Smith, Acton called the classic English philosophy of history. His logical effect is the French Revolution and socialism. Burke fails because he does not reconcile national and universal. Acton's own formula, the sovereignty of the developed

---

[1] Consult Lord Lindsay's Introduction to Professor Woodhouse's *Puritanism and Liberty*. Cf. Add. 4954: "Harrington first thoroughly understood Liberty as it may be. A really free democracy." See also Add. 4945: "What the several Sects contributed: Independents, local self-government, Quakers, reign of Conscience, Socinians, Toleration." In Add. 4940 Acton notes anticipations of the Quaker attitude to military service: "Condemn military service: Lactantius, Inst. V. 18, vi 20. Jerome to Nepotian: LX. 8. 9. Paulinus of Nola, Ep. Victircio vxiii 7. But the Council of Arles 314 decided the other way: De his qui arma projiciunt in pace, placuit abstineri eos de communione." I have found in Acton no reference to Tolstoy. This is probably because his later work had not been translated.

[2] Add. 4870.   [3] *Hawarden Letters*.

[4] Acton recognizes the organic element in Rousseau's thought implicitly, but not explicitly. In Add. 4950 he writes: "Idea of organism applies to forms—not to ideas."

conscience, was an attempt to succeed where Burke failed. Of Jefferson Acton wrote: "How development of nations keeps the reality a little behind the wish and the will. That is, the people live under a rule made by others. Each generation is governed, necessarily, by a former generation. Jefferson's great idea: Let it be governed by its own ideas." (Add. 4942.) Hamilton and Jefferson Acton valued as the greatest theorists of federalism apart from Rousseau, Kant for the reconciliation of empiricism and rationalism, historical causation, and personal autonomy. One of Herder's correspondents wrote: "*La pensée de Kant était constamment en Angleterre, parceque Rousseau et Hume s'y trouvaient réunis.*"[1] Hegel Acton appreciated for his luminous treatment of continuity in ideas, the French Doctrinaires, Royer-Collard, Guizot, and Constant for the modern formulation of the doctrine of separation of Church and State. Bentham is one of the "Fathers of the Liberal Church."[2] The day on which he decided that every part of the judicial and administrative system must be subjected to the closest scrutiny is memorable in the political calendar beyond the entire administration of many statesmen. Tocqueville is "as just as Aristides." Three of Tocqueville's ideas specially interested Acton: (1) the need to reconcile democracy and religion; (2) democracy leads to centralization[3]; (3) the idea, "which Tocqueville made a corner-stone," that nations that lack the self-governing force of religion are unfit for freedom. Mill's great merit was the defence of the minority, and of the rights of minorities. But in another manuscript (Add. 4943) Acton wrote: "What does Brougham know in his political philosophy? or even Macaulay, Mackintosh, Mill. Now that is what had to be done—just as Puchta did Roman law, or Stubbs the Constitution, or Freeman Federalism, or Baur for theology." Vinet forged the alliance between liberalism and conscience. Acton bracketed Vinet with Butler and Kant. He regarded his *Manifestation des Convictions Religieuses* as one

---

[1] Add. 4916. This passage is dated 16 August 1766.
[2] In Add. 4954 there is a highly significant comment: "Hegel omits America." Cf. Add. 4939: "Hegel sees extension of Liberty as the law of history—but not its deeper conception."
[3] This, it will be remembered, is the theme of the concluding chapters of *Democracy in America*.

of the world's decisive books, and Astié's *Esprit de Vinet* as one of the most important. Vinet's key-note may be illustrated from a passage in the *Convictions Religieuses*: "*Tout devoir emporte un droit; il n'est pas de droit plus sacré que celui de remplir son devoir; c'est même ice-bas le seul droit absolu; car le droit s'appuie sur une nécessité primitive; or le devoir est la première des nécessités, et, à la rigueur, la seule nécessité.*"[1] The consonance of this view with Acton's fundamental beliefs needs no emphasis. The same may be said of Vinet's doctrine of the separation of Church and State.

Dr. Vernon Bartlett concluded an encyclopaedia article on Vinet by saying that Acton ranked him with Rothe. In a sense Acton ranked him even higher. A passage from Vinet, which is copied in Acton's manuscripts, runs: "Conscience is not ourselves; it is against us; therefore it is something other than ourselves. But if it is other than ourselves, what can it be but God? And if it be God, we must give it the honour due to God; we cannot reverence the Sovereign less than the ambassador."[2] Still more revealing is a later passage in the same manuscript: "Note that all parties met, from different regions, to accept Conscience—Sarasa, Butler, Rousseau, Kant, Fichte, Vinet."

Yet Acton thought that even Vinet was open to objections so obvious that they must occur to anyone. In one of his letters, Acton wrote: "[Pascal and Vinet] raise more doubts than they answer."[3] The great point is that conscience must be guided by experience and knowledge.

Rothe Acton termed the greatest moral theologian of modern times—in spite of the fact that he ejected the term "conscience" from the second edition of his *Ethics*. Trendelenburg Acton respected for his resolute founding of politics on ethics, Roscher and Cournot for their economics and sociology. Acton's judgment on Roscher is an especially interesting illustration of his insight as a critic. Marshall calls Roscher "acute and well-balanced." Acton, who ranked Roscher in economics as high as Burke in politics, wrote that Roscher's "interest was first in history, next in government, only in the third place for his own science of economics."[4] In the same manuscript he writes: "Formerly P[olitical] E[conomy] was deductive, or

[1] P. 183, 2nd ed., Paris, 1858.
[2] Add. 4901.
[3] *Corr.*, 227 (1896).
[4] Add. 5481.

deeply influenced by local causes, by unscientific, contingent elements. They were great practical men, De Witt and Turgot, great theorists and observers, Smith and Malthus. But their science was like Descartes' philosophy—Roscher turned on the waters of history. History of the doctrine, history of the determining facts." Most succinctly: "Since 1865, the great event is the incorporation of political economy in the historical domain."[1]

As a political theorist Acton stands between T. H. Green and Lord Lindsay.[2] Like Green and Lord Lindsay Acton found his inspiration in Plato, and in the thinkers of the Puritan revolution.[3] There is a very obvious resemblance between Green's conception of the function of the State as "the hinderer of the hindrances to the good life," and Acton's conception of the meaning and conditions of freedom, and between Lord Lindsay's emphasis on the function of discussion in a democratic community, and Acton's endorsement of the same doctrine in Sieyès. With less critical power than T. H. Green or Lord Lindsay, Acton had greater historical knowledge, and his value is that his thinking is historical. This gives his thought an extra dimension which no other philosopher has possessed in the same degree.

In political science Acton stands between Mill and Sir Ernest Barker, in sociology between Roscher, and Hobhouse,

[1] Add. 5481.
[2] Very curiously the only reference Acton makes to T. H. Green in his published writings appears to be in a letter where he refers to him as the editor of Hume. There are two references to T. H. Green in the MSS. (Add. 4943): "Green, of Balliol, full of politics . . . very weighty. Strictly, a philosopher, not a man of science." And: "His conscience was equally exacting in speculation and in practice. Ritchie on Green. Cont[emporary] R[eview]. LI.843." (*Ibid.*) Herbert Paul has written that Green contributed to one of the periodicals that Acton edited, but I have not checked this statement. For Lord Lindsay, see *Theory of the Modern Democratic State*, Vol. I, the article on *Individualism* in *E.S.S.*, the paper on Sovereignty in *Proceedings of the Aristotelian Society*, 1923, *Karl Marx's Capital* (1925), *The Philosophy of Immanuel Kant* (n.d.), and the articles on Aristotle and Hobbes prefixed to the Everyman edition of the *Politics* and the *Leviathan*. See also Professor G. D. H. Cole's Inaugural on Social and Political Theory. Professor Cole's position is in some ways rather like that of Fénelon.
[3] Cf. Lord Lindsay's Introduction to Professor Woodhouse's *Puritanism and Liberty*, and T. H. Green's lectures on the commonwealth period printed in his *Collected Works*.

whose argument in the *Metaphysical Theory of the State* he anticipated. As a philosophic historian Acton stands between Tocqueville and Croce. In another way he is the philosophic analogue of Dicey. Fundamentally he is the complement of Burke, the answer of the nineteenth century to the eighteenth century, giving the philosophy of liberal development without breach of continuity.

It is in Acton that the great transition is made at the deeper level from the negative to the positive conception of the State. Acton obeyed the same movement as the great jurist Ihering, whom he so immensely admired. Like Acton, Ihering placed his primary emphasis on the distinction between society and the State, on the idea of duty, and the sociology of law which these concepts entail. For Ihering it is society which is the supreme concept. Projecting his ideas into the international field, he maintains that nations exist for the purposes of the world, and that private property must be subordinated to social needs. One is reminded of the terms in which Acton wrote to contributors to the Cambridge Modern History: "Universal History moves in a succession to which the nations are subsidiary." Professor Toynbee's work is really an enlargement of this theme. In 1886 Acton said that Ihering's insight was deeper, and his dialectics keener than Hegel's. As a jurist, Ihering stood to the late nineteenth century as Savigny to the earlier.

Acton exhibits in the highest degree the tension and the reconciliation between moral idealism and the facts of history. The sovereignty of the developed conscience is the analogue of the sovereignty of God. Acton is the antithesis of Hobbes, and avoids his confusion of authority and power. Acton restates the theory of the universal community, of the conscience of humanity. As Lamartine said: "*La liberté est plus que l'esprit humain, c'est la conscience humaine.*"[1] Acton's centre of interest is the common fortunes of mankind, his ideal a world of federal democracies, a world of real freedom based on the twin foundations of real comfort for the masses, and the sharing of a common moral ideal. It is the Christian alternative to Communism, an undenominational universalism, informed by the lessons of experience. It is a true fusion of philosophy and

[1] Cited by Acton, Add. 4901.

history. If it needs a name it must be termed rational empiricism. The subject of Acton's study was the ethical structure of the universe, and what he stood for was the principle of order in the social sciences. The queen of the sciences is ethics. It is ethics which is the real marrow of history. Acton's ultimate ethical principle is the sanctity of human life. War is only murder unless it is inescapable in defence of freedom.

Liberal ideas are now the common property of every party in the State. It is significant that the most doctrinaire of liberals should also have been the profoundest, as well as the most learned of historians. In two respects there is some analogy between Acton's experience and that of the present generation. It is clear that the dictatorship of Napoleon III played a part in Acton's psychology which to some extent resembles that of Hitler in our's. Secondly, the criticism of classical economics by Marx and Lassalle, by the academic socialists and Roscher, and the light of comparative statistics influenced Acton's judgment in a way comparable to that in which the writings of Keynes and his successors have influenced economic opinion in our own day.

Acton's philosophy was based on a mastery of many disciplines as well as of many periods—economics, ethics, politics, history, jurisprudence, philosophy, sociology. As Lord Morley said, Acton was extraordinary both in the depth and compass of his mind. His knowledge was matched by a character which has been described as heroic.[1] It is not without reason that his Cambridge editors wrote that Acton's real masterpiece was himself.

Acton was a Platonist, and what he really believed in was knowledge, which, with experience, is the guide to conscience. The term he uses most frequently is science, by which he means knowledge which is certain. It is knowledge of the truth that makes us free. The sovereignty of the developed conscience therefore means the final authority of conscience resting upon convictions based on certain knowledge. Conscience is "the indestructible soul of revolution"; but conscience cannot prevail in politics without "science," that is certain knowledge of the true ethics of politics. The true ethics of politics involve effective securities for freedom, that is, freedom to do one's

[1] *Edinburgh Review*, April 1903.

moral duty. Moral responsibility entails political responsibility. The "science of conscience" therefore involves the science of constitutional government. Its conditions are experience, conviction, knowledge, morality, education, courage, self-restraint. The outward signs are representation, the extinction of slavery, the reign of opinion, the security of the weaker groups, and freedom of conscience "which, effectually secured, secures the rest." The growth of freedom has to be traced in the growth of knowledge as much as in the acts of political assemblies. It is ideas which give wings and motion. The sovereignty of the developed conscience is Acton's testament as a political thinker. As a Christian he could not say less, as a thinker he would not say more. But as the ethics of politics cannot rest on a denominational basis they must be based on an autonomous discipline, that is, undenominational ethics. He wrote in his manuscripts: "Morality associated with either Catholicism or Protestantism was vitiated by that dependence. The one approved persecution, etc. As soon as Toleration prevailed, orthodoxy faded. That followed—If persecution, sorcery, etc., were wrong, then the religions that promoted them were not to be trusted. Conscience must look elsewhere. Ethics gave up orthodoxy. Scepticism, in the revolt of morality."[1]

The supreme moral principle is the sanctity of human life, a principle which can only be violated if absolutely necessary for the sake of freedom, because freedom to do one's moral duty is dearer than life itself.

If we ask what is the practical meaning today of Acton's doctrine, we find it in human rights, partial, that is, not totalitarian socialism, administrative decentralization, and federalism. Federalism, in Acton's view, is the necessary safeguard in a democracy, otherwise democracy will be corrupted by its own possession of unlimited power. In practice, the division of power, which is what federalism means, is the supreme political principle.[2]

Acton's political thought is only a small part, though the most important part of his sociology. The contemporary sociologists he especially valued were Roscher, Cournot,

---

[1] Add. 4916.
[2] The autonomy of local authorities represented a kind of "restricted federalism" in Acton's sense of the term.

Ihering, Vinet, and Lewis Henry Morgan, the last the single example of a writer who is both a Marxist and an Actonian classic.[1] But Acton's thought as a whole is so closely knit together that one can only compare it with a kind of transformed monadology, in which the monads, so far from being "windowless," all mirror his entire universe of thought in their own unique individuation. It is this which Acton refers to when he calls universal history an illumination of the soul. Acton studies history philosophically, and philosophy historically, and all the social sciences both historically and philosophically.[2] He gives us an interpenetration of disciplines, the cross-fertilization which results from the mastery of the fields of knowledge adjacent to history. His ultimate presupposition is the existence of God. Faith is achieved, as Acton once put it, by a deliberate suspense of the critical faculty, or, in Collingwood's words, the business of a presupposition is not to be questioned, but to be presupposed. This is primarily an ethical presupposition, and is nearly identical with Kant's. As Figgis and Laurence, Acton's Cambridge editors, wisely observed, Acton's generation lived in and breathed the atmosphere of Kant. In one other particular Acton makes us think of Kant. If it be true, as it has been said, that no one reads the *Critique of Pure Reason* once until he has read it four times, a similar remark would be justified of Acton's writings, and most of all of the *Inaugural*, which is so tightly packed with meaning as to be virtually inexhaustible.

Many of Acton's judgments would require a lifetime's research to examine. This truth is part of his endless fascination, for no book on Acton can ever be more than an agenda for further study.

[1] At the time of his death Marx was writing a book on Morgan. This was completed by Engels. Among earlier writers Acton recognized the importance of Vico. Cf. Add. 4916: "the philosophy of history ... its results from Bossuet and Vico to Buckle and Ferrari are not comparable, in solidity and completeness, to those of inductive science." See also *F.R.*, 17-18: "the Italians, through Vico ... had an eighteenth century of their own." See also *H.F.*, 590, where Vico is bracketed with Hegel.

[2] Cf.: "History, the patrimony of mankind, carry the accumulated knowledge along ... History of philosophy ... History of religion ... History of political economy. This is progress. Without this, we move in a circle—the stone is always rolling back." (Add. 4943.)

One of Acton's favourite quotations comes from Landor: Few scholars are critics, few critics are philosophers, few philosophers look with equal care on both sides of a question. Because Acton always made it a rule to look with equal care on both sides of a question there are two sides to this thought on every question at every date. As he wrote in his manuscripts: "The retarding process is as necessary to vitality, safety and endurance, as the progressive."[1] But the progressive principle, represented by the developing conscience, is nearer to the purposes of God. It is the emphasis on both elements, tradition, and ethical and political progress without breach of continuity, supported by profound learning in many different fields that constitutes Acton's greatness as a political thinker.[2] He is one of the deepest interpreters of the English philosophy of politics.

Acton's ultimate thought is that it is the truth that makes us free. And the ultimate truth is that Caesar and God are different. His philosophy is the philosophy of freedom. It might be argued that, in the last analysis, Acton's system contains two indefinables, liberty, which is a thing that grows, and depends on innumerable conditions, and social evolution, which is charged with interminable consequences. But Acton's philosophy is not strictly a system, it is rather a developing spirit. It is really the English blending of empiricism and rationalism.[3]

Acton once criticized a Scottish philosopher for not raising Hegel to a higher level and a wider view. This was what Acton attempted. The higher level is the sovereignty of the developed

[1] Add. 4870. Therefore, Acton concluded, the legitimate forms of party are permanent. In the same manuscript Acton wrote: "Party needful to practise true ideas, contrary, to find them."

[2] Cf. "Ideas entirely derived from the past, superfluous. Ideas disconnected from the past, unripe and ineffective. One must have tradition and independency." (Add. 4943). Acton studied dozens of economists, hundreds of philosophers, and thousands of historians. An American computes his reading as 22,000 volumes.

[3] Rationalism is represented by conscience, empiricism by development. "System," he wrote, "means a view of only certain truths" (Add. 4955). If Acton's formula, the sovereignty of the developed conscience, involves a system, it is an open, not a closed system. There is more than a hint of his own view in what he says of Döllinger's aversion from "pretentious" systems.

conscience; the wider view is, in his own words, "All that goes to weave the web of social life." In the inexhaustible list of competing philosophies which includes "fatalism and retribution, race and nationality, the test of success and of duration, heredity, and . . . the law of progress," it is the sovereignty of the developed conscience which holds the highest place, liberty that occupies the final summit. It is the sign and the prize and the motive in the upward advance of the race for which Christ was crucified. It is the refined essence which draws sustenance from all good things.

Acton has been compared to Plato. The judgment is excessive, but it is not pointless. What Acton shares with Plato is the capacity to think out his thought to the end without flinching, and the application of an ideal standard. And Plato was the greatest single influence on Acton's thought.[1] Acton believed that the most powerful political amalgam in the world is true liberalism in a conservative spirit, and this is the secret of freedom.

Acton's essential significance and value could be expressed by saying that Acton stands to Marx as the New Testament stands to the Old Testament,[2] and to Hegel as Christianity to pantheism.

Acton had reached in thought the problems with which we are now faced in experience—nationality and power, freedom and socialism, decentralization and administration. And he is not only a great English prophet: he is a prophet of America also. America, he said, has assigned a new course to history. America stands for ideas "rooted in the future," reason cutting clean as Atropos. America is the freest as well as the most powerful country in the world. Acton is a prophet of the Atlantic community, one of the great interpreters of the heritage which is Western civilization. Above all Acton is a Christian prophet. The supreme quality of his thought is that it is just.

[1] Excluding sacred writings of east and west. It is from Plato Acton first takes the ideas of division of sovereignty and constitutional government.
[2] In principle this is easily shown. Orthodox Marxism leads to the identification of Church and State—the Communist State and the Communist religion. This is contrary to Acton's first principle, Render unto Caesar, which he takes from the New Testament. *Das Kapital* is a *Koran* as Acton said. Cf. Add. 4943: "How far the ideas of Christianity are established—apart from its system—The ethical and social, without the religious aspects."

It is for this reason that he has been universally recognized as the Magistrate of history.

Acton had a universal outlook, encyclopaedic knowledge, a judicial method, sincerity, and a capacity to go on learning, which remained to the end. His intensity of conviction, illumination, and vision lifts his work to the level of art. There too we can find in Acton a quality which, in its own way, recalls Plato.

Acton's essential work was to show, with a more than German weight of learning, that the German philosophy of history (we may add, and its derivatives, now so common) was false. It is better, said Acton, to be a citizen of a humble republic in the Alps, than a subject of the superb autocracy which overshadows half of Europe and of Asia. In this judgment he was not referring primarily to the material standard of living. The action of Providence is shown, not in the perfection, but in the improvement of the world. It is still a tenable view that mankind has made some, if not great, progress since the stone age. Acton's view of Providence is not, as some suppose, a paradox. It is simply a necessary tautology.

Acton's doctrine is the Christian doctrine of the unity of theory and practice. As he once quoted, "No one has a true idea of right until he does it"; or, in Acton's words, "conscience cannot prevail in politics without science."[1] The pursuit of knowledge is also a moral obligation.

[1] Cf. "The end of knowledge is power. Hobbes. Elem. 1.1. Roger and Francis Bacon." (Add. 4944.)

Appendix I

THE ECONOMIC FACTOR

It is sometimes suggested that only conscious or unconscious Marxists, or those under their influence, give adequate attention to the relations between economic and political power. From this point of view it is worth examining how far Acton attended to the economic factor in history in his writings. It has indeed been doubted whether Acton saw sufficiently clearly what were the relations between economic and political power.[1] The evidence I should like to submit shows that the economic factor in history was constantly present in his mind. What is true is that Acton was more interested in the influence of ideas (including economic ideas) than in the specialized study of economic history. It will be convenient to begin with two decisive illustrations of the importance Acton attached to economic history, and especially to its bearing on general history.

In his celebrated article on German Schools of History[2] Acton wrote:

> The academic socialists are proceeding to reconstrue history, making property and the social condition the determining factor, above the acts of government or the changes of opinion; and this is by many degrees the most important addition made of late years to historic science.

This judgment is preceded by a passage of appreciation and criticism of Roscher, and of his place in German historiography. "Forty years," he wrote, "after Savigny's *Vocation* made Germany a nation of historically-thinking men, every branch of knowledge had felt its influence. It had penetrated jurisprudence . . . language . . . geography . . . philosophy . . . art . . . theology . . . canon law." Acton continues:

---

[1] E.g. by Professor Woodward in *Politica*, September 1939. Professor Woodward's criticism is worded with studious moderation.
[2] *English Historical Review*, 1886, reprinted in *Historical Essays and Studies*.

The change came when Roscher, who had been the ripest of Ranke's scholars, a man more perfectly endowed with historic instinct than Niebuhr or Baur, was set to train practical economists for the kingdom of Hanover. . . . If the full-blown precepts of developed science which accompany the mature, the normal, and therefore industrial epoch of national life were not clear formerly, Roscher explains the defect not by the fault of men groping in the dark, but by the fact that political economy, which exists for mankind, varies with the progress of events, and is subject to the conditions of youth and age. He distinguishes physiology from pathology, insists on the phenomena proper to epochs of decline, and notes with especial care the teaching of nations that have carried the experiment of existence to its conclusion. Starting with the idea that the ancients understood distribution better than we do, and that truth is often older than error, he has expanded and enriched professional literature with the study of all the economic notions in the civil and the ecclesiastical code, in Erasmus and Luther, Bacon and Burke.

With less than Buckle's appreciation of Adam Smith, Roscher's memory, crowded with instances of the power of self-sacrifice, disinclines him from the doctrine which refers economic facts to the simplest and most universal of human motives, and he derives laws and theories from causes deep in the entire structure of society, and from combinations of human and spiritual influence. He came at a time when several candid generalizations of primitive liberalism were withering under the mathematical touch of comparative statistics, and is always ready to find a grain of wisdom in the oddities of our ancestors; and the saying of ancient practitioners that the lancet produced much the same results upon the generation that is past as its disuse upon the generation that is passing, is Roscher all over. Though he deems protection a mark of weakness, and its prolongation a mark of incapacity, he admits the use of temporary sacrifices in the training of resources. With Adam Smith he rejoices at the enactment of the navigation laws, and with Cobden at their repeal; he feels with Garrison about emancipation but is vividly conscious of conditions in which slavery is an instrument of civilization. He expounds with intelligent admiration the colonial system by which this country has changed the face of the world, he admires in another way the system by which Spain preserved where we destroyed. Absolute monarchy is the note of first or second childhood, but absolute monarchy rescued the peasants. Monopolies are a mistake; but the monopoly of the Oporto Company saved port wine.

A further passage in Acton's discussion of Roscher is illuminating:

> The best of the economists who last preceded Roscher admitted that in dealing with poverty their science failed. Mill thought that want in any sense implying suffering may be completely extinguished; and Roscher added that precept must be modified by fact. His disciples went on to argue that the principles of the classic teachers on the theory of population, of rent, of the source of wealth, lead beyond their conclusions. With Roscher's doctrine of relative truth, the impregnable stronghold was hard to keep against the assault of sympathy and the prickings of a delicate conscience, which is defined, a conscience unequal to the struggle of life. He dwells complacently on the immeasurable progress of this age, on the enlarged sphere and accepted duties of the State in respect of misery, education, overwork, health, and help to the weak, and judges that the social advance cancels the socialist programme. "Socialism," said Dunoyer, "is merely the present system logically carried out." On the other side, if it is right that the State should do so much, the reign of the log was usurpation and the ancient ways were wrong. Then the indictment brought by Considérant and Engels against the society of 1840 is just, and the order of things which produced so much sorrow was criminal. So vast a change is not development but subversion, the departure of one principle, the development of another. In all that pertains to the past, the party now dominant in the universities, and destined, after calculable intervals, to dominate in literature and law, pursues the ideas of Roscher, and completes his work. In practical things it does not accept, as he does, the Frenchman's saying, "*Je n'impose rien; je ne propose même pas: j'expose.*" His contemplative, retrospective spirit, borne backward by sheer weight of knowledge, is not easily roused by the spectacle of error, suffering, and wrong, and is slow to admit the guilt of omitted acts and the responsibility of States for all they might prevent or cure. He has attended as much to problems and their solutions in other times as to the problems and solutions of his own; and the service done by his enormous influence to political

economy, which Mr. Cliffe Leslie and Mr. Ingram have described, is far less than his services to the cause of intelligible history.

Acton thought Roscher's work so important that in his letters to Mary Gladstone he repeatedly refers to him and to the other "socialists of the chair," and tried very hard to get Mary Gladstone to persuade Mr. Gladstone to read their books.[1]

The second decisive preliminary illustration of Acton's attitude to the economic interpretation of history is that Harrington, the modern pioneer in the application of economics to politics, not only heads the list of Acton's "little band of true theorists,"[2] but, over a period of twenty-five years, is a favourite subject of quotation in his writings:

> Harrington is the author of what Americans have called the greatest discovery since the printing-press. For he has given the reason why the Great Rebellion failed, and was followed by the reaction under Charles II. He says that it failed because it omitted to redistribute the property of the kingdom. The large estates constituted an aristocratic society, on which it was impossible to construct a democratic state. If the great estates had been broken up into small ones, on a definite plan, the nation would have been committed to the new order of things, and would have accepted the law of equality. Poverty would have been diminished on one side, and nobles would have been abolished on the other. A timorous conservatism and legal scruples made this impossible, and government, by a law of nature, took its shape from the forms and forces of society.[3]

It is true that Acton goes on to say that it is unnecessary to go quite so deep as this to see that the Cromwellian system, which was the work of a minority, led by a man of pre-eminent services and talents, crumbled when the necessary leader was gone.

In another place[4] Acton writes:

> [Treitschke] had attacked, and it was thought had refuted, the notion of a separate science of society, as the sphere

---

[1] *L.M.G.*, pp. 89, 90, etc., etc. [2] *H.E.*, p. 492 (1892).
[3] *L.M.H.*, p. 204. See also *H.F.*, p. 50 (Freedom in Christianity, 1877), and *L.M.G.*, p. 139. [4] *H.E.*, p. 380 (1886).

of religion, morality, economy and knowledge, as a vast community, organically distinct from the State and able to control it. The idea, which comes from Harrington, and was pronounced by John Adams the greatest discovery in politics, had been made by Lorenz von Stein the key to the Revolution, in a work exposing the economic cause of political science.

Acton's practice is as good as his precept, and some examples may be given of the use he himself made of the economic key to events. In his famous *Inaugural* he said: "In those days Columbus subverted the notions of the world, and reversed the conditions of production, wealth, and power."[1] Elsewhere he writes: "[The discovery of the New World] influenced the position of classes in Europe by making property obtained from afar, in portable shape, predominate over property at home. ... These events shifted the centre of political gravity from land to sea. The resources of the ocean world extended the physical basis of modern History; and increase of wealth involving increase of power, depended thenceforward on the control of distant regions."[2]

Going back to the Middle Ages, he writes:

> The opening of the East by the Crusades had imparted a great stimulus to industry. A stream set in from the country to the towns... The townspeople not only made themselves free from the control of prelates and barons, but endeavoured to obtain for their own class and interest the command of the State. The fourteenth century was filled with the tumult of this struggle between democracy and chivalry. The Italian towns, foremost in intelligence and civilization, led the way with democratic constitutions of an ideal and generally impracticable type. The Swiss cast off the yoke of Austria. The citizens of Paris got possession of the King, reformed the State, and began their tremendous career of experiments to govern France. But the most healthy and vigorous growth of municipal liberties was in Belgium, of all countries on the Continent that which has been from immemorial ages the most stubborn in its fidelity to the principle of self-government. So vast were the resources concentrated in the Flemish towns, so widespread was the movement of democracy, that it was long doubtful whether the new

[1] P. 3 (1895). [2] *L.M.H.*, p. 70 (1901).

interest would not prevail, and whether the ascendancy of the military aristocracy would not pass over to the wealth and intelligence of the men that lived by trade.[1]

"Venice," Acton notices, ". . . was a republic not of landowners but of shipowners."[2]

In his *Lectures* (1901) Acton wrote:

> The Portuguese were the first Europeans to understand that the ocean is not a limit, but the universal waterway that unites mankind. Shut in by Spain, they could not extend on land, and had no opening but the Atlantic. Their arid soil gave little scope to the territorial magnate.[3]
>
> The secret of Portuguese prosperity was the small bulk and the enormous market value of the particular products in which they dealt. . . . A voyage sometimes lasted two years, out and home, and cost, including the ship, over £4,000. But the freight might amount to £150,000.[4]

Thirty years earlier he said:

> Nowhere, perhaps, was the position of the Jews, during the Middle Ages, so favourable as in Portugal. They constituted a very respectable portion of the community; trade and industry were almost entirely in their hands; they had large landed properties; and the flourishing and prosperous condition of Portugal in the fifteenth century was in a great measure their work.[5]

Acton continues:

The Kings of Portugal, like the Kings of Spain, seeing in the Inquisition above all things a means of filling their treasury, refused obedience to the Papal decree abolishing the Inquisition. The consequences were the rapid impoverishment of the land, and absence of all literary culture, and a vigorous rise in the prosperity of Ferrara, Livorno, Amsterdam, and Hamburg, to which towns the Jews managed to convey their wealth and industry.[6] Later, referring to the third quarter of the seventeenth century, Acton writes: "The merchants of Amsterdam, . . . were now the second Power in Europe politically, and commercially by far the first."[7]

---

[1] *H.F.*, p. 38 (1877).　　[2] *L.M.H.*, p. 52.
[3] *Ibid.*　　[4] *Ibid.*, p. 58.
[5] *Chronicle*, 10 Aug. 1867, p. 475.
[6] *Ibid.*　　[7] *L.M.H.*, p. 241.

Of the indulgence revived by Leo X in 1517, which was the spark which occasioned Luther's explosion, Acton notes that "half the proceeds [were] to go to the Archbishop of Mainz, that he might pay back a loan to Fugger of Augsburg. The banker's agent went round with the appointed preacher and kept the strong box."[1]

After the Peasants' Revolt in Germany, Acton writes: "Even the industry of the towns was struck down by the blow which crushed the country people. The decline of trade led to new restrictions on the freedom of labour, intended to make up for the diminished production, but really oppressive to the community and injurious to industry. One reason for the falling-off of commerce was the independence of Holland; for the commercial policy of the Dutch was narrow in spirit, and selfish towards their Continental neighbours."[2]

"In the sixteenth century," Acton writes, "throughout the North of Europe ... the peasantry, by a long series of enactments, extending to the end of the seventeenth century, was reduced to servitude; the population grew scanty, and much of the land went out of cultivation."[3]

[On the eve of the Civil War in England] "The quick increase of the middle class, which was the seat of sectarianism, could not well be discovered from the returns of taxation."[4]

Of the Puritan Revolution we have already noticed that Acton constantly quoted Harrington's economic explanation of the cause of its failure.

Turning to Europe he notices that "Conring was the first, according to Roscher, who found an adequate ideal of political economy, of statistics, and of political observations; he was certainly the first university professor who lectured on statistics and defined properly their notion and object."[5]

Of the Revolution of 1688 ("the greatest thing done by the English nation") Acton writes that the war to which it gave rise brought "The National Debt, the Bank of England, the growth of the moneyed interest." Acton continues:

> But the agrarian interest still largely predominated, and the landlords, as the ruling class, required a reward for their

[1] *L.M.H.*, p. 92. [2] *H.F.R.*, Jan. 1863, p. 234.
[3] *Rambler*, Vol. VI, p. 25. [4] *L.M.H.*, p. 197.
[5] *N.B.R.*, Jan. 1871, p. 565.

share in the elevation of William. Nineteen years earlier the Corn Laws had been invented for their benefit. Protection against foreign importation did much; but in 1689 a premium on the exportation of English-grown corn was added, and it is this which caused the immense prosperity of English agriculture in the eighteenth century, enriching the landlord with capital at the expense of the yeoman without it.[1]

By the war of the Spanish succession "We acquired Newfoundland, Nova Scotia, and the Hudson Bay territory, and, in addition to the *asiento*, the right of trading in the possessions of the House of Bourbon—in fact, the commerce of the world."[2]

"[Walpole] was quite content to preserve the government of the country by the rich, in the interest of their own class."[3]

Coming to the French Revolution, Acton writes of Turgot and the Physiocrats:

> They are of supreme importance to us, because they founded political science on the economic science which was coming into existence. . . . They said: A man's most sacred property is his labour. It is anterior even to the right of property, for it is the possession of those who own nothing else. Therefore he must be free to make the best use of it he can.[4]

Acton notes: "The sovereignty of public opinion was just then coming in through the rise of national debts and the increasing importance of the public creditor." "Adam Smith says that to prohibit a great people from making all they can of every part of their own produce, or from employing their stock and industry in the way that they judge most advantageous for themselves, is a manifest violation of the most sacred rights of mankind." To the French peasants privileges were "relics and remnants of feudalism, and feudalism meant power given to land and denied to capital and industry. It meant class government."[5]

When Necker took office "the funds rose 30 per cent. in one day.[6] . . . He was the earliest foreign statesman who studied and

[1] *L.M.H.*, p. 230.   [2] *Ibid.*, p. 263.   [3] *Ibid.*, p. 274.
[4] *F.R.*, p. 11.   [5] *Ibid.*, p. 41.   [6] *Ibid.*, p. 46.

understood the modern force of opinion; and he identified public opinion with credit, as we should say, with the city. He took the views of capitalists as the most sensitive record of public confidence."

Behind a political reform "there was a social revolution."

Most clearly of all: "The assault on the restricted distribution of power involved an assault on the concentration of wealth. The connection of the two ideas is the secret motive of the Revolution. At that time the law by which power follows property, which has been called the most important discovery made by man since the invention of printing, was not clearly known."[1]

Other instances of Acton's clear perception of the interaction of economic with political forces in the French Revolution are: "The France of history vanished on August 4, and the France of the new democracy took its place. The transfer of property from the upper class to the lower was considerable. The peasants' income was increased by about 60 per cent." "There was little concentration yet of the working class in towns, for the industrial age had hardly dawned, and it was hard to understand that the Third Estate contained divergent interests and the material of a coming conflict." "The masses were becoming conscious that they were not the Third Estate, that there was a conflict of interest between property and labour, and they began to vent their yet inarticulate rage upon the middle class above them."[2] "The hard kernel of the revolutionary scheme, taken from agrarian Rome, was that those who till the land shall own the land."[3] Of the effect on England of the war against revolutionary France, Acton writes: "It brought increase of rents to the class that governed, and advantage to the trader from the conquest of dependencies and dominions over the sea."[4]

Acton puts the economic factor on the first page of his *French Revolution*:

> The revenue of France was near twenty millions when Louis XVI, finding it inadequate, called upon the nation for supply. In a single lifetime it rose to far more than one hundred millions, while the national income grew still more

[1] *F.R.*, pp. 53–54. [2] *Ibid.*, p. 129.
[3] *Ibid.*, p. 301. [4] *Ibid.*, p. 321.

rapidly; and this increase was wrought by a class to whom the ancient monarchy denied its best rewards, and whom it deprived of power in the country they enriched. As their industry effected change in the distribution of property, and wealth ceased to be the prerogative of a few, the excluded majority perceived that their disabilities rested on no foundation of right and justice, and were unsupported by reasons of State.

Writing to Mary Gladstone in April, 1881, Acton said:[1]

We are forced, in equity, to share the Government with the working class by considerations which were made supreme by the awakening of political economy. Adam Smith set up two propositions—that contracts ought to be free between capital and labour, and that labour is the source, he sometimes says the only source, of wealth. If the last sentence, in its exclusive form, was true, it was difficult to resist the conclusion that the class on which national prosperity depends ought to govern instead of the useless unproductive class, and that the class which earns the increment ought to enjoy it. That is the foreign effect of Adam Smith—French Revolution and socialism. We, who reject that extreme proposition, cannot resist the logical pressure of the other. If there is a free contract in open market, between capital and labour, it cannot be right that one of the two contracting parties should have the making of the laws, the management of the conditions, the keeping of the peace, the administration of justice, the distribution of taxes, the control of expenditure, in its own hands exclusively. It is unjust that all these securities, all these advantages, should be on the same side. . . . Before this argument, the ancient dogma, that power attends on property, broke down. Justice required that property should—not abdicate, but—share its political supremacy.

In the *Rambler* in May 1861, Acton quoted a memorial of the merchants of Salem in 1820:

Nothing can be more obvious than that many of the manufacturers and their friends are attempting, by fallacious statements, founded on an interested policy, or a misguided zeal, or very short-sighted views, to uproot some of the fundamental principles of our revenue policy. . . . If we are

[1] *L.M.G.*, pp. 91–92.

unwilling to receive foreign manufactures, we cannot reasonably suppose that foreign nations will receive our raw materials. We cannot force them to become buyers when they are not sellers, or to consume our cotton when they cannot pay the price in their own fabrics.[1]

Acton quotes Cobbett (*Political Register* for 1853):

The heavy duties imposed by the Congress upon British manufactured goods is neither more nor less than so many millions a year taken from the Southern and Western States, and given to the Northern States.[2]
(*Cobbett's Political Works*, VI, 662.)

"The yeoman farmers of the United States," Acton pointed out, "have always been the strength of the republic."[3]

Acton notes that "[Talleyrand] said . . . that a sound political economy was the talisman which made England, for thirty years, the first of European powers."[4]

Acton had carefully read and appraised Samuel Smiles's *Lives of the Engineers*.[5]

He notes that "the permanent unsettlement of the Spanish Republics is caused by the economic defects of the old Spanish system."[6]

One of the most interesting examples of Acton's treatment of the relations between the economic and political factors in history is what he says about the July Monarchy:

[The ministers of Louis Philippe] acted as if the intelligent middle class was destined by heaven to govern. The upper class had proved its unfitness before 1789; the lower class, since 1789. Government by professional men, by manufacturers and scholars, was sure to be safe, and almost sure to be reasonable and practical. Money became the object of a political superstition, such as had formerly attached to the land, and afterwards attached to labour. The masses, of the people, who had fought against Marmont, became aware that they had not fought for their own benefit. They were still governed by their employers. . . . In 1836 . . . the term Socialism made its appearance in literature. . . . Towards 1840, in the recesses of secret societies, republicans and

---

[1] Pp. 35–36.
[2] *Rambler*, May 1861, p. 37.
[3] *N.B.R.*, April 1870, p. 268.
[4] *H.E.*, p. 409.
[5] *Chronicle*, 28 Dec. 1867, p. 253.
[6] *Ibid.*, 1 June 1867, p. 235.

socialists coalesced. Whilst the Liberal leaders, Lamartine and Barrot, discoursed on the surface concerning reform, Ledru Rollin and Louis Blanc were quietly digging a grave for the monarchy, the Liberal party, and the reign of wealth. They worked so well . . . that in 1848, they were able to conquer without fighting. The fruit of their victory was universal suffrage. From that time the promises of socialism have supplied the best energy of democracy.[1]

This passage was written in 1878, when Acton was forty-four. Fifteen years earlier he wrote (*Rambler*, Oct. 1862):

The violent and revolutionary condition of France . . . is founded primarily on the antagonism between rich and poor, property and labour; and hence the socialist character of the revolution of 1848. But the government of July, and its theorist, Guizot, added to the envy of the rich the hatred of privileges, and increased the natural distinction which separates poverty from wealth, by the artificial protection of capital against aristocracy. It united the two worst qualities of government by a class.

In 1864 (April) in the *Home and Foreign Review* (pp. 723–724), Acton referred to Guizot as "unwilling fairly to consider the great economical motives of the schism between the people and the middle class on which despotism is founded in France."

"Democracy," writes Acton, "is a gigantic current that has been fed by many springs. Physical and spiritual causes have contributed to swell it. Much has been done by economic theories, and more by economic laws."[2]

Referring to 1874, he writes: "[In Switzerland] the railways, and the vast interests they created, made the position of the cantonal governments untenable."[3]

In regard to the Irish question, "the land question has been from the beginning the great difficulty in Ireland."[4]

Most generally, "a people averse to the institution of private property is without the first element of freedom."[5]

Acton quotes Cavour apparently with approval: "The political regeneration of a nation is never separate from its economic regeneration."[6] He refers to the need "to make the

[1] *H.F.*, p. 92.   [2] *Ibid.*, pp. 61–62 (1878).   [3] *Ibid.*, p. 91 (1878).
[4] *Ibid.*, p. 236.   [5] *Ibid.*, p. 297.   [6] *H.E.*, p. 179.

laws of economic science subservient to considerations of policy,"[1] and to the Master of University, "who knows the unpolitical cause of much political effect."[2] Acton writes: "Ranke is always concrete, seldom puzzling over predestination or the balance of trade."[3]

Finally, "If, taking other examples and other methods into account, historians occupy themselves with all that goes to weave the web of social life then the work of Giesebrecht, like the work of Ranke, will appear neither sufficient nor efficient, but characteristic of a passing stage in the progress of science."[4]

Perhaps the argument may conveniently stop at this point. Enough has been quoted to show that Acton did emphasize repeatedly the economic factor in history, to the limit of the knowledge of his own day.

It is, however, true that Acton was more interested in the analysis of history in terms of ideas. Many instances could be given, but perhaps two will suffice. "There may be," he writes, "perhaps a score or two dozen decisive and characteristic views that govern the world, and that every man should master in order to understand his age."[5] This is a recurrent view in Acton's writings.

In the *Inaugural* he speaks of "the advance of knowledge and the development of ideas, which ... are the charter of progress and the vital spark in history." In this, Acton was at one with the late Lord Keynes, whose last recorded sentence was a tribute to the supreme importance of ideas. It is a mark of the liberal spirit.

Perhaps we may conclude with an extract from Mr. Rostow's *British Economy of the Nineteenth Century*:[6]

> a reviewer has recently criticized a study in which a rather rigid and wholeheartedly economic interpretation was applied to a complex set of political and social events.[7] The reviewer concluded:
> Now, such an extreme position is neither science nor history. It is merely a new theology—not even good theology,

---

[1] *H.E.* p. 179.   [2] *Ibid.*, p. 473 (1888).   [3] *Ibid.*, p. 489 (1888).
[4] *Ibid.*, p. 502 (1890).   [5] *F.R.*, p. 268.
[6] Oxford, 1948, pp. 126–127.
[7] F. Tannenbaum, "A Note on the Economic Interpretation of History," *Political Science Quarterly*, June 1946.

because it is uninspired. It has faith in nothing but a verbal formula. It would rule Christ out of the Christian Church, Lincoln and the idea of national unity out of the Civil War, Roosevelt and the concept of human dignity out of the battle against the Nazis ... even a great scholar knows only a very little and may not understand the little he knows. Facts are easily acquired by industry and diligence. The meaning of the facts, all their meaning, is beyond the ken of any scholar —perhaps beyond the ken of mortal man.

Acton would doubtless have accepted Mr. Tannenbaum's implied doctrine of plurality of causes. But so far from neglecting the economic factor in history, Acton regarded its recognition as the crowning achievement of historical science, and endeavoured to apply its lessons, and notably in his Cambridge lectures.

Mr. Rostow has attempted, in the work from which I have quoted, to outline an acceptable scheme of relations between economic, social, and political history. But he confesses historians received it with scepticism. We have to remember that for the proper appreciation of the relation between economic and political power, not only must the general historian appreciate the significance of the work of the economic historian; the economic historian must have some understanding of the economist: and, not least, the economists must understand each other.

In his latest book, on dynamic economics, Mr. Harrod makes economic growth (as defined) his fundamental idea. Very obviously this must be of supreme concern to all historians. But at least one of Mr. Harrod's reviewers (in the *Economist*) has confessed his inability to understand this important book. It is to be hoped that historians writing in 1949 will not be severely blamed half a century hence for not having digested what, apparently, not all economists find plain sailing.

It goes without saying that Acton did not give exactly the same proportions as the plan for the new *Cambridge Modern History* does to the price revolution of the sixteenth century, and to other economic factors less understood fifty years ago than now. But it will be found that Acton gave greater weight to the economic factor than any of the other general historians of his day.

Acton is the only writer who gives the first place to national income in his account of the English, American, and French Revolutions.[1] In beginning his account of the first he writes: The House of Commons voted (i.e. to James II) a revenue which, by the growth of trade, soon rose to near two millions.[2] Of the American Revolution: Between 1727 and 1761 many things had changed, and the Colonies had grown to be richer, more confident, more self-respecting.[3] He quotes with approval an American: "The real foundation of the discontent that led to the Revolution was the effort of Great Britain, beginning in 1750, to prevent diversity of occupation, to attack the growth of manufactures and the mechanic arts."[4] Of the French Revolution (the first two sentences of the book): "The revenue of France was near twenty millions when Louis XVI, finding it inadequate, called upon the nation for supply. In a single lifetime it rose to far more than one hundred millions, while the national income grew still more rapidly."[5] The significance of these examples is increased by the fact that in his first lecture at Cambridge after his formal *Inaugural* he dwelled at length on the services of Turgot in emphasizing that political science is based on economic science.[6] In the first half of the *Inaugural* itself he spoke of "commerce having risen against land, labour against wealth."[7]

[1] Not necessarily, of course, the greatest weight.
[2] *L.M.H.*, p. 219.　　[3] *Ibid.*, p. 307.
[4] *F.R.*, p. 22.　　[5] *Ibid.*, p. 1.
[6] *F.R.*, p. 11. "They [the Physiocrats] are of supreme importance to us because they founded political science on the economic science which was coming into existence."
[7] *L.M.H.*, p. 13. Cf. also: "Un grand historien me disait un jour: 'Si j'avais à faire une histoire universelle, je ferais deux chapitres: le monde avant les chemins de fer; le monde après les chemins de fer.' Richet, Revue Scientifique, xlviii, 780." (Cited in Add. 4938.)

Appendix II

ACTON'S CRITICS

THERE has been a long line of distinguished critics of Acton, from Gladstone to Professor Butterfield. As already noticed, Gladstone greeted the article on the American Civil War with the words, "Its principles of politics I embrace, its wealth of learning I admire, its whole atmosphere is that which I desire to breathe." Matthew Arnold noticed that Gladstone influenced everybody except Acton: it was Acton who influenced Gladstone. Grant Duff wrote: "Acton the Great." The late Mr. R. L. Poole, whose authority will not be questioned, said that Acton was equally master of mediaeval and modern times,[1] and that his influence in politics was often decisive. Maitland, the most learned of Acton's English contemporaries, stood amazed at his range. Mary Gladstone wished to apply to Acton himself Acton's judgment on Burke, that systems of scientific thought have been built upon the crumbs that fell from his table. This is only one of Acton's many judgments which cannot but seem to have at least some reference to himself, as for instance, when he says of Döllinger that everyone felt that he knew too much to write, that he would not write with imperfect materials and that the materials were always imperfect; most significant of all, when he writes of Leibniz that the fertility of his genius was such that the harvest could never be completely gathered.

Mr. Herbert Paul emphasized Acton's mastery of Greek philosophy, and his appreciation of the stupendous importance of Rousseau. Morley has given the most just of concentrated judgments in the words, "Acton was extraordinary in the depth and compass of his mind." Bryce relates as one of the greatest experiences of his life an occasion on which for six or seven minutes Acton outlined how the theme of liberty ought to be treated, comparing the experience to a vision from a high

[1] Obituary in *E.H.R.*, 1902. Cf. Add. 4943: "Mediaeval philosophy of History. Examine Leo, Augustine, Salvianus, Orosius, Cassiodorus, Bede, Malmesbury, William of Tyre, Frisingensis, Ragewin, Sanuto, Matthew Paris, Pavo, Simeon Dunelm, Dlugoss, Meyer, Tubero, Spaniards, French."

Alpine peak. H. A. L. Fisher concentrated on the function of the idea as the seminal principle in all Acton's thought. Figgis and Laurence emphasized the ideal of constitutional government. More recent critics have fastened upon other facets of Acton's philosophy. Professor Noack makes a valuable contribution to Acton studies in the very title of his third volume: "Politics as Security for Freedom."[1] Professor Woodward has rightly emphasized his insistence on the ethical criterion as his supreme merit. Mr. Lally has noticed Acton's complementary judgments. Miss Himmelfarb stresses Acton's conception of the autonomy of science, Dr. G. N. Clark has written of Acton's part in planning the Cambridge Modern History, Archbishop Mathew on the influence of Burke, Professor Butterfield has stressed Acton's unique historical knowledge, and Dr. Gooch has elucidated Acton's significance as The Future in Retrospect. Professor Toynbee has acknowledged Acton as his inspiration.

Since the present volume was written Miss Gertrude Himmelfarb has published a valuable study of the place of the American Revolution in Acton's political thought.[2] Some of the reasons why I dissent from the conclusions of this article have appeared already. Here I ought to record some of the reasons for differing from Miss Himmelfarb on the following points: (1) Acton did not regard conscience as infallible, as Miss Himmelfarb states. He pronounced the doctrine of the infallibility of conscience "indefensible."[3] (2) Acton did not regard the facts of history as all so well established that little more remains to be done. On the contrary, in the passage to which Miss Himmelfarb refers, Acton says: "The topics indeed are few on which the resources have been so employed that we can be content with the work done for us and never wish it to be done again."[4] (3) Acton was not contemptuous of the Revolution of 1688: on the contrary he said it was the greatest thing done by the English nation,[5] the point at which the Englishman became the leader

---

[1] Professor Noack has collected 240 of Acton's aphorisms on liberty from his published writings, but not this one, which appears in the MSS. and is a tribute to Professor Noack's insight: "Definition [of Liberty]: Security for the future" (Add. 4945). Cf. also Add. 4951: "Liberty as an idea—as a condition enjoyed—as an established security."
[2] *Journal of Modern History*, Dec. 1949.
[3] *Corr.*, p. 79 (1895; *aetat.* 61).
[4] *L.M.H.*, p. 7.   [5] *Ibid.*, p. 231.

of the world. He goes on: "The consequences ripened slowly, and a time came, under George III, when it seemed that they were exhausted. It was then that another and a more glorious Revolution, infinitely more definite and clear-cut, with a stronger grasp of principle, began to influence England and Europe." (4) Miss Himmelfarb wishes to deny that Acton's views developed—in spite of the double warning to the contrary in his *Inaugural*.

Appendix III

MORAL JUDGMENTS

ACTON has been criticized for his insistence on the moral criterion in history. In his last illness he himself regretted the severity of some of his judgments. But, in fact, Acton's moral judgments, though severe, are both realistic and restrained in expression, and they are not obtrusive. An excellent example is his judgment on Napoleon, which is given in a remarkable passage:

> Few things denote him more than the manner of his regret for his greatest crime: "La mort meritée du duc d'Enghien nuisit à Napoléon dans l'opinion et ne lui fut d'aucune utilité politique." An entire book of Retractations might be made of avowals such as this. In 1805 he said to Talleyrand: "Je me suis tant trompé en ma vie que je n'en rougis pas." And in 1813 to Roederer: "Une faute! C'est moi qui ai fait des fautes." He confessed at various times that he had done wrong in crowning his relations, in raising his marshals above the level of their capacity, in restoring the confiscations. The concordat was the worst fault of his reign; the Austrian match was his ruin; the birth of his son an onerous complication. The unlucky attack upon Spain was not only a wholesale blunder, as the irrevocable event proved, but a series of blunders in detail. The invasion of Russia was hopeless during the Spanish war. He ought to have restored Poland; he ought not to have remained at Moscow; he

ought to have stopped at Smolensk; he ought not to have crossed the Niemen. At the Beresina he cried: "Voilà ce qui arrive quand on entasse fautes sur fautes!" He regretted the attempted conquest of San Domingo, the annexation of Holland, the rejection of Talleyrand's warning that France would show less energy than himself. He wished that he had not concluded the armistice after Bautzen, that he had followed up his victory after Dresden, that he had made peace at Prague, at Frankfort, at Châtillon. It would have been better if he had employed Sieyès, if he had never trusted Fouché, if he had not sent Narbonne to Vienna. When he heard of the treaty of February 1815 between England, Austria and France, he said that that would have been his true policy. He repented his moderation as sincerely as his violence. He lamented that he had twice shrunk from making himself dictator, and had swerved too soon from the scheme of making his dynasty the oldest in Europe, which it might have become if he had had the resolution to dethrone the house of Brandenburg after Jena, and to dissolve the Austrian monarchy after Wagram.

There is that which bars the vindication of his career. It is condemned by the best authority, by the final judgment of Napoleon himself. And this is not the only lesson to be learnt from the later, unofficial, intimate, and even trivial records which the two biographers incline to disregard. They might have enabled one of the two to admire without defending, and the other to censure without disparaging, and would have supplied both with a thousand telling speeches and a thousand striking traits for a closer and more impressive likeness of the most splendid genius that has appeared on earth.[1]

It seems to me that Acton's doctrine about moral judgments has been misunderstood. The critical passage comes at the end of the *Inaugural*, and begins by asking whether there is any "neglected truth" that requires emphasis. The answer suggested is that we should never "debase the moral currency." To do so only enables writers to "tamper with weights and measures." The point is elucidated by a quotation from Goldwin Smith to the same effect. Acton's really characteristic doctrine is sincerity. In discussing the science of history Acton

[1] *H.E.*, pp. 457-458 (1887). Article on the biographies by Seeley and Ropes.

says that the main thing is to discern truth from falsehood, certainty from doubt.[1] The responsible writer's character, position, antecedents and probable motives have to be examined into.[2] A historian has to be treated as a witness and not believed unless his sincerity is established.[3] Sincerity means making out for our opponents a stronger and more impressive case than they present themselves.[4] The impartiality of the scientific school is not the whole truth. A more robust impartiality is sincerity.[5]

Appendix IV

ENGLISH HISTORIANS

It has been said that Acton did not value sufficiently highly the writings of English historians. The matter is sufficiently important to call for a short examination of the evidence. Apart from the dozens of English historians he reviewed in the periodicals he edited, there is decisive evidence the other way in the study of German schools of history (where he refers to twenty-five English historians) and in the *Inaugural*. I will quote a very few examples from these two sources:

"Like all men before Shirley, he [Neander] entirely mistook Wyclif. In our day Lechler and Arnold, Matthews, Buddensieg, and Loserth have published a new Wyclif, and a new pedigree of Hus."[6]

"During many years Pauli regularly introduced the Rolls publications which were undermining the work of his life, and admitted that there were points on which the *History of the Norman Conquest* surpasses everything yet written on the Middle

---

[1] *L.M.H.*, p. 15.   [2] *Ibid.*, p. 16.   [3] *Ibid*.
[4] *Ibid.*, p. 18.
[5] *Ibid.* Cf. *F.R.*, p. 373: "the man . . . who can be liberal towards those who have erred, who have sinned, who have failed. . . ."
[6] "German Schools of History" (*H.E.*, p. 360). Acton regarded the German school as derived from Burke.

Ages. Ewald preferred Selden to all his followers in Syriac. Lehrs declared that he could make nothing of the political life of Greece until he read Grote. The Prolegomena to Tischendorf's last text have, I believe, been committed to an English hand; Bailleu says that the best lives of the greatest modern Germans, of Frederic, Stein, and Goethe, are those which have been written in England."[1]

"The topics ... are few on which the resources have been so employed that we can be content with the work done for us and never wish it to be done over again. Part of the lives of Luther and Frederick, a little of the Thirty Years War, much of the American Revolution and the French Restoration, the early years of Richelieu and Mazarin, and a few volumes of Mr. Gardiner, show here and there like Pacific islands in the ocean."[2]

"When we are told that England is behind the Continent in critical faculty, we must admit that this is true as to quantity, not as to quality of work. As they are no longer living, I will say of two Cambridge professors, Lightfoot and Hort, that they were critical scholars whom neither Frenchman nor German has surpassed."[3]

"More satisfactory because more decisive has been the critical treatment of the mediaeval writers, parallel with the new editions, on which incredible labour has been lavished, and of which we have no better examples than the prefaces of Bishop Stubbs."[4]

Elsewhere Acton wrote of Freeman that he was "a first-rate man."

In the letters to contributors to the *Cambridge Modern History* he wrote: "Froude spoke of 100,000 papers consulted by him in manuscript, abroad and at home; and that is still the price to be paid for mastery, beyond the narrow area of effective occupation."[5]

The reviews of the works of English historians in the *English Historical Review* (Bryce, Creighton, Seeley, Bright, Stephens, Flint), of Erskine May in the *Quarterly Review*, and elsewhere of Goldwin Smith, Burd, and others are evidence that Acton took the greatest care to give credit where credit was due.

[1] *H.E.*, p. 385. [2] *Inaugural*, p. 7. [3] *Ibid.*, p. 17.
[4] *Ibid.*, p. 16. [5] *L.M.H.*, p. 316.

And, once again, the fact that he regarded the entire German school as derived from Burke is significant. Acton goes out of his way to praise English writers and scholars whenever he can.

Appendix V

PROBLEMS OF ACTON INTERPRETATION

THE major clues to the problems of Acton interpretation are:

A. that he was a (1) Christian, (2) Liberal, (3) Historian, (4) Learned, (5) Sincere, (6) Developing;
B. the evidence is of different kinds and of different dates and very large—essays, reviews, popular lectures, university lectures, letters, manuscripts (the last about fifty thousand pages); marked passages in the books in the Acton Library;
C. Acton never says in one place all that he thinks on any topic;
D. Acton intentionally made statements that appear to be grossly inconsistent[1];
E. Acton believed that some truths need supplementing by others.
F. No one has yet mastered the whole of the evidence.

Appendix VI

NATURAL SCIENCE

ACTON claimed to be ignorant of natural science, but the claim can hardly be allowed in respect of the history of science. For example, among the scientists whose importance Acton

[1] *H.F.*, xxxviii–xxxix.

specifically recognized were: Hippocrates, Archimedes, Ptolemy, Pliny, Roger Bacon, Copernicus, Kepler, Galileo, Harvey, Newton, Lavoisier, Priestley, Laplace, Cuvier, Darwin, Oersted, Faraday, Liebig. This list, which could be extended, omits mathematicians and statisticians, for example Conring, Quetelet, Ball and others, and historians of science, for instance, Valentin, Kopp, Du Bois Reymond.[1]

Appendix VII

ANALYSIS OF ACTON MS. Add. 4955[2]

In Acton's view, it was the Whigs, from the Trimmers to Gladstone, who were the party of real freedom. They were lacking in originality, deficient in ideas, prone to compromise, often taken "in tow" by others, frequently in the wrong. But they are the central feature in "that great movement of the human mind," still unfinished, which begins with Grotius, Bacon, and Descartes. They took their rise in the age which saw the beginnings of modern science and modern philosophy. That climate of thought must be understood first. Its dominant idea is the idea of clearness of thought.

The "doctrine of Clearness . . . took deep root in the seventeenth century," and, though most familiar in its Cartesian form, it was an idea that "was generally current. It entered into the view of Whig philosophy" and proved the "greatest source [both] of power and of error." "[It is] remarkable that

[1] Also cf. the following: "Why it is that, between 1841 and 1847, Grove, Joule, Meyer, Helmholtz, knowing nought of each other, made the same discovery" (Add. 4943). This is an example of a general problem which is examined in the Provost of Oriel's *Science and Social Welfare in the Age of Newton*, 2nd ed. 1950. See also Add. 4943: "Arago enumerates—estimates—the number of really great mathematicians at 10. Humboldt, advised by Dirichlet, in the translation, reduced them to eight. Leben A. by H. 11., 173."

[2] In this Appendix I have inserted the necessary brackets and commas to show how this manuscript has been used in Chapter III. The order of the excerpts is not the same as in the MS.

the most eminent Englishmen of that age inclined to Socinianism—Milton, Locke, Newton"—another sign of the same influence. And one of its results was that "it reduced the dogmatic quality of the State religion." The "doctrine of clearness [was also] necessary for popular action. [The] masses only understand what is quite clear. If they are to decide, things must be made clear—and only such things submitted to them. Hence, limitation of the Whig doctrine. Science goes on clearing things up. The domain of certainty extends, and [also the domain] of evidence. [Later, the] doctrine of clearness [was to be] applied by Say, and [by] Bastiat. [But] truths that are obvious to children are good only for children. The principles of the wealth of nations lie rather deeper." The danger of the doctrine of clearness is that "it gives the victory to those things which nobody can fail to see over those which belong to the intelligent."

"[Another of the] philosophic ideas then in the air [was the idea of] Progress, [represented by] Bacon, Descartes, Malebranche, Pascal [and] Leibniz." This is the doctrine that the "Moderns are not inferior to the Ancients, that progression is not in a circle, that the world is not gradually getting worse and worse, that God is stronger than the devil, [and] the spirit than the flesh." "The two principles, tradition, . . . and progress, [are met] in all countries and [all] ages." "Each attracts certain natures, [certain] ages, [certain] classes. Party divided them [the Whigs] from the Conservatives, gave them onesidedness, and made them more familiar with their liberal half. So they never combined the two sides properly, continuity and progress." "Locke has no [notion of] Devel[opment]. . . . [That came with] Leibniz," of whose ideas on the subject Locke shows no knowledge. "Until then the appeal to the past was traditional. . . . Now, not the law that was permanent, but the principle of the law. . . . [This is] Conservatism spiritualized." It is the idea "which Lessing, Herder, Humboldt, Savigny, Hegel and Baur made a patrimony of the Germans." Though "[the Whigs] never combined the two sides properly, continuity and progress," they "introduced the principle of continuity" though they did not fully grasp its underlying law.[1]

[1] That is to say, the Revolution of 1688 was carried out without breach of continuity.

But the "real force and value" of tradition "in society [was] known [at that time] to none, not even to Leibniz."

Newton's philosophy of nature, the "philosophy of observation," also had its influence on Whiggism. Later that influence was revived and increased by Scottish philosophy, by "Hutcheson, Reid, Ferguson, Brown, Playfair, Stewart, Mackintosh, Jeffrey, Napier," the *Edinburgh Review*. "The three greatest Whigs were Scotsmen—Brougham, Macaulay, and Gladstone."

"[The] contributory currents [were many—beyond] experimental [science, with] Newton, Boyle, [and] Sydenham, [and] Bacon, [and] Descartes, [there were the] Cambridge [Platonists, such as] More, [and] Whichcote, [independent thinkers such as] Cumberland, [the lawyers], . . . Selden [and] Pym, [the] Puritan[s], Penn, Marvel, Milton, Church[men like] Leighton, Chillingworth, Hales [and] Burnet, [and the] revolutionary [thinkers such as] Lilburne [and] Harrington." "It was the age of mechanics of mathematics. Those were the prevailing discoveries. Not the formation of languages, physiology, ethnology, the forms and laws of growth. The mechanism, not the organism. But Harvey had thrown the deepest discredit on the ancients—For they had been so near it, and had not seen it."

"[To the Whigs, politics] was an experimental and progressive science—not to be shut up in the formulas of doctrinaires." "They perceived that the State cannot judge Dogma, and need not. [It] requires only moral convictions. But there are exceptions: [(1) the] unity of mankind [(2)] immortality." "Science . . . points to cosmopolitanism. The sources of error most to be guarded against are national pride and prejudice, ambition, [and the] interests of classes, of churches, of races." "Up to then politics alone were insufficient. Religion had always been needed to stimulate men, and to cause progress. But now there was a purely political force at work. Even without religious impulses political theory henceforth made its own way."

"Certainty had just begun, and people learned to see clear. [This was shown not only by] Newton in astronomy, Sydenham, Boyle [and the] Royal Society; Mabillon had done it with history, . . . Bentley with the classics," [not to speak of] Henschen, and . . . Holstenius." "England had more than her share of all this. [At the same time] Political Economy also came up."

"[The] idea [of the Whigs] was that there is such a thing as political science, that it is clear and certain, that it is [as] sacred as morality, that it is imperfect, progressive, and increasing, as essential to the welfare of society as religion or private morals, and as demonstrable as the truths of science." But "[the Whigs] might say [that although] there is a science of politics . . . it is not yet determined, the elements do not exist. . . . Criminal law, . . . international law, political economy— all this was in its infancy. So the past retained a hold, [which it was] destined to relax. Things might be gradually determined. Codes might develop themselves, practice [and] experience might be reduced to theory. Meantime, [the Whigs] accept things as they are, without respect or authority, but for want of certainty." "Political science travels slowly. . . . It was not treated scientifically, any more than polit[ical] economy or criminal law [at that time]." The Whigs had "not a very energetic system of ideas." "Algernon Sidney's supply of information [was] very scanty. Locke [was] tolerably superficial." "Burnet, Hoadly, Addison, Toland [were] all on the surface." But the Whigs "began the emancipation of politics from religion—at least it was the first party that lived on purely political considerations. So it had to put religious arguments aside. It lost the sectarianism of 1641."

The Whigs lack depth "because they go back to no one principle." The "Whigs took things as they found them, accepted the results of history, [and] decided to build from the foundations. If [they had] any principle it was what will practically promote freedom. . . . they afterwards canonized those inherited forms. This was the work of Montesquieu, who idealized them, and of Burke. . . . This canon was shaken by America."

"Rationalism was one thing that prepared the way for them [the Whigs]. [They] dreaded the force of orthodoxy. They relied a little on scepticism." "Influence of [Lord] Herbert of Cherbury on the early Whigs. Other sceptical influences . . . [were] Spinoza [and] Bayle. So we find a great religious unbelief . . . Shaftesbury, Sidney, Halifax, Somers, Locke, Toland." "Metaphysics do not decide against religion, for faith is stronger than metaphysics. But conscience is stronger than faith, so Whiggism put aside speculation, admitted only ethics." "Penn [was] the most liberal mind of the age," and Coleridge thought that "Penn on toleration [was] better than Locke." Though "Locke is the Whig classic for propaganda," he is "not the complete Whig," and he had a "weak notion of the judiciary." There were "other currents," including the idea of the "supremacy of conscience."

"Locke derived all knowledge from experience, [as] Leibniz [did] from intellect. The Whigs grew under the former influence. Then came Rationalism, and rejected that method, claiming to produce everything from the reason. This is the revolutionary doctrine, distinguishing 1789 [the French Revolution] from 1688 [the English Revolution]. Lambert[1] (Nov. Organon) and Kant corrected and combined the two." "Grotius [had produced the] theory of doing without God, [and it was] on this basis that Locke constructed his theory." "The eighteenth century developed their [Whig] ideas, worked on their lines [and] built up on their foundations. Voltaire, Montesquieu, Condillac, [and] Rousseau, [who were] the greatest forces, [are] only popularized Locke. Even Turgot and [Adam] Smith [are] largely founded on him, [and] also Hume and Kant and Lessing. It took long to make them [the Whigs] scientific—to deliver them from their age." "As Locke displays the metaphysical basis [of Whiggism], Somers [and] Holt the legal, who the ecclesiastical? Burnet. Leibniz the universal." "Writers later introduced deductive and *a priori* doctrines which were not indigenous in Whiggism. Mill [for instance] treats pol[itical] econ[omy] as a deductive science."

The definition of Whiggism is "morality applied to politics." "Other parties represent class interests, or religions. They represent a principle, bound by no interest, attached to no class." Their rule was to consider the past, but to be ready, if need be, to break with it. "[There was] no quite new idea [among the Whigs]." "[They] desired the predominance of no class, of no religion, of no form. [They] obeyed [at once] experience, . . . [and] the ideal. But both ideas were undeveloped. No part of the science of gov[ernment] was so well

[1] [For Lambert see *Critique of Pure Reason*, passim.]

established as to make the ideal triumph. When that came, with Quesnay, [and] with Beccaria, the ideal element gained strength from it. Nor was continuity, progress, [or] the method of growth ascertained. So that history was also [to them] an uncertain, unregulated force. So Whiggism was destined to be transformed."

"The transition from the Roundheads to the Whigs" is occupied by the Trimmers, who were "moderators of" the extremes of the former. "The Shaftesbury party were, we know, in the right. Charles deserved to be deposed [and] James to be excluded. But the doctrine of acquiescence in forms had to prevail." They "tried to make the throne, the church, the aristocracy innocuous, [and to make] a king who should not oppress, a church that should not persecute, a nobility that should not injure trade." "If men gave up enforcing their religion, they [the Whigs] gave up more. They could not stand by other interests more firmly. So they were ready, for the sake of liberty, to see their faith suffer. In the same way, they had to sacrifice to Liberty their country and their class. The repudiation of class purposes was as strong in the Whigs as the repudiation of sectarianism. How could patriotism resist the contagion?" "Their rule [was] to promote whatever promoted liberty, [and] to prevent the domination of class." They "adopted the idea of party, allowed what they claimed to their adversaries. This is the idea of being liberal—not to proscribe."

"Liberty regarded as security—security of property [appears in] Locke, Hume [and] Fox. No consideration of a more spiritual kind. But this was the character of [the Revolution of] 1688, that it was spiritual." The Whigs were "not in the service of a particular Church, . . . not in the service of any class, land, labour or capital; but independent of special interests. [They were] not in the service of one part of society, at the expense of any others." At the time of the Revolution "there were hardly any great towns. . . . The poor people [were] not represented, could not read, and were dependent on the preacher for ideas, [and] on [their] employers for pay." "Dem[ocracy was then] without roots in England. Vane [had been] put to death, Baxter retracted, Harrington forgotten in prison, Prynne an eager royalist, Milton in obscurity. How completely [democracy had disappeared] appeared afterwards. [Yet] Harrington's law [that power follows property] governed the Rev[olution] of 1688. Somers, Locke, Davenant, Defoe, Temple, all proclaim the dominion of land—The right divine of freeholders."

"[The] Whigs [were] the first party that made liberty its object. Therefore [they were] opposed to Dem[ocracy]. It desires the union of elements, that is the division of power." "So far then, [there was] a lurking tenderness for aristocracy." "They seek it [liberty] by ways propounded by others. So they were made to follow, not to lead—[this is the story in the time of Adam] Smith, Bentham, Mill, [Gibbon] Wakefield, Cobden [and] O'Connell."

"What was neither aristocratic nor puritan, etc., etc., etc. [*sic*] was somewhat general. . . . The supreme principle was liberty—not anything else. The time might come when landed aristocracy would become obnoxious, when monarchy would stand stubborn in the way, when religion would be an obstacle to liberty. When that day came,[1] the foundations of the British Constitution would be dug up, for the sake of a principle which is above the nations, and does not depend on tradition." "It [the Whig party] subsisted on condition of not multiplying party dogmas and party tests. It accepted only what was common to Churchman, and Nonconformist, royalist and republican, freeholder and capitalist. All this tended to detach them from the soil."

"The fundamental principle, the *raison d'être* of the Whigs was Liberty, and not for anybody in particular. For the whole nation. This was the first time this principle was established. It is the beginning of that intense force—Liberty for its own sake. So it was for the sake of those who do not govern. Hence, Whig compromise, [and] Division of power, Division [that is] between those who exercise power and those who do not. [There was a] tendency gradually to exalt the controlling forces outside [to] gravitate towards the circumference. The forms of State tend to yield to the substance of the nation."

"[It was the] idea [of the Whigs] to preserve the existing Powers, to renounce speculation and radical improvement

[1] I.e. in the American Revolution.

apart from tradition. To accept the results of history, and make them tolerable. Crown, Church, aristocracy, army, Judges, magistrates, Corporations—[were all] preserved, but not allowed to injure. All [were] brought under control, for the benefit of those outside. [It was] not [the] dominion of any favoured class or sect, but [the] safety of all [those] outside from all inside—of the governed from the governing elements, safety ag[ain]st privilege and power. What is that? That is liberty." "They resolved to avoid extremes [and] to make King, Church, [and] Lords innocuous and acceptable. Land was the one thing untouched."

"Every doctrine, to become popular, must be made superficial, exaggerated, untrue. We must always distinguish the real essence from the conveyance, especially in political economy." "[In the Whig view] the people, the constituencies, [were] quite incompetent to decide a policy—the balance of power, the colonial trade, the Bank question, the currency question. They are not informed. There is no way to inform them. They must choose their members. Having chosen, they must let them act as they think best."

"The people choose men—or have the choice of measures. The first is the Whig theory, the people have the choice only of men. As to measures they can petition, they can hold meetings. But they cannot control their representatives. Therefore the debates were secret, there were no instructions, and the Lords were able to balance the Commons. Parliament might do what the nation did not wish. If all this disappears, then there is democracy, as in America, as in Switzerland. That divides Whigs and Democrats."

"To be of one accord a community must be small. . . . [There are] important passages in Waddington [illustrative of this]." "The Independents, wiser than almost all their imitators, wished to deliver the individual, not to create an irresistible force for the collective individuals. One democracy sets no limit to the general will. The Ind[ependents] set the most definite limits." "Defoe argued that all powers conferred by the people could be resumed. All depends not on those who represent, but on those who are represented." "The Act of Succession forbad the King to pardon a man accused by the Commons. They represented the people, and it must be assumed that they would undertake nothing unjust. This is very curious, as a beginning of Infallibility."

"As to the standing army, they [the Whigs] said: If we cannot protect our liberties ourselves, we are not a free people."

"The masses had no part in the Revolution [of 1688]. . . . The Democracy of 1650 was theoretic. It came from Independency. It hardly grew on English soil. It was American."

The early Whigs were beaten by Charles II. It was "the moderate party [that] survived. [There is a great] contrast between the two generations," the Roundheads, and the early Whigs with their "doctrine of Compromise," making the best of things, and progressing slowly. They came to subsist "on condition of not multiplying party dogmas and party tests, accepting only what was common to Churchman and Nonconformist, royalist and republican, freeholder and capitalist. All this tended to detach them from the soil." "As it [the Whig system] was a delicate system of compromises, there was no eagerness to push enquiry to logical consequences—Rather some reluctance. The Whigs took their lead from outside—never shut the door against ideas that would promote freedom, but [would] not open it with alacrity. They were always in tow, [as witness] Negro slavery, American taxation, political economy, Bentham, [Parliamentary] Reform, Religious Liberty, [the] Colonies, Criminal Law, [the] Factory Laws, Grote, Mill."

"[The Whigs] accepted existing forms without discussion. So far [they were] not scientific. Compromise between fact and theory was their object. And they were driven to consider the essence, not forms—to leave these, and to decide what is good in principle, apart from forms. This means [the] negation of Radicalism. [It meant] make the best of realities. So [the Whigs] were driven to find excuses for what they accepted. They canonized what they could not disturb. That is Burke. That is the glorification of country gentlemen, broad establishments, Constit[utional] Monarchy."

"There is no Whig pr[inciple] which the Whig party has not repudiated. Fox against [Parliamentary] Reform, Walpole agst Dissenters, Chatham agst America, Russell agst Free Trade, Grey agst [the] Factory Laws, Fox agst [the] French treaty, Melbourne agst [the] Charter, Palmerston agst [the] Ballot."

"[The Whig] want of system broke down at last. America began it, with Camden and Chatham, France with Fox, Ireland with Grattan. Ricardo pushing forward Adam Smith, Bentham developing Beccaria. . . . [There was also the influence of] independent thinkers—Grote, Wakefield, Mill, Cobden, Plunket. It [the Whig party] was taken in tow and went reluctantly."

"Whiggism [was] influenced by [the] Economists, [the] Liberals, [the] Radicals, in succession." "[English] Liberalism rose out of [Adam] Smithianism."

The "rise of Liberalism" in Europe, "in France and Germany," followed the "suppression of [the Spanish] Constitution" in 1823. "So an international system was gradually formed [which was] not Whig. Its basis was the inheritance, the lesson, of the [French] Revolution—the ideals of 1789 controlled by ten years—equal to centuries—of experience, [together with the] example—idealized—of England—[and the] practical [example] of America."

"[The] term [liberalism was] first used about 1807—of Chateaubriand and [of Madame] de Staël. Then in Spain [in] 1811. [Other instances are the] Irish members in the British Parliament, [the] *Edinburgh Review*, [the] influence of the Scots philosophy. [It was an] epoch of little faith. The general tendency [is] proved, outside of politics, by the poets . . . Schiller, Alfieri, Monti, the Freiheitsdichter in Germany, even the Lake school at first, and Heine, . . . Grün, Byron, Shelley, Landor, Tennyson, Browning, Swinburne, Campbell, Rogers, Moore, Quintana, Mickiewicz, Delavigne, Manzoni, Pushkin, Hugo."

"Liberalism . . . rose and spread: Jovellanos, Arguelles, Toreno, the Americans and South Americans, the English opposition—Brougham, Romilly, Bentham, Dumont, Mill, Ricardo, Huskisson, Senior, Mill, Wakefield, Whately, Hare, Arnold, Cobbett, Frost, C[harles] Buller."

Continental Liberalism meant "the residuum of the [French] Revolution—Daunou, De Staël, Constant, Broglie, Chateaubriand, Courrier, Fiévée, Foy; [the] Doctrinaires—De Serre, R[oyer]-Collard, Guizot, Barante; Rossi, Rémusat; Comte,

Thierry, and the recovery of the Saint Simonians; Chevalier, Say, Sismondi, Bastiat, Cousin, Thiers, Tocqueville, the rep[resentative] School, the Socialist school, Comte's school; Lamennais."

"All these schools, towards 1848, combined together—when the lines of Lamennais, Chateaubriand, Daunou, S. Simon, A. Comte, Lafayette, R[oyer-]Collard, Berryer, Sismondi, came to much the same general result, to a common ground, very near Constant, Rémusat, Tocqueville, Laboulaye, etc. That idea is evidently very powerful. Follow it up out of France, under French influence. How it grew in Germany, Italy, Spain, Switzerland."

The "stages of . . . [the] progress" of the ideas of Liberalism are marked by the following names: in France—"Constant, Fiévée, Guizot, Sismondi, Rossi, Tocqueville, Le Play, Broglie, Cormenin, Bastiat, S. Simon"; in Germany—"Kant, Humboldt, Savigny, Hegel, Radowitz, Fröbel, Heine, Dahlmann, Vollgraff, Schmoller, Ihering."

The Tories might argue that "Whig concessions would be limited by no principle.[1] It might become democratic, revolutionary, Socialist. . . . They would resist for a time, [but] not on principle. [They would judge by] expediency. [There would be] a process of incessant, indefinite change. . . . Ideal Toryism [was] prepared by Burke's dislike of [Parliamentary] Reform. . . . [Their great prize was the] prize of tradition. [According to] ideal Toryism Burke was right in rejecting the [French] Revolution as [the] enemy of liberty." "On this basis [Ideal Toryism] legitimacy arose on the Continent." "[Ideal Toryism was] against [the] new Poor Law. Favourable to [the] Factory Laws." "[The] Tories . . . had the common ground of Conservatism—government by tradition, by property, by religion, that is, acquired rights are sacred. Property [in their view] is the safest ruler, because it has the greatest stake [in the country], also because it is educated. [They could argue that] if political power is given without property, it will oblige property to follow it. Therefore, to avoid spoliation, give power to property."

But "system means [a] view of only certain truths." What the Whigs represent is "not a system, [but] a spirit." "Liberty is

---
[1] This page of the MS. is headed "Tories."

one. It is the same cause always—but the opposition varies." But the "desire of doing the enemy justice [is] a mark of scientific sincerity." The saying that the terms "Whig and Tory belong to natural history" was made by Jefferson and was "adopted by Adams."

"[At one time] the Whigs—Fox [and] Turgot, etc., admit the supreme right of property. That is the liberty they most attend to. It is the old mediaeval view—the physical, not the moral basis of freedom.[1] [It was] revived by Locke—and [it] continued as long as toleration was not recognized. The insufficiency of it came out in the American Revolution. The right to tax was denied. The right to govern was admitted. This is the position of Chatham, Camden, Franklin. It was necessary to go one step further—and that was revolution." "In reality, a Whig cannot think other gov[ernmen]ts legitimate. [In him is a] principle of revolution, if not of aggression. . . . An attempt to upset them [i.e. governments resting on a basis he deems illegitimate] must attract him."

"[There is] not an absolute contradiction between liberal and conservative. It is a question of time and place and expediency. Liberals admit that men are not always ripe for freedom. Conservatives wish to preserve it lest it be imperilled. But Whigs and Tories really mean contrary things, excluding each other. One wishes to preserve things for their own sake. The other will sacrifice every institution that does not stand the test of liberality."

"Parties [abroad] that have adopted Whig principles—Federalists, Feuillants, Cavour. . . . But no constitutions [have emulated the example of the Whigs]. All [have been drawn] on the French models—[in] Spain, Portugal, Holland, Belgium, Denmark, Austria, Prussia, Italy."

That they proposed the partition of Poland, maintained the penal laws, that they were responsible for the treatment meted out to the Dissenters, and to Ireland; their record in regard to slavery—that is the case against the Whigs.[2]

[1] This does not represent the whole of Acton's view of course.
[2] *L.M.H.*, p. 274. Cf. Add. 4955: "They persecuted Ireland," and "oppression of Ireland" (*Ibid*).

Appendix VIII

ADAM SMITH

Acton called *The Wealth of Nations* the "classic English philosophy of history." The following list, headed "Adam Smith," illustrates the thoroughness of his economic studies: "D. Stewart, Blanqui, Macculoch, Jouffroy, Cousin, Janet, Haldane, Kautz, Hildebrand, Roscher, Bluntschli, Rösler, List, Eisenhart, J. Karczynski, Schönberg, Held, Wagner, Bagehot, Stephen, Kettner, Cadet, Brougham, T. Brown, Chevalier, Cossa, A. Carlyle, Carey, Buckle, Hallam, Ingram, Franck, McCosh, Liser, Mackintosh, Neurath, Rogers, C. Leslie, Oncken, Puynode, Stöpel." (Add. 4943.)

Appendix IX

GROTIUS

In Add. 4945 there is a note: "Sidgwick tells Maine that Hobbes really was attacking Grotius." Acton called Grotius the founder of "real political science." Below are two lists which illustrate how profoundly Acton studied him.

"Grotius anticipated. Althusius, Barclay, Arnisaeus, Bodinus, Tolosanus, Molina, Contzen, Stinzing." (Add. 4939.)

(An adjoining list headed Grotius.) "Vives, Victoria, Brunus, Soto, Ayala, Castropalao, Suarez, Belli, Gentili, Oldenburg, Hunning, Languet, Janet, Tiercelin, Cauchy, Wheaton, Kaltenborn, Mohl, Stahl, Gierke, Hinrichs."

(Add. 4939.)

In another MS. Acton noted that Grotius's doctrine of natural law may be found in Gratian. He was aware in principle of what has since become familiar in detail since the publication of the six volumes of *Mediaeval Political Theory in the West* by A. J. and R. W. Carlyle.

Appendix X

ROTHE AND VINET

ACTON regarded Rothe as the greatest moral theologian of modern times. His chief work was *Theologische Ethik* (2nd ed. 1867). See Nippold, *Rothe*; Holtzmann, *Rothe's Speculative System* (1899), Troeltsch in the Memorial volume dedicated to Kuno Fischer, and Merz, *History of European Thought in the Nineteenth Century*, Vol. IV.

Vinet was a great Swiss moralist much admired by Acton. His chief work was *Manifestation des Convictions Religieuses* (2nd ed. Paris, 1858). Its keynote is the following (p. 183): "Tout devoir emporte un droit; il n'est pas de droit plus sacré que celui de remplir son devoir; c'est même ice-bas le seul droit absolu; car le droit s'appuie sur une nécessité primitive; or le devoir est la première des nécessités, et, à la rigeur, la seule nécessité." See also Astié, *Esprit de Vinet* (2 vols.), which Acton listed as one of the world's great books.

Acton was once asked what book he would give to anyone he wished to convert to Catholicism. He replied: Rothe's *Ethics*. Rothe was a Protestant theologian! It is also highly characteristic that Acton ranked Vinet with Rothe. But in his heart of hearts he seems almost always to prefer a French writer (including French-Swiss) to a German. He really prefers Calvin to Luther, Fénelon to Leibniz, Tocqueville to Ranke, and Cournot to Roscher. In the last analysis he prefers Vinet to Rothe. This is because Vinet makes conscience supreme, while Rothe deleted the term from his theological vocabulary in the second edition of his *Ethics*.

Appendix XI

FURTHER EXTRACTS FROM THE ACTON MANUSCRIPTS

The following passages, found in Acton's manuscripts after the present book was completed, may form a fitting conclusion.

Democracy without a moral standard . . . could no more stand than a Republic governed by Marat. (Add. 5504.)

The later democracy of 1848, Universal Suffrage, Socialism in its new forms—not founded on equality—but a scientific modification of political economy. (Add. 4895.)

There is no liberty where there is hunger. . . . The theory of liberty demands strong efforts to help the poor. Not merely for safety, for humanity, for religion, but for liberty.
(Add. 5500.)

the poorer class . . . their interests are the most sacred.
(Add. 5500.)

Liberality . . . The principle must gradually eventuate in Equality. Equality only limited by necessity. This is the higher equality. (Add. 5486.)

Only since Socialism is there a thorough conception of the financial character of the State. (Add. 5486.)

America started with the habit of abstract ideas . . . It came to them from Religion, and the Puritan struggle . . . The Rights of Man grew out of English toleration. It was the link between tradition and abstraction. (Add. 4897.)

The great revelation of America was that of a revolution effected by conservative politicians.
Hamilton and Adams and Washington.
In our days, Deak, Cavour.
Nobody can measure their force. (Add. 4898.)

Federalism . . . Allows of different nationalities, religions, epochs of civilization to exist in harmony side by side.
Capable of unlimited extension. (Add. 4895.)

Remedy

The most efficacious are, sovereignty of reason, and the sense of continuity with the past.

One, idea of what is constitutional, apart from legal—the other, the idea of what is right, apart from will.

(Add. 5504.)

End with the kingdom of God, which is liberty.
How far from the end? Africa not begun, Asia, how little.
But America and Australia, South Africa, governed by the ideas of our revolution. The ideas that went out there, govern the world—Their reaction in Europe. (Add. 5504.)

End

Reasons for Hope. Ignorance was at the bottom of it.
This century has produced great securities.
    It strengthens and enlightens conscience.
    Discovered anthropology, statistics, political economy.

(Add. 5504.)

End

Liberty grows as conscience grows. For the conscience of man becomes more sensitive and more true by culture.
So also the notion of liberty—and it varies with facts.

(Add. 5504.)

Political Science [is] in its infancy. (Add. 5504.)

Conclusion—or upshot—

Politics, as a science of collective life, stand not by themselves.
Involve so much besides.
Determined not only by actual political conditions—
    Economic, national character, interests, needs, passions, but by ideas deep down elsewhere, in religion, in philosophy, in science. (Add. 4991.)

Federalism—The only way of avoiding war. (Add. 5415).

BIBLIOGRAPHY

A LIST of Acton's writings is given in Dr. W. A. Shaw's *Bibliography of the Historical Works of Dr. Creighton, Dr. Stubbs, Dr. S. R. Gardiner, and The Late Lord Acton*, published by the Royal Historical Society in 1903. The part relating to Acton has twice been reprinted, (1) by Mr. F. E. Lally in *As Lord Acton Says* (1942) and (2), with additions, by Miss G. Himmelfarb in a selection of Acton's essays published in the United States under the title *Essays on Freedom and Power* (Glencoe, Ill., 1948). The first list supplementing Dr. Shaw was given in *The History of Freedom and Other Essays*, particulars of which are given below.

Acton's *Inaugural* on *The Study of History* was published separately in 1895, and was reprinted in *Lectures on Modern History* (1906).

In 1904 Mr. Herbert Paul edited, with an Introduction, *Letters of Lord Acton to Mary Gladstone*, of which a second edition with additional letters appeared in 1913.

In 1906 Cardinal F. A. Gasquet published a volume of letters under the title *Lord Acton and his Circle*.

In the same year a beginning was made of the publication of Acton's collected lectures and essays. These appeared as follows: *Lectures on Modern History* (1906), *The History of Freedom and other Essays* (1907), *Historical Essays and Studies* (1907), and *Lectures on the French Revolution* (1910). The first two of these contain valuable introductions by J. N. Figgis and R. V. Laurence, as also does *Lord Acton's Correspondence*, Vol. I (1917).[1] Mr. Lally prints some extracts from articles in periodicals not previously collected, and Miss Himmelfarb reprints the essay on the political causes of the American civil war also not previously reprinted. This article Acton entitled "Political Causes of the American Revolution." Professor E. L. Woodward published, with most valuable comments, short extracts from unpublished letters in an article in *Politica*, September 1939, under the title "The Place of Lord Acton in the Liberal Movement of the Nineteenth Century." Professor H. Butterfield has printed extracts from an early note-book in the *Cambridge Historical Journal* (1946). Since this bibliography was compiled a selection of Acton's uncollected essays, edited with an introduction by Mr. Douglas Woodruff, has been announced under the title, *Essays on Church and State*.

[1] **The** full title is: *Selections from the Correspondence of the first Lord Acton*.

Two of Acton's lists of books are given in *Some Hawarden Letters* (1917), edited by L. March-Phillipps and B. Christian, and *Immortal Memories* by Clement Shorter (1907).

It was not until the publication in 1942 of Mr. Lally's book that it became known that the second volume of Acton's Correspondence would not be published.

These particulars explain why Acton's political thought has not previously been studied as a whole.

Beyond the foregoing works, criticism and appreciation of Acton can be found principally in the following:

R. L. Poole, *English Historical Review* (October 1902).
Annual Register, 1902.
Dictionary of National Biography.
Encyclopaedia of the Social Sciences.
Sir Mountstuart Grant Duff, *Out of the Past* and also *Diaries*.
F. W. Maitland, *Independent Review*, 1904.
Bryce, *Studies in Contemporary Biography* (1903).
Mary Gladstone (Mrs. Drew), *Acton, Gladstone and Others* (1924).
H. A. L. Fisher, *Studies in History and Politics* (1920).
Professor H. Butterfield, *The Whig Interpretation of History* (1931), and *Lord Acton* (Historical Association pamphlet G.9 (1948)).
H. Finer, Preface to G. Himmelfarb, *Essays on Freedom and Power* (1948).
G. Himmelfarb, Introduction to above.
G. N. Clark in *Cambridge Historical Journal*, 1945 (on Acton's part in the planning of the Cambridge Modern History).
G. P. Gooch in *Foreign Affairs*, July 1947. (This is the only reliable account of Acton's thought in English), and *Chambers' Encyclopaedia*, 1950.
Professor U. Noack, *Politik als Sicherung der Freiheit* (1947).

An extremely large number of biographies contain material relating to Acton. Most of these are listed in two volumes of the Oxford History of England, viz. E. L. Woodward, *The Age of Reform*, and R. C. K. Ensor, *England 1870–1914*.

In addition the Life of Döllinger by C. Friedrich should be mentioned, and also Dr. G. P. Gooch's *Annals of Politics and Culture*, which has an Introduction by Acton. (First ed. 1901, reprinted 1905).

The biography of Acton's pupil and editor, J. N. Figgis, by M. G. Tucker, and Miss G. Himmelfarb's study, "The American Revolution in the Political Theory of Lord Acton" (*Journal of Modern History*, Dec. 1949, Vol. XXI, No. 4), appeared too late to be utilized.

See also *Cambridge Historical Journal*, Vol. X, No. 1, 1950, *Gasquet and the Acton-Simpson Correspondence*, by A. Watkin and Professor H. Butterfield, Dr. Gooch's study of Acton now available in *Maria Theresa and Other Studies* (1951), Archbishop Mathew's *Lord Acton, the Formative Years* (1945), and Lady Blennerhassett's fine obituary article in *Edinburgh Review*, 1903.

THE ACTON MANUSCRIPTS

THE Acton manuscripts are in the Cambridge University Library. They consist mainly of note-books, folders, and boxes. The folders contain up to about 170 slips, the boxes up to about 370. There are about 180 note-books and about 275 boxes and folders. In the writing of the present volume use has been made of the following: Add. 4867, 4868, 4869, 4870, 4871, 4901, 4916, 4955, 4956, 4965, 4983, 4991, 5389, 5390, 5393, 5395, 5434, 5470, 5481, 5487, 5495, 5581, 5582, 5583, 5609, 5670, 5696, 4937–4954, 4894–4898, 5499, 5500, 5504, 4992, 4993, 5389, 5415.

INDEX

Abbott, Dr., Bacon scholar, 137
Abelard, 144, 187
Absolutism, 104, 139, 142, 146, 166, 167, 170, 171, 172, 180, 181, 187, 198
Act of Settlement, 72
Act of Succession, *see* Act of Settlement
Acton, J. E. E. D., 1st Baron (1834–1902)
   Political theory, 33–80, 81–139
   Sources, 140–206
   Standpoint, 1–32
Acton Library, 12, 125, 228
Acton Manuscripts, 7 n. 2, 11 n. 5, 33, 54, 64 n. 3, 115–116, 119, 124, 131, 134, 194 n. 2, 195–196, 199 n. 2, 226, 243–244
Adams, John, President of the United States, 12, 13, 15, 75, 211, 240, 243
Addison, Joseph, 67, 232
Administration, 177, 197, 205
Africa, 244
Agriculture, 213, 214
Albertus Magnus, 144 n. 2, 187
Alcuin, 12, 55 n. 2, 106, 187
Alfieri, Count Vittorio, 73, 238
Alfred the Great, 31
Almagest, the, 144
Alphonso X (the Wise) of Castile, 144
Althusius, A. J., 241
America, 19, 23, 62, 64, 76–80, 99, 114, 144, 162, 168, 172, 173, 174, 175, 176, 181, 182, 184, 191, 192, 193, 195, 197 n. 2, 204 n. 2, 205, 210, 211, 217, 243, 244
American Civil War, 101 n. 3, 220, 222
American Commonwealth, Bryce's, 100, 101
American Constitution, 58, 77, 100, 174 n. 1
American Revolution, 24, 58, 59 and n. 4, 64, 68, 70 n. 1, 75, 76 ff, 104, 109, 110, 142, 145, 148, 167, 171, 174 n. 1, 181, 184, 193, 221, 223, 224, 227
Amsterdam, 212
Anabaptists, 121
Ancestry, 163
Andocides, 186
Anglicanism, 141, 145

Anselm, 144, 187
Anthropology, 244
Anti-Dühring, 17, 125
Antiquity, 82, 91, 144, 165
Antonius Augustinus, 49
Appeal from the New to the Old Whigs, Burke's, 7, 145, 190
Aquinas, St. Thomas, 22, 26, 34, 35 n. 4, 85, 91, 144 and n. 2, 166, 187 and n. 8, 195
Arago, 140 n. 1, 229 n. 1
Archimedes, 144, 229
Arguelles, Augustin, 73, 238
Arianism, 144
Aristocracy, 63, 69, 70, 102, 169, 174, 175, 218
Aristophanes, 106, 186
Aristotelian Society, 199 n. 2
Aristotle, 14, 21, 85, 115, 144, 154, 166, 185, 186 and n. 1, 199 n. 2
Arkwright, Sir Richard, 59
Arles, Council of (A.D. 314), 196 n. 1
Arminians, 169
Army, 72, 182
Arnisaeus, 241
Arnold of Brescia (d. 1155), 121
Arnold, English opposition leader, 74, 238
Arnold, Matthew, 222
Arnold, Dr. Thomas, 74, 226
Art, 158, 206, 207
Asia, 206, 244
Asiento, 214
Asoka, Buddhist king, 40
Associations, 90, 121, 124, 141, 167
Astié, 198, 242
Athanasius, 144
Athens, 25, 106, 165, 186
Atlantic, the, 132, 205, 212
Augustine, St., 34, 144, 187, 222 n. 1
Augustinus, Jansen's, 145
Aulard, A., 164
Austin, John, 28, 62
Australia, 244
Austria, 76, 122, 129, 133, 179, 211, 224, 225
Authority, 5, 7 n. 1, 46, 89, 133, 146, 166, 167, 168, 170, 171, 174, 189, 200, 201
Autocracy, vii, 206
Autonomy, personal, 197
Avesta, the, 143

249

Ayala, Pedro de, 241

Bacon, Francis, 62 and n. 1, 64, 65, 66, 77, 135, 137, 145, 154, 155, 206 n. 1, 208, 230, 231
Bacon, Roger, 144, 206 n. 1, 229
Bagehot, Walter, 241
Bailleu, 227
Bain, T., 135
Balance of trade, 219
Ball, Sir Robert, 229
Balliol College, xiii, 199 n. 2
Bank of England, 19, 213
Bankers, 180
Banking, 171, 213
Barante, Baron de, 44 n. 1, 74, 161, 238
Barclay, William, 241
Barker, Professor Sir Ernest, 91 n. 3, 105, 199
Barnave, Antoine, 176, 178
Baronius, Cardinal, 23, 145
Barrot, Camille, 113, 218
Bartlett, Dr. Vernon, 198
Bastiat, 65, 74, 120, 230, 239
Bastille, 110
Baur, F. C. von, 53, 66, 153, 154, 197, 208, 230
Bautzen, battle of, 1813, 225
Baxter, Richard, 70, 234
Bayle, Pierre, 4, 68, 145, 169, 188, 232
Beatitudes, 5, 22
Beccaria, Cesare, Marquis di, 27, 69, 73, 136, 145, 234, 238
Bede, 222 n. 1
Belgium, 76, 91, 182, 211
Bellarmine, Roberto, Cardinal, 169
Belli, 241
Bentham, Jeremy, 4, 27, 61, 70, 72, 73, 74, 88, 136, 146, 182, 180 n. 10, 197, 235, 237, 238
Bentley, Richard, 67, 231
Beresina, 225
Berlin, 17, 101 n. 2, 155
Bernhardi, 156
Berryer, Pierre Antoine, 74, 239
Berthold of Ratisbon (d. 1272), 120
Bible, 54, 130, 143 n. 3, 145, 195
Binkley, Professor R. C., 126
Birmingham, 184
Bismarck, 133, 139, 163
Blanc, Louis, 113, 159, 185, 218
Blanqui, L. A., 241
Blennerhassett, Lady, 2, 99 n. 5
Blondel, 49
Bluntschli, 241
Böck, 154
Bodin, 22, 241
Bohemian Brethren, 121
Bolingbroke, Henry St. John, 1st Viscount, 61 n. 1, 160, 172

Bologna, jurists of, 84
Bonar, Dr., 142 n. 2
Bopp, 150
Borghesi, Bartolommeo, Count, Italian archaeologist, 50, 188
Bosanquet, Bernard, 21 n. 1
Bossuet, 49, 106, 203 n. 1
Bourdillon, A. F. C., 81 n. 5
Boyle, Hon. Robert, 66, 67, 231
Brandenburg, house of, 225
Brentano, Professor L., 120, 123 n. 2, 125
Brethren, the, *see* Bohemian Brethren
Bright, John, 107
Bright, J. F., Master of University College, 8, 140, 219, 227
Brisson, Henri, 2
British Constitution, 4, 5, 23, 70, 76, 82, 99, 163 and n. 1, 197
British Economy of the Nineteenth Century, Rostow's, 219
British Museum, 159
Brodrick, William St. John Fremantle, 9th Viscount Midleton, 5 n. 4
Broglie, Duc de, 74, 238, 239
Brougham, Henry Peter, Baron, 62, 66, 74, 191, 197, 231, 238, 241
Brown, T., Scottish philosopher, 66 231, 241
Browning, Robert, 73, 238
Brunus, 241
Brussels, 101 n. 2
Bryce, James, Viscount, 27, 101, 102, 222, 227
Buckle, H. T., 141, 150 n. 1, 164, 203 n. 1, 208, 241
Buddensieg, German writer on Wyclif, 226
Buddha, 143
Bull, Stuart, theologian, 49
Buller, Charles, 74, 238
Burckhardt, Jacob, 48 n. 2, 158
Burd, L. A., editor of Machiavelli, 227
Burke, Edmund, 7, 8, 10, 20, 23, 24, 27, 28, 33, 49, 50, 60 and n. 5, 61–63, 68, 73, 74, 89, 90, 98, 127, 132, 135, 145, 150, 151, 155, 157, 173, 179, 186, 190–195, 196, 197, 198, 200, 208, 222, 223, 226 n. 6, 228, 232, 239
Burnet, Gilbert, Bishop of Salisbury, xi, 66, 67, 68, 231, 232, 233
Butler, Bishop, 1, 2, 33, 36, 37, 38, 39, 62, 188, 197, 198
Butler, Sir Harold, First Warden of Nuffield College, vii, viii, xiii
Butterfield, Professor Herbert, 222, 223
Buzot, François, 177

INDEX

Byron, George Gordon Noel, 6th Baron, 73, 238

Cabinet, 172
Cabot, 168
Cadet, 241
Cadiz, 101 n. 2, 112
Calhoun, John Caldwell, 90, 93–95, 103, 114, 190 n. 10
Calixtus, George, 36
Calvin, 144, 169, 242
Calvinism, 108, 170
Cambridge, 9, 58, 103, 114, 125, 134, 189
Cambridge Modern History, 200, 220, 223, 227
Cambridge Platonists, 66, 231
Cambridge University Library, 119
Camden, Sir John Pratt, 1st Marquis of, 73, 75, 192, 238, 240
Camisards, 121
Campbell, Thomas, 73, 238
Camus, Armand Gaston, 176
Canada, 173
Canning, George, 60, 62, 132
Canon law, 121, 207
Cantillon, Richard (d. 1734), 190
Capital, 70, 102, 172, 175, 214, 215, 216, 218
Carey, Henry Charles, American economist, 241
Carlyle, A., 241
Carlyle, The Rev. A. J., 241
Carlyle, R. W., 241
Carlyle, Thomas, 136, 157
Carnot, L. N. M., 181
Carolina, 15
Carr, Professor E. H., 126
Carritt, E. F., xiii, 2, 40, 134
Casaubon, Isaac, 22
Cassiodorus, 222 n. 1
Castellio, Sebastian, 169
Castropalao, 241
Catholicism, 2–4, 133, 145, 153, 202, 242
Catholics, 120, 192
Cauchy, 241
Caucus, 106
Causation, 148, 163, 197
Cavour, Camillo, Count di, 75, 218, 240, 243
Centralization, 99, 162, 180, 197, 202, 205
Certainty, idea of, 65, 67, 145, 158, 183, 195, 201
Chamberlain, Joseph, 18, 118
Channing, William Ellery, 4, 39
Character, 63
Charlemagne, Emperor, 31

Charles II, King of England, 13, 69, 210, 234, 237
Charles V, Emperor, 138
Charles X, King of France, 160
Charron, Pierre, 22, 188 and n. 9
Charter of 1814, French, 44, 122
Chateaubriand, François Auguste, Vicomte de, 73, 74, 238
Chatham, William Pitt, 1st Earl of, 73, 75, 192, 237, 238, 240
Châtillon, Conference at (1814), 225
Chemistry, 145
Cherbuliez, 43 n. 2, 125
Chevalier, Michel, French economist, 74, 113, 117, 239, 241
Chillingworth, William, 66, 231
Christianity, 3–4, 11, 20, 28, 31, 39, 51, 52, 54, 55, 58, 65, 82, 122, 130, 144, 146, 147, 148, 153, 166, 170, 186, 187, 200, 202, 205 and n. 2, 206
Church, the, 3–4, 41, 69, 72, 91, 102, 139, 144, 145, 146, 161, 166, 169, 178, 181, 187, 220
Church and State, relation of, 9–10, 42–46, 64, 81, 86, 108, 141, 144, 145, 170, 178, 196, 197, 198, 205 n. 2
Churches, 67, 81
Cicero, 22, 186, 187
City of God, St. Augustine's, 187
Civil Constitution of the Clergy, 42–43, 178
Civil Service, 184
Civil War, English, 213
Civilization, 157, 158, 168, 172, 205, 243
Clark, Dr. G. N., Provost of Oriel, xiii, 223, 229 n. 1
Classes, 60, 67, 69, 70, 71, 95–96, 110, 112, 113, 120, 121, 124, 125, 130, 132, 140, 148, 159, 164, 166, 167, 168, 171, 172, 174, 182, 183, 184, 186, 200, 211, 213, 214, 215, 216, 217, 218
Classical economists, 123, 209
Clay, Sir Henry, xiii
Clearness, importance of doctrine of, 65–67, 176, 229–231
Clergy, 174, 177, 178
Climate, 148
Cobbett, William, 74, 217, 238
Cobden, Richard, 70, 73, 107, 208, 235, 238
Cole, Professor G. D. H., xiii, 199 n. 2
Coleridge, Samuel Taylor, 15, 68, 233
Collingwood, Professor R. G., 40 n. 4, 203
Columbus, Christopher, 211
Commercial Treaty of 1786, 182

INDEX

Committee of Public Safety, 180
Common law, 56
Commonwealth, 64, 142
Commune, 114, 118, 183
Communism, 117 n. 5, 146–147, 200, 205 n. 2, *see also* Marx, Socialism
Communities, 5, 156, 200, 211
Commynes, Philip de, 57
Compromise, 64 ff., 66 n. 1, 72 and n. 1, 140 n. 1, 170, 192
Comte, Auguste, 74, 113, 117, 146, 153, 158, 163, 183, 238, 239
Concordat, of Leo X, 42
  of Napoleon, 42, 161, 181, 224
Condillac, Étienne de, 41, 68, 233
Condorcet, 145
Confessionalism, 134
Confucius, 143
Congregationalism, 141
Congregationalists, 14, *see also* Independents
Congress, United States, 217
Conring, Hermann, 213, 229
Conscience, 2, 19, 21, 24, 32 n. 4, 33–47, 62, 63, 64 and n. 4, 68, 90, 97, 115, 138, 145, 146, 147, 148, 150, 151, 152, 157, 165, 166, 167, 168, 169, 170, 183, 186, 187, 188, 189, 195, 196, 197, 198, 199 n. 2, 200, 201, 202, 204, and n. 3, 205, 206, 209, 223, 244
Consent, 87, 90, 103, 188, 194
Conservatism, 60, 65, 66 and n. 1, 102, 115, 120, 145, 150, 151, 160, 168, 177, 178, 180, 182, 184, 191, 192, 194, 243
Considérant, Victor, 119, 209
Constancy, 95–96
Constant, Benjamin, 4, 30, 43, 45, 74, 104, 132, 190 n. 10, 197, 238, 239
Constituent assemblies, 101 n. 2
Constitution of Poland, Rousseau's, 196
Constitution of 1812, Spanish, 112, 182
Constitutional monarchy, 73, 93, 142, 170, 172, 177, 178, 184
Constitutionalism, 141, 145, 166, 188, 195, 202, 205 and n. 1, 244
Constitutions, 19, 93–103, 141, 151, 160, 165, 174, 175, 176, 177, 179, 180, 181, 182, 189
Contemporary Review, xiii, 199 n. 2
Contemporary Socialism, Rae's, 123 n. 2
Continuity, 48, 51, 60, 61 and n. 1, 63, 66, 69, 145, 153, 195, 196, 197, 200, 204, 244
Contract theory, 165, 171, 175, 188, 195, 196
Contzen, 241
Convention, the, 146, 161, 179, 180, 181

Conviction, 1, 62, 63, 189, 195, 201, 202, 206
Coornhert, D. V., 169
Copernicus, 144, 158, 229
Cormenin, Viscomte de, 74, 239
Corn Laws, 19, 214
Corporate personality, 5, 83
Corporations, 37 n. 8, 83, 84, 85, 96, 124
Cossa, 241
Cotton, 217
Courmenin, 160
Cournot, 12, 18, 54, 125, 146, 148, 198, 202, 242
Courrier, French politician, 74, 238
Cousin, Victor, 74, 121, 136, 239, 241
Crécy, 57
Credit, 215
Creighton, Mandell, Bishop of London, 28, 134, 147, 227
Creuzer, G. Friedrich, 150, 154
Criminal law, 27, 67, 145, 172, *see also* Beccaria, Bentham
Critias, 26
Critique of Political Economy, Marx's, 117 n. 2, 125
Critique of Practical Reason, Kant's, 145
Critique of Pure Reason, Kant's, 68 n. 2, 203, 233 n. 1
Croce, Benedetto, 112 n. 2, 200
Cromwell, Oliver, 108, 210
Cromwell, Thomas, 169
Crown, the, 102, 169, 170, 172, 178
Crusades, 166, 211
Cumberland, expositor of Grotius, 66, 231
Custom, 23, 25, 56, 89, 102, 148, 162, 167
Cuvier, Georges, 146, 148, 229
Cyprian, 144

Dahlmann, F. C., 51, 74, 152, 155, 239
Dante, 144
Danton, 160, 179, 180
D'Argenson, René Louis, Marquis, 89, 174
Darwin, Charles, 5, 48, 51, 136, 146, 153, 196, 229
Daunou, Pierre, 74, 238
Davenant, Sir William, 70, 235
Deak, 243
Declaration of American Independence, 77, 100
Definition of liberty, 1–2, 47 n. 1, 223 n. 1
Defoe, Daniel, 19, 70, 72, 109, 235, 236
Deism, 145
Delavigne, Jean François Casimir, poet, 73, 238
Delhi, 133

INDEX

De Maistre, Joseph-Marie, Comte, 146
Democracy, 8, 10, 17, 34, 63, 70, 78, 85–89, 98, 99, 103–116, 117, 131, 133, 141, 145, 154, 160, 162, 165, 166, 168, 169, 170, 174, 175, 176, 177, 181, 182, 183, 184, 186, 196 and n. 1, 197, 199, 200, 202, 211, 218, 243
Democracy in America, Tocqueville's, 197 n. 3
Demosthenes, 61, 186
Denmark, 76
Departments, 177
De Revolutionibus (Copernicus), 144
Descartes, René, 64, 65, 144 n. 2, 145, 199, 229, 230, 231
De Serre, Comte Pierre, 74, 97, 238
De Staël, Madame, xii, 43 n. 2, 73, 74, 92, 238
Development, idea of, 48–63, 123 n. 2, 146, 153, 165, 167, 185 n. 2, 195, 196, 197, 200, 202, 204 and n. 3
De Witt, John, 199
Dicey, A. V., 200
Dictatorship, 99, 180, 184, 201
Diderot, Denis, 32, 148, 174
Dilke, Sir Charles, 27
Diplomacy, 27
Directory, 161, 181
Dirichlet, mathematician, 229 n. 1
Discorsi, Machiavelli's, 134
Discussion, 86, 196, 199
Dissenters, 76
Dissolution, right of, 176, 177
Distribution, 17, 122
Divine Comedy, Dante's, 144
Divine right, 28, 70, 76, 109, 141, 144, 166, 170, 182
Division of power, 70, 71, 77, 89, 97, 124, 176, 177, 179, 180, 205
Dlugoss, 222 n. 1
Doctor and Student, 35
Doctrinaires, 43–46, 161, 162, 197, 238
Doctrine, 146, 153, 171, 178, 179, 187, 189, 199, 202
Dogma, 67, 145, 166, 192
Döllinger, Dr., 49, 204 n. 3, 222
Domat, Jean, 23, 174
Dove, 152
Dresden, battle of (1813), 225
Droysen, J. G., 152, 155, 156
Droz, 159
Du Bois Reymond, 158, 229
Duff, Sir Mountstuart Grant, 143 n. 3, 222
Dümmler, 154
Dumont, 43 n. 2, 74, 238
Duncker, M. W., 156
Dunoyer, Barthélemy, 119, 209
Du Pape (De Maistre), 146

Duperron, Cardinal, 50
Dupont de Nemours, Pierre, 176
Duration, test of, 205
Dutch East India Company, 19
Dutch jurists, 61
Dutch Republic, 19
Dutch Revolution, 24, 167, 184
Dutens, 49 n. 2
Duty, 19, 28, 57, 116 n. 1, 124, 144, 145, 164, 166, 167, 175, 188, 189, 198, 200, 202, 209
Duvair, Guillaume, 22, 188
Duvergier de Hauranne, Abbé de St. Cyran, 162

Eastern Asia, 168 n. 2
Ecclesiastical Polity, Hooker's, 22, 145
Eckhart, 35 n. 4
Eclectics, 52
Economics, 12–19, 27, 67, 118, 119, 125, 141, 142, 146, 156, 176, 183, 196, 198, 199, 201, 203 n. 2, 204 n. 2, 207–221, 243, 244
Economist, The, 220
Edinburgh Review, 66, 73, 196, 231, 238
Education, 121, 124, 145, 173, 175, 184, 189, 203, 209
Eisenhart, 241
Elections, 183
Electorates, size of, 105
Eliot, George, 75
Emancipation, 60, 63
Emerson, Ralph Waldo, 100, 157
Emigration, 121
Emigrés, 111
Empiricism, 68, 197, 201, 204 and n. 3
Enchaînement des Idées Fondamentales Cournot's, 148
Encyclopaedists, 141
Encyclopédie, 145
Engels, Friedrich, 17, 119, 203, 209
Enghien, Duc de, 224
England, 56, 57, 63, 67, 108, 121, 133, 134, 136, 142, 146, 168, 169, 170, 171, 172, 173, 174, 175, 176, 179, 180, 182, 183, 184, 193, 194, 195, 197, 204, 205, 217, 224, 225, 227, 231, 241, 243, 244
English Historical Review, 120, 194, 207 n. 1, 222 n. 1, 227
English Revolution, 19, 24, 59 and n. 4, 63, 64, 68, 70, 72, 77, 109, 127, 142, 147, 167, 170, 171, 184, 213, 221, 223, 244
Ensor, R. C. K., xiii
Equality, 89, 111, 120, 121 n. 1, 141, 145, 162, 170, 175, 184, 196, 243
Erasmus, 22, 144, 208
Esprit de Vinet, Astié's, 198, 242
Essays, Hume's, 190

Essenes, 121
Ethical and Political Thinking, Mr. Carritt's, 40 n. 6, 134
Ethics, 9, 19–32, 52, 145, 147, 153, 154, 156, 165, 188, 191, 200, 201, 202, 204, 223, 224–226, 244
Ethik, Rothe's, 198
Ethnology, 66
Euripides, 34, 186
Europe, 109, 121, 127, 128, 131, 138, 139, 146, 150, 164, 167, 168 and n. 2, 171, 172, 173, 178, 179, 181, 194, 206, 211, 212, 213, 224, 227, 244
European war of 1792, 178, 179
Eusebius, 144
Evolution, 50, 53, 146
Ewald, G. H. A., 155, 227
Experience, 1, 195, 198, 200, 201, 202
Experts, 173
Exports, 214

Factory laws, 72, 73, 74, 121, 209
Faguet, Emile, 43 n. 2, 44, 45
Family, the, 184, 190
Faraday, Michael, 7, 229
Farmers, 217
Fatalism, 205
Fathers, the, 34, 120, 121
Feast of the Supreme Being, 181
Federalist, The, 102, 145
Federalists, 75
Federation, 5 and n. 4, 58, 76, 93, 98, 99, 100, 101–103, 105, 165, 177, 183, 184, 195, 197, 202 and n. 2, 243, 244
Fénelon, 145, 146, 174, 189–190 199 n. 2, 242
Ferguson, Adam, philosopher, 66, 231
Ferrara, 212
Ferrari, Giuseppe, 203 n. 1
Feudalism, 56, 108, 174, 214
Feuerbach, Ludwig Andreas, 38
Feuillants, 75
Fichte, Johann, 38, 39, 120, 137, 198
Fiévée, Joseph, 74, 238, 239
Figgis, J. N., 203, 223
Finance, 243
Fischer, Kuno, 137, 158, 242
Fisher, H. A. L., 223
Fleurus, battle of, 181
Flint, Robert, 227
Force, 46, 136, 175, 176, 179
Fortescue, Sir John, 57
Fouché, Joseph, 225
Fourier, François, 117, 121, 145
Fox, Charles James, 47 n. 1, 60, 70, 73, 75, 234, 237, 238, 240
Foy, Maximilien, 74, 238

France, 18, 61, 62, 63, 64, 110, 114, 121, 150, 155, 161, 168, 169, 171, 174 and n. 1, 175–181, 182, 183, 193, 194, 195, 211, 218, 222, 225, 227
Franchise, 160
Francis II, Emperor, 179
Francis, St., 144
Franciscans, 49, 120, 121
Franck, political economist, 241
Frankfort, 101 n. 2, 225
Frankfort Parliament of 1848, 132, 155
Franklin, Benjamin, 4, 75, 88, 240
Frederick the Great, 139, 155, 156, 172, 227
Frederick William I, King of Prussia, 139, 172
Freedom, *see* Liberty
Freedom of trade, 60, 189
Freeholders, 19
Freeman, Edward Augustus, 137, 197, 227
Free will, 51, 55, 106, 163, 186 n. 1
Freiheitsdichter, 73
French Revolution, 16, 19, 24, 30, 64, 68, 86, 92, 110–111, 112, 122, 126, 127, 128, 140, 142, 145, 146, 148, 150, 155, 156, 158, 159–164, 167, 174–181, 184, 189, 190, 192, 193, 196, 211, 214, 215–216, 221
French Revolution, Acton's, 14, 105
Friedländer, Ludwig, 158
Frisingensis, *see* Otto of Freising
Fröbel, 74, 239
Frost, John, Chartist leader, 74, 238
Froude, James Anthony, 227
Fugger of Augsburg, 213

Gabourd, Amédée, 161
Galileo, 145, 229
Gallicanism, 42, 144
Gallicans, 42
Gans, 152
Gardiner, Samuel Rawson, 227
Gardiner, Stephen, Bishop of Winchester, 169
Garrison, William Lloyd, 208
Gasquet, F. A., Cardinal, 142
Gass, 154
Gaul, 87
Gazette de France, 160
General will, 72, 129
Geneva, 101 n. 2
Genoa, 14
Genoude, A. E., 160
Gentili, Alberico, 241
Geographical discovery, 168
Geography, 207
George, Henry, 16, 17, 118
George III, 224

German Empire, 133, 163
Germany, 114, 118, 122, 125, 128, 131, 132, 134, 136, 150, 151, 152, 154, 155, 156, 163, 181, 183, 194, 195, 206, 227
Gerson, 144, 188
Gervinus, G. G., 154, 155
Ghibellinism, 188
Gierke, Otto, 83 n. 2, 154, 241
Giesebrecht, Wilhelm von, 219
Gieseler, J. C. L., 152
Girondins, 111, 159, 177, 180
Gizycki, 39
Gladstone, Mary, 3, 6, 8, 9, 14, 16, 18, 25, 95, 97, 107, 134, 141, 143, 148, 191, 210, 216, 222
Gladstone, W. E., 3, 10, 12, 18, 25, 64, 66, 101 and n. 4, 107, 115, 117, 118, 124, 131, 146, 184, 191, 210, 222, 229, 231
Gneist, H. R. von, 156
God, 65, 84, 145, 157, 167, 175, 189, 194, 198, 200, 203, 204, 233, 244
Godwin, Independent, 40
Goethe, 51, 158, 227
Goldsmith, Oliver, 8, 191
Gooch, Dr. G. P., xiii, 14 n. 3, 223
Göttingen, 155
Government, 89–103, 146, 147, 173, 189, 194, 198
Grant, Ulysses, 102
Gratian, 144, 187, 241
Grattan, Henry, 73, 238
Greece, 55, 143, 150, 152, 186, 222, 227
Greeks, 58
Green, T. H., 21 n. 1, 199 and n. 2, 3
Gregorovius, Ferdinand, 48 n. 2
Grenville, George, 60
Grey, Charles, 2nd Earl, 73, 135, 237
Grimm, Jacob, 146, 150
Grote, George, 72, 73, 152, 227, 237, 238
Grotius, Hugo, 22, 23, 33, 36, 64, 68, 85, 97, 145, 188, 195, 229, 233, 241
Groups, 2, 45, 46, 202, see also Associations, Churches, Classes, Communities, Corporations, Religion, Society, Trade Unions
Grove, English physicist, 229 n. 1
Grün, 73, 238
Guicciardini, 138
Guild Socialists, 124
Guilds, 124
Guizot, François, 43, 45–6, 74, 84, 87, 102, 161, 162, 183, 197, 218, 238, 239
Gurth, 87
Guyau, Madame, French moralist, 39

Habit, 177
Hahn, 116 n. 1
Haldane, 241
Hales, John, Canon of Windsor, 66, 231
Halifax, George Savile, 1st Marquis of, 68, 232
Hallam, Henry, 74, 241
Haller, Karl Ludwig, Swiss writer, 48, 51
Hamburg, 212
Hamilton, Alexander, 13, 24, 85, 93, 102, 145, 186, 190 n. 10, 197, 243
Hampden, John, 138
Hanover, 208
Hare, Thomas, advocate of proportional representation, 74, 105 n. 4, 190 n. 10, 238
Harrington, James, 12–15, 47 n. 1, 64, 66, 70, 85, 88, 107, 115, 170, 188, 196 n. 1, 210, 211, 213, 231, 234, 235
Harrison, William, 60
Harrod, R. F., 220
Hartmann, Edward von, 39
Harvey, William, 66, 145, 229, 231
Health, 209
Hébert, 180
Hegel, G. W. F., xi, 5, 24, 48 and n. 2, 51–52, 61 and n. 3, 66, 74, 88, 112, 136, 146, 152, 153, 163, 185, 196, 197 and b. 2, 200, 203 n. 1, 204, 205, 230, 239
Heidelberg, 14 n. 3, 155
Heine, Heinrich, 73, 74, 238, 239
Held, German economist, 125, 241
Helmholtz, Hermann von, German physicist, 229 n. 1
Helvetius, 106, 135, 141, 145
Henry VIII, King of England, 169
Henschen, ecclesiastical historian, 67, 231
Heraclitus, 89, 185 and n. 2, 195
Herbert of Cherbury, Lord, 68, 232
Herder, Johann Gottfried, 48, 51, 61, 66, 145, 197, 230
Heredity, 205
Herford, Professor C. H., 48 and n. 2
Herodotus, 143 and n. 3
Hibbert Journal, xiii
Higher law, see Law of Nature
Hildebrand, Bruno, German economist, 123 n. 2, 241
Himmelfarb, Miss Gertrude, 223–224
Hinrichs, 241
Hippocrates, 143, 229
Historical jurisprudence, 11, 60, 151, 153, 201, 207
History, 2, 52–53, 55, 60 n. 5, 61, 63, 67, 69, 107, 133, 134, 136, 138, 140 and n. 1, 141, 143 and n. 3,

256 INDEX

History—*continued*
146, 148, 150–164, 169, 187, 188, 190, 191 and n. 3, 194, 195, 196, 197 n. 2, 198, 199, 200, 201, 203 and n. 1, 2, 204 n. 2, 205, 206, 207–221, 222 n. 1, 223, 225, 226–228
History of the Girondins, Lamartine's, 159
History of the Norman Conquest, Freeman's, 226
History of Prussian Policy, Droysen's, 156
History of the World, Raleigh's, 18
Hitler, Adolf, 131, 201
Hoadly, Benjamin, Bishop of Bangor, 67, 232
Hobbes, Thomas, 14, 77, 137, 188, 199 n. 2, 200, 206 n. 1, 241
Hobhouse, L. T., 199
Holbach, 141
Holland, 14, 76, 121, 213, 225
Holmbury, 121 n. 1
Holst, German historian of American federalism, 102
Holstenius, ecclesiastical historian, 67, 231
Holt, Lord Chief Justice, xi, 68, 233
Holtzmann, 242
Home and Foreign Review, 58
Home Rule, 27, 131 n. 3
Hooker, Richard, 22, 106, 145, 188
Hort, theological scholar, 227
Hossbach Memorandum, 131
House of Commons, 5, 194, 221
House of Lords, 95–97
Hudson Bay, 214
Hugo, Victor, 73, 238
Humanists, 120, 168
Humanitarianism, 141, 145, 173
Humanity, 200, 243
Humboldt, Baron Alexander von, 51, 66, 74, 154, 229 n. 1, 230, 239
Hume, David, 15, 27, 68, 70, 143, 145, 148–149, 190, 196, 197, 199 n. 2, 233, 234
Hunger, 243
Hunning, 241
Hunter, John, 7
Hus, John, 226
Huskisson, William, 60, 74, 238
Hutcheson, Francis, 66, 136, 231
Huxley, T. H., 153

Ideas, 64, 140–149, 153, 156, 163, 165, 167, 170, 182, 183, 196 n. 4, 197, 200, 201, 202, 204 n. 1, 2, 205, 207, 211, 219, 223 and n. 1, 243, 244
Ignorance, 182, 244
Ihering, Rudolf von, 24, 52, 74, 82, 116, 151, 200, 203, 239

Imitatio Christi, 144
Impartiality, 226
Imperialism, 144, 145, 155
Imports, 214
Inaugural, Acton's, 7, 19, 29, 53, 76, 79, 101 n. 2, 115, 125, 134, 140, 148, 189, 190, 203, 219, 224, 225
Incas, 122
Independents, 23, 40, 71, 89, 91, 169, 170, 196 n. 1
India, 27, 133, 150
Individualism, 37 n. 8, 199 n. 2
Induction, 27
Industry, 172, 176, 211, 212, 213, 214, 215, 216
Ingram, J. K., 17, 118, 210, 241
Inquisition, 212
Institutions, 100, 146
Insurrection, right of, 167
Interests, 182, 184, 244, *see also* Classes
International law, 67, 145, 166, 168, 195
International relations, 138, 146
Ireland, 28, 76, 131 n. 3, 192, 218, 240 n. 2.
Isocrates, 186
Israel, 21
Israelites, 165
Italian Revolution, 136
Italy, 76, 128, 131, 136, 137, 168, 181, 211

Jacobins, 62, 111–112, 161, 177, 178, 180
James I, King of England, 170
James II, King of England, 69, 221, 234
Janet, Paul, 241
Jansen, 145
Jansenism, 141
Jefferson, Thomas, 4, 13, 15, 27, 75, 85, 102, 103, 197, 240
Jeffrey, Francis, Lord, 4, 66, 231
Jena, 225
Jerome, St., 196 n. 1
Jesuits, 85, 135
Jesus Christ, 3, 4, 65, 82, 116, 194, 205, 220
Jews, 133, 144, 152, 187, 212
John of Salisbury, 35 n. 2, 187
Jones, Sir William, 192
Joseph, H. W. B., 59 and n. 3
Jouffroy, T. S., 241
Joule, James Prescott, 229 n. 1
Journal of Modern History, 79 n. 1, 223 n. 2
Jovellanos, Spanish dramatist, 73, 238
Judges, 44, 45, 71, 88, 96, 98, 174, 177
July Monarchy, 117, 217, 218
Jurieu, Pierre, 174
Jurisprudence, 51, 53

Jurists, 176, 182, 200
Juste milieu, 45, 115
Justice, 30 n. 1, 135, 136, 152, 182, 194, 216
Justin, 123
Justinian, 166

Kaltenborn, 241
Kampschulte, F. W., 154
Kant, Immanuel, 1, 2, 33, 36-39, 74, 145, 190 n. 10, 197, 198, 203, 233, 239
Kapital, Das, Marx's, 117, 124, 205 n. 2
Karczynski, J., 241
Kautz, German economist, 241
Keble, John, 27
Kepler, 145, 229
Kettner, 241
Keynes, John Maynard, Baron, 201, 219
Kierkegaard, 11 n. 5, 39
King's Friends, 172
Kingsley, Charles, 142
Knies, Karl, German economist, 123 n. 2
Knowledge, 1, 125, 134, 150 n. 1, 155, 156, 164, 195, 198, 201, 202, 203 and n. 2, 206 and n. 1, 207, 211
Kopp, 229
Koran, the, 144
Kurtz, 157

La Boétie, 22
Laboulaye, Édouard de, 74, 103, 114, 162, 239
Labour, 16, 70, 113, 121, 122, 123, 183, 213, 214, 215, 216, 217, 218, 221
Labour theory of value, 18, 209
La Bourdonnaie, Comte François de, 113
Lactantius, 196 n. 1
Lafayette, Marquis de, 27, 74, 113, 179, 239
Lally, F. E., 223
Lamartine, Alphonse de, 113, 159, 160, 200, 218
Lambert, *see* Saint-Lambert
Lamennais, 54, 74
Land, 19, 70, 71, 96, 102, 113, 122, 165, 168, 182, 183, 213, 214, 217, 218, 221
Landlords, 19, 138, 213
Landor, W. S., 7, 73, 204, 238
Landowners, 212
Lanfrey, Pierre, 154
Langer, Professor W. L., 126
Languet, 241
Laplace, Pierre-Simon, Marquis de, 140 n. 1, 145, 229

Lasker, 154
Laski, Professor H. J., 43 n. 2
Laspeyres, E., 18
Lassalle, Ferdinand, 120, 201
Laurence, R. V., 203, 223
Laurent, 137
Laveleye, 17, 118
Lavoisier, 145, 229
Law, 55, 58, 61-62, 97, 100, 115, 125, 139, 151, 152, 157, 163, 165, 166, 172, 174, 176, 180, 181, 185, 186, 189, 194, 197 n. 2, 200, 205, 209, 244, *see also* Canon law, Common law, Criminal law, Grotius, Historical jurisprudence, International law, Laws of Manu, Law of Nature, Legislation, Municipal law, Roman law, Statute law
Law of Nature, 22, 23, 52, 76, 90, 105, 141, 152, 165, 166, 167, 173, 187, 188 and n. 9, 192, 194, 195, 241
Laws of Manu, 34
Laws, Plato's, 21, 85, 166, 185, 195 n. 2
Learning, xii n. 1, 150-164
Lechler, G. V., authority on Wyclif, 226
Lecky, W. E. H., 15, 164
Ledru-Rollin, Alexandre, 113, 218
Legislation, 56, 151, 175, 194
Legitimism, 74, 160
Lehrs, Greek scholar, 227
Leibniz, Gottfried Wilhelm von, xi, 2, 5, 20, 48-51, 61, 65, 68, 132, 134, 145, 153, 188, 196, 222, 230, 233, 242
Leighton, Robert, Archbishop, 66, 231
Leo I (the Great), Pope (A.D. 440-461), 222 n. 1
Leo X, Pope (1513-1521), 213
Le Play, Pierre, 74, 119 and n. 2, 125, 239
Leslie, Cliffe, 17, 118, 210, 241
Lessing, Gotthold Ephraim, 61, 66, 68, 154, 230, 233
Lessius, Leonard, S. J., 108, 168
Letters Concerning Toleration, Locke's, 41
Letters to Mary Gladstone, Acton's, 26, 120
Lettres sur les Anglais, Voltaire's (1733) 41
Leviathan, Hobbes's, 199 n. 2
Leys, The Rev. K. K. M., v, xiii
L'Hospital, 22
Liberal Catholics, 42
Liberalism, 3, 4, 25, 28, 39, 47 n. 1, 55, 60, 63, 68 n. 1, 69, 73, 74, 75, 111, 120, 127, 132, 133, 140 n. 1, 145, 148, 150, 160, 161, 167, 176, 177, 179, 181, 182, 184, 190, 197, 200, 201, 208, 218, 238-239

INDEX

Liberty, 1–2, 3, 5, 6, 11, 19, 20, 24, 29–32, 38, 40, 55, 59, 60, 64–80, 84, 88, 89, 92, 97, 104, 106, 111, 114, 116 and n. 1, 120, 122, 123, 124, 125, 128, 130, 131, 138, 139, 146, 148, 150 n. 1, 151–2, 153, 155, 156, 162, 165–184, 186 and n. 1, 189, 192, 193, 194, 196 and n. 1, 197 and n. 2, 199, 201, 202, 204, 205, 218, 222, 223 and n. 1, 229–240, 243, 244
Library of Congress, 15
Liebig, Justus, Baron von, 229
Lieven, Princess, 135
Life, mean duration of, 18
Lightfoot, Joseph Barber, Bishop of Durham, 227
Lilburne, John, 13, 66, 107, 108, 122, 170, 188, 231
Liljegren, G. B., 14 n. 3
Lincoln, Abraham, 220
Lindsay of Birker, Lord, xiii, 37 n. 8, 81 n. 5, 188, 196 n. 1, 199 and n. 2, 3
Liser, 241
List, Friedrich, 241
Literature, 158, 162, 164, 209
Littré, M. P. E., 74 n. 1
Liverpool, 2nd Earl of, Prime Minister, 182
Lives of the Engineers, Smiles's, 217
Livorno, 212
Local government, 5 n. 4, 170, 196 n. 1, 202 n. 2
Locke, John, xi, 4, 10, 13, 18, 38, 40, 41–42, 47 n. 1, 65, 67, 68, 69, 70, 85, 121, 135, 145, 148, 168, 169, 188, 190, 196, 230, 232, 233, 234, 235, 240
Logic, 136, 176
Lollards, 121
London, city of, 171, 215
Löning, 154
Lord Acton on Nationality and Socialism, xiii
Loserth, authority on Wyclif, 226
Louis XIV, King of France, 141, 190
Louis XV, King of France, 190
Louis XVI, King of France, 111, 174, 178, 179, 180, 215, 221
Louis Philippe, King of the French, 113, 182, 217
Lowe, Robert, 17
Loyola, Ignatius, 144
Lucretius, 50
Lully, Raymond, 144
Luther, 144, 168, 170, 208, 213, 227, 242
Lutheranism, 141
Lysias, 186

Mabillon, Jean, 48, 50, 67, 188, 231
Mably, Abbé Gabriel de, 117, 141
Macartney, C. A., 126
Macaulay, Thomas Babington, Lord, 4, 10, 62, 66, 191, 231
Macculoch, *see* McCulloch, J. R.
Machiavelli, 22, 123 n. 2, 134–139, 144, 149, 168, 169, 170, 188, 190
Mackintosh, Sir James, 62, 66, 191 n. 3, 197, 231, 241
Macmurray, Professor John, 59 and n. 3
Madison, James, 102
Maimonides, 144 and n. 2, 187
Maine, Sir Henry, 17, 27, 241
Mainz, Archbishop of, 213
Maitland, F. W., 37 n. 8, 83 n. 2, 222
Major, John, of St. Andrews, 85
Malebranche, Nicolas de, 65, 230
Mallet, 17
Malmesbury, William of, 222 n. 1
Malouet, Pierre Victor, Baron, 176
Malthus, Thomas, 121, 123, 199
Management, 176
Manchester, 184
Mandragola, 136
Manifestation des Convictions Religieuses, Vinet's, 38 n. 2, 197–198, 242
Manlius, 152
Manufacture, 80, 173, 183, 216, 217, 221
Manzoni, Alessandro, 73, 238
Marat, Jean Paul, 110, 141, 160, 179
Marche des Idées, Cournot's, 148
Mariana, Juan, Jesuit writer, 108, 169
Marie Antoinette, 62, 178, 179
Marlborough, Duke of, 171
Marlo, pseudonym for Winkelblech, German economist, 124, 125
Marmont, A. F. L. V. de, 113, 217
Marshall, Alfred, 12, 18, 198
Marshall, John, American jurist, 102, 125, 173
Marsilius, 85, 91, 166, 187 n. 8, 188
Martignac, Jean, Vicomte de, 112
Martineau, James, 4, 136
Marvell, Andrew, 66, 231
Marx, Karl, 11 n. 5, 12, 17, 18, 117 and n. 2, 120, 125, 146, 201, 203 n. 1, 205 and n. 2, 207
Materialism, 141, 145
Mathematics, 66, 229 and n. 1
Mathew, Archbishop David, 223
Matthews, F. D., historian of Wyclif, 226
Maultrot, 174
Maurice, F. D., 142
May, T. Erskine, 55, 227
Mazarin, Cardinal, 227
Mazzini, Giuseppe, 129 and n. 4
McCosh, 241

INDEX

McCulloch, J. R., 241
Mechanics, 66, 144
Mediaeval Political Theory in the West, by A. J. and R. W. Carlyle, 241
Medicine, 145
Mediterranean, the, 172
Melbourne, William Lamb, 2nd Viscount, 73, 238
Mendicant orders, 121
Menzel, 152
Mercier de la Rivière, F. F. J. H., 190
Merv, 147
Merz, 242
Metaphysical Theory of the State, Hobhouse's, 200
Metaphysics, 147, *see also* Philosophy
Meyer, Dr., German jurist, 61
Meyer, German physicist, 229 n. 1
Meyer, Dr., theologian, 187, 222 n. 1
Michelet, Jules, 160, 162
Mickiewicz, Adam, Polish poet, 73, 238
Middle Ages, 72 n. 1, 85, 91, 103, 108, 124, 139, 166–167, 212, 222 and n. 1, 226–227
Middle class, 110, 166, 213, 215, 217, 218
Military science, 156
Mill, James, 38, 74
Mill, John Stuart, 4, 13, 39, 62, 69, 70, 72, 73, 74, 85, 114, 129, 131, 136, 197, 199, 209, 233, 235, 237, 238
Milton, John, 4, 65, 66, 70, 168, 230, 231, 234
Mind, 54–55, 64
Minorities, 62, 165, 167, 197
Mirabeau, Count, 86, 100, 111, 152, 177
Mohl, 241
Molina, Luis, 108, 169, 241
Molinari, Belgian economist, 117
Moltke, Count H. K. von, 156
Mommsen, Theodor, 133, 137, 156, 157
Monadology, 203
Monarchy, 69, 152, 159, 161, 171, 172, 173, 174, 175, 177, 179, 183
Monasticism, 121
Money, 19, 80, 113, 165, 168, 178, 183, 213, 217
Monopolies, 209
Monroe, James, President, 182
Montaigne, 22, 145
Montcalm, 173
Montesquieu, 23, 32, 41, 60 n. 5, 61, 68, 100, 121, 135, 141, 145, 148, 174, 190 n. 10, 196, 232, 233
Monti, Vincenzo, 73, 238
Moore, Thomas, 73, 238
Moralia, Plutarch's, 144

Morality, 1, 69, 202, 211, 225, 243, 244
More, Henry, Cambridge Platonist, 66, 231
More, Sir Thomas, 117 n. 5
Morellet, André, Abbé, 27
Morelly, 117
Morgan, Lewis Henry, American sociologist, 50, 188, 203 and n. 1
Morley, John, Viscount, 4, 19, 20, 27, 28, 135, 192, 201, 222
Mornay, Duplessis, 85
Moscow, 224
Moslems, 144, 187
Mounier, 176
Müller Otfried, 150
Municipal law, 22, 89
Murder, 5, 6, 201
Mystics, 121, 141
Mythology, 150

Nantes, Edict of, 169, 171
Napier, Sir William, 66, 231
Napoleon I, Emperor, 42, 57, 99, 112, 128, 136, 139, 154, 156, 175, 176, 177, 180, 181, 224–225
Napoleon III, Emperor, 8, 99, 107, 118, 119, 183, 201
Narbonne, Comte Louis de, 225
National Assembly of 1789, 50, 87, 175, 177, 178
National character, 159, 244
National Debt, 19, 213, 214
National income, 215, 221
Nationality, 50, 52, 126–134, 141, 163, 181, 205, 243
Natural law, *see* Law of Nature
Natural rights, *see* Rights
Navigation laws, 173
Nazis, 220
Neander, J. A. W., 226
Necker, Jacques, 100, 214
Nelson, Robert, 49
Nepotian, 196 n. 1
Netherlands, 64, 169
Neurath, 241
New Jersey, 15
New Testament, 4–5, 17, 22, 28, 34, 54, 195, 205 and n. 2
Newfoundland, 214
Newman, J. H., 27, 38, 106
Newmarch, William, 17
Newton, Isaac, 41, 51, 59, 65, 67, 145, 229, 230, 231
Niebuhr, B. G., 48 n. 2, 49, 51, 146, 152 and n. 1, 208
Niemen, 225
Nippold, 242
Noack, Professor Ulrich, xiii, 223 and n. 1
Nova Scotia, 214

Nuffield College, xiii, 81 n. 5
Numbers, political importance of, 19, 113, 165

Obligation, 21 n. 1, 24, 28, 175, 206, *see also* Duty, Ethics, Liberty, Politics
Oceana, Harrington's, 14 n. 3, 15
O'Connell, Daniel, 70, 235
Oersted, Hans Christian, Danish scientist, 146, 229
Old Testament, 12, 34, 121, 195, 205
Oldenburg, 241
Oliver, F. S., 145
Oncken, 241
Opinion, 63, 98, 116 n. 1, 137, 169, 202, 207, 214
Oporto Company, 209
Opus Majus, Roger Bacon's, 144
Order, 177
Oriel, Provost of, *see* Clark, Dr., G. N.
Origen, 144
Orleanists, 160
Orleans, Duke of, 3
Orleans dynasty, 159
Orosius, Bishop, 222 n. 1
Otis, James, 15, 23, 173
Otto of Freising, 222 n. 1
Owen, Robert, 117
Oxford, 136
Oxford University Press, xiii

Paine, Tom, 104, 145
Palmerston, Henry John Temple, 3rd Viscount, 73, 238
Pantheism, 51, 141, 205
Papacy, 168
Paraguay, 123
Paris, 101 n. 2, 110, 111, 159, 175, 176, 177, 181, 182, 211
Paris, Matthew, 222 n. 1
Parliament, 85, 138, 141, 194
Parliament Act (1911), 97
Parliamentary, debates, publication of, 98, 172
Parliamentary Reform, 60
Party, 69, 71 n. 1, 148, 157, 164, 171, 172, 183, 191, 192, 195, 204 n. 1
Pascal, 50, 65, 135, 198, 230
Paschalis II, Pope (1099-1118), 121
Pasquier, Estienne, 22
Passavant, 39
Paul, Herbert, 199 n. 2, 222
Pauli, German historian, 226
Paulinus of Nola, 196 n. 1
Pauperism, 79, 182
Pavo, 222 n. 1
Peace, 124, 184, 244
Peasants, 175, 213, 214, 215
Peasants' Revolt in Germany, 213

Peel, Sir Robert, 60
Pelagius, 144, 187
Penn, William, 4, 36, 37, 47, 55 and n. 2, 66, 68, 109, 169, 188, 189, 196, 231, 233
Pennsylvania, 15, 31, 37, 109
Perfectibility, 141, 145
Periander, 34
Pericles, 19, 106, 165
Persecution, 28, 41, 178, 189, 202
Pessimism, 141
Petavius, 48-50
Peter the Great, 138-139, 172
Peter Lombard, 144, 187
Philadelphia, 101 n. 2
Philip II, King of Spain, 169
Philo of Alexandria, 22, 187
Philology, 53, 66, 146, 150, 151, 153, 207
Philosophical Theory of the State, Bosanquet's, 21 n. 1.
Philosophy, 11, 28, 51, 54-55, 65-68, 73, 125, 137, 142, 143, 145, 148, 157, 158, 159, 183, 185 n. 2, 187, 190, 192, 195, 196, 199 and n. 2, 200, 201, 203 and n. 1, 2, 204 and n. 2, 205, 206, 207, 222 and n. 1, 229, 244
Physiocrats, 15, 214, 221 n. 6
Physiology, 66, 146
Pibrac, Guy du Faur de, 22, 188
Pilgrim Fathers, 145
Pitt, William, 172, 180
Plain, the, 181
Plato, 21, 85, 106, 115, 131, 144, 154, 166, 185, 186 and n. 1, 195, 199, 201, 205 and n. 1, 206
Playfair, William, 66, 231
Plebiscite, 106, 175
Pliny, 144, 229
Plotinus, 154
Plunket, William Conyngham, 1st Baron, 73, 238
Plutarch, 144
Poland, 76, 126, 127, 128, 133, 182, 224
Polignac, Auguste, Prince de, 112
Politica, 207 n. 1
Political economy, *see* Economics
Political Register, Cobbett's, 217
Political Science, xi, 5, 84, 85, 156, 171, 185, 188, 211, 214, 221 and n. 6, 241, 244, *see also* Constitutions, Economics, Ethics, Politics
Political Science Quarterly, 219 n. 7
Politics, 8, 9, 26, 66, 67, 69, 89 n. 5, 125, 137, 138, 139, 140, 145, 149, 153, 155, 157, 163, 166, 167, 168, 170, 173, 177, 183, 188, 191, 192, 195, 196, 201, 202, 204, 223

INDEX

Politics, Aristotle's, 21, 85, 166, 186, 199 n. 2
Polybius, 186
Poole, R. L., 222
Poor, the, 121, 122, 123, 125, 166, 182, 184, 189, 218, 243
Poor Law Amendment Act (1834), 74, 118
Pope, Alexander, 61 n. 1
Pope, the, 133
Population, theory of, 209
Port Royal, 44
Portugal, 76, 121, 168, 212
Posen, 133
Positivism, 141, 153, 183
Potomac, 102
Pouthas, 45 n. 1
Poverty, 13, 17, 122, 173, 174, 175, 186, 209, 210, 218
Power, 12, 19, 91, 121 n. 1, 130, 134–139, 144, 145, 155, 156, 158, 160, 162, 165, 167, 168 and n. 2, 169, 170, 171, 173, 174, 175, 176, 177, 178, 180, 184, 188, 189, 200, 202, 205, 207, 211, 215, 216, 220
Prague, 225
Prairial, law of, 181
Precedent, 170
Predestination, 141, 219
Premier, 172
Presbyterians, 14
Press, the, 45, 172, 175, 176
Price, 217
Price revolution, 220
Priestley, Joseph, 136, 229
Primogeniture, 96
Prince, The, Machiavelli's, 134, 149
Principia, Newton's, 145
Principles, 63, 97, 170, 171, 173, 174, 175, 178, 186, 191, 192, 193, 194, 195, 201, 202, 209, 211
Printing, invention of, 168
Privilege, 174, 194, 218
Probability, 158
Production, 19, 211
Progress, 2, 6, 18, 24, 48 n. 1, 50, 51, 54, 56, 59, 60 and n. 1, 61, 65 and n. 1, 69, 83, 116 n. 1, 121, 125, 137, 140 and n. 1, 145, 153, 165, 167, 195, 203 n. 2, 204, 205, 206, 219
Proletariat, 122, 133
Property, 16, 19, 47, 69, 75, 97 n. 1, 117, 121 and n. 1, 123, 168, 170, 174, 175, 178, 180, 200, 207, 211, 214, 215, 216, 218
Proportional representation, 105, 183
Protagoras, 26, 185
Protestants, 120, 141, 202
Proudhon, Pierre Joseph, 120
Providentialism, 135, 157, 206
Prussia, 76, 128, 132, 133, 134, 154, 155, 156, 162, 163, 172, 179
Prynne, William, 70, 234
Pseudo-Dionysius, 144
Psychology, 35, 201
Ptolemy, 144, 229
Public works, 119, 173
Puchta, authority on Roman law, 197
Puritan Revolution, 57, 196, 199, 213
Puritanism and Liberty, Professor Woodhouse's, 199 n. 3
Puritans, 36, 141, 243
Pushkin, Alexander, 73, 238
Puynode, 241
Pym, John, 66, 231
Pythagoreans, 185

Quakers, 36–37, 109, 169, 196 n. 1
Quarterly Review, 227
Queen's College, Oxford, 136
Quesnay, François, 27, 69, 234
Qu'est-ce que le tiers état (Sieyès), 145
Quetelet, 146, 229
Quintana, Manuel José, Spanish poet, 73, 238

Rabelais, 22
Race, 67, 131, 138, 205
Radicalism, 60, 66, 73, 154, 184
Radowitz, Joseph von, 74, 239
Rae, 123 n. 2
Ragewin, continuator of Otto of Freising, 222 n. 1
Railways, 182, 218, 221 n. 7
Raleigh, Sir Walter, 12, 18
Rambler, 216
Ramsay, William Mitchell, 39
Ranke, Leopold von, 132, 136, 137, 152, 153, 154, 208, 219, 242
Rationalism, 39, 68, 141, 145, 173, 197, 204 and n. 3
Realism and Nationalism, Professor Binkley's, 126
Reason, 25, 39, 45, 89, 144, 145, 161, 162, 165, 166, 167, 182, 185, 195, 205, 244
Referendum, 106
Reform Bill, 182
Reformation, 34, 152, 168, 169
Réforme Sociale, Le Play's, 119
Reid, Thomas, 44, 66, 231
Reign of Terror, 179, 180, 181
Religion, 9, 10, 11, 22, 51, 67, 69, 86, 120, 125, 128, 137, 138, 140, 145, 146, 147, 153, 156, 169, 170, 178, 187, 188, 197, 202, 203 n. 2, 205 n. 2, 211, 243, 244

262   INDEX

Rémusat, Comte Charles de, 74, 131, 238, 239
Renaissance, 2, 35, 53, 151, 168
Renan, Ernest, 79, 136
Renouvier, Charles-Bernard, 39
Rent, theory of, 209
Rents, 215
Representative government, 167, 175, 176, 180, 202
Responsibility, 125, 202
Restoration, the, 122, 129, 162, 182, 227
Resurrection, the, 53, 153
Retribution, 205
Retz, Cardinal de, 135
Revenue, 215, 216, 221
Revolution, 61, 64, 78, 85, 109, 130, 146, 169, 182, 184, 189, 201
Revolution of July, 1830, 182
Revolution of 1848, 118, 155, 159, 161
Revue Scientifique, 221 n. 7
Ricardo, David, 73, 74, 238
Richelieu, 136, 139, 227
Richet, 221 n. 7
Riehl, W. H. von, 158
Rights, 19, 47 n. 1, 77, 100, 116 n. 1, 145, 166, 170, 171, 175, 194, 198, 202, 214, 244, *see also* Duty, Rights of Man
Rights of Man, 23, 27, 28, 31, 62, 78, 138, 141, 145, 175, 177, 189, 197, 243
Rights of Man, Tom Paine's, 104
Ritchie, A. D., 199 n. 2
Robespierre, 160, 176, 177, 179, 180, 181, 190
Robinson, John, 37 n. 8, 48, 50, 145
Rodbertus, Johann Karl, 120, 123 n. 2, 190 n. 10
Rödet, 116 n. 1
Roederer, Comte Pierre Louis, 224
Rogers, J. E. Thorold, 241
Rogers, Samuel, 73, 238
Rolls Series, 226
Roman History, Niebuhr's, 152
Roman jurists, 22, 166, 187
Roman law, 83, 84, 153, 166, 197
Romans, 58
Rome, 133, 150, 157, 166, 215
Romilly, Sir Samuel, 4, 74, 238
Roosevelt, F. D., 220
Ropes, John Codman, biographer of Napoleon, 225
Roscher, Wilhelm, 12, 17, 18, 24, 63, 118, 119, 123 n. 2, 146, 154, 186, 198, 199, 201, 202, 207–210, 213, 241, 242
Rösler, Austrian economist, 241
Rosmini, Antonio, 39

Rossi, Count Pellegrino, 43 n. 2, 74, 238, 239
Rostow, W. W., 219, 220
Roth, Dr. Leon, 144 n. 2
Rothe, 24, 38, 154, 198, 242
Rotteck, Karl von, 132
Rousseau, 12, 13, 32, 37, 38, 39, 41, 55 and n. 2, 68, 85, 86, 100, 103, 105, 106, 118, 121, 141, 145, 148, 168, 174, 188, 190 n. 10, 191, 196 and n. 4, 197, 198, 222, 233
Royal Institute of International Affairs, 126
Royal Society, 67, 231
Royer-Collard, Pierre-Paul, 43–45, 74, 197, 238, 239
Rush, Richard, American Minister to Great Britain, 102
Ruskin, John, 196
Russell, Lord John, 73, 237
Russia, 121, 128, 146, 172, 181, 206

St. Bartholomew, massacre of, 160
St. Just, 105 n. 4
Saint-Lambert, Jean François, Marquis de, 68 and n. 1, 233 and n. 1
Saint-Simon, Comte de, 74, 121
Saint Simonians, 74
Salem, 216
Salic Law, 144
Salvianus of Marseilles, 222 n. 1
San Domingo, 225
Sand, Georges, 113, 117
Sanuto, 222 n. 1
Sarasa, Alphonso Antonio de S. J. (1618–67), 1, 33, 36, 168, 198
Saskatchewan, 133
Savigny, F. K. von, 48 n. 2, 51, 52, 53 n. 4, 61, 66, 74, 146, 151, 155, 190 n. 10, 200, 207, 230, 239
Say, J. B., 65, 74, 230, 239
Scepticism, 68, 202
Schaarschmidt, 158
Schäffle, Albert, 125
Schelling, Friedrich Wilhelm von, 51, 151
Scherer, Edmond Henri, Adolphe, 135
Schiller, J. C. F. von, 73, 238
Schleiermacher, F. E. D., 48 n. 2
Schmidt, Michael Ignaz, German historian, 116 n. 1
Schmoller, Gustav, 74, 123 n. 2, 125, 239
Schönberg, 241
Schopenhauer, 51, 154
Schumpeter, 123 n. 2
Science, 51, 54, 65–67, 118, 137, 140, 143, 144, 145, 148, 153, 154, 157, 158, 183, 190, 199 n. 2, 201, 202, 203 n. 1, 206, 210, 219, 225, 228–229 and n. 1, 243, 244

INDEX

Science and Social Welfare in the Age of Newton, Dr. G. N. Clark's, 229 n. 1
Scotland, 66, 170, 204
Second Chamber, 95–97, 101–2, 176, 177
Sects, 121, 169, 196, 213
Secularism, 141
Securities for freedom, 92, 136, 173, 175, 177, 201, 223 and n. 1, 244, *see also* Constitutions
Security, 94, 123, 175, 202
Seeley, Sir John Robert, 225, 227
Selden, John, 66, 227, 231
Self-defence, 175
Self-government, 24, 46, 56, 59, 64, 90, 124, 130, 165, 166, 169, 170, 196 and n. 1, 197, 211
Seneca, 22, 35, 50, 187
Senior, William Nassau, 74, 238
Serfdom, 121
Sermon on the Mount, 5, 22
Services, the, 27, 102
Seven Years War, 173
Seward, William Henry, 77, 100
Shaftesbury, Anthony Ashley Cooper, 1st Earl of, 68, 69, 232, 234
Shaftesbury, Anthony Ashley Cooper, 7th Earl of, 152
Shaftesbury, English moral philosopher, 39
Shakespeare, 186
Shelley, Percy Bysshe, 73, 238
Sherman, William, 102
Shipowners, 138, 212
Shirley, J., writer on Wyclif, 226
Sidgwick, Henry, 241
Sidney, Algernon, 67, 68, 232
Sieyès, Abbé, 13, 18, 23, 27, 30, 32, 85–89, 103, 145, 176, 177, 190 n. 10, 196, 199, 225
Sigonius, Italian historian, 49, 50, 188
Simeon of Durham, 222 n. 1
Simon, Richard, 145
Simpson, Richard, 4, 37 n. 8, 141
Sincerity, 7, 164, 206, 225
Sismondi, Jean, 43 n. 2, 74, 239
Slavery, 22, 28, 63, 72, 121, 139, 166, 167, 168, 171, 172, 173, 194, 202
Smiles, Samuel, 217
Smith, Adam, 4, 5, 10, 12, 15, 16, 18, 27, 37 and n. 7, 38, 41, 62, 68, 70, 73, 86, 99, 121, 123, 145, 148, 173, 182, 188, 190 and n. 10, 196, 199, 208, 214, 216, 233, 235, 238, 241
Smith, A. L., 14
Smith, Bosworth, 27
Smith, Goldwin, 136, 225, 227
Smith, H. F. Russell, 14 n. 3
Smolensk, 225
Social Contract, The (Rousseau), 105 n. 7
Social revolution, 215
Social sciences, the, 158, 201, 203 and n. 2
Socialism, 16, 17, 113, 114, 117–125, 133, 141, 146, 148, 159, 183, 184, 190, 196, 201, 202, 205, 207, 209, 210, 217, 218, 243
Societies, 41, 182
Society, 67, 81–82, 114, 116 n. 1, 120, 122, 125, 156, 167, 169, 174, 180, 190, 194, 200, 204, 205, 208, 209, 210, 219
Society of Friends, *see* Quakers
Socinianism, 49, 65, 141, 169, 196 n. 1
Socinus, 23, 32, 40, 144, 169
Sociology, 150, 198, 200, 201, 202–203
Socrates, 33, 34, 89, 90–91, 166, 186 and n. 1
Solon, 61, 165
Somers, John, Lord, xi, 10, 68, 70, 232, 233, 235
Sophocles, 34, 186
Sorel, Albert, 162, 163, 164
Soto, 241
South Africa, 244
South Sea Bubble, 172
Sovereignty, 45, 46 n. 1, 101, 160, 166, 169, 173, 175, 176, 183, 185, 195, 196, 199 n. 2, 200, 201, 202, 204, and n. 3, 205 and n. 1, 214, 244
Spain, 76, 91, 112, 121, 122, 128, 168, 181, 182, 208, 212, 217, 222 n. 1, 224
Spanish America, 172, 217
Spanish Succession, war of, 171, 214
Spencer, Herbert, 39, 63, 154 and n. 1
Spinoza, 68, 145, 232
Stahl, F. J., 241
Stanley, A. P., Dean of Westminster, 152
State, 5, 20, 23, 58, 67, 81–89, 96, 119, 120, 124, 125, 128, 130, 138, 139, 146, 147, 151, 156, 160, 166, 167, 168, 169, 170, 171, 172, 178, 183, 186, 187, 190, 199, 200, 201, 205 n. 2, 209, 211, 243
State rights, 58
States-General, 174
Statistics, 146, 201, 208, 213, 229, 244
Statute law, 172
Stein, Lorenz von, 13, 156, 211, 227
Stephen, Leslie, 4, 27, 38, 39, 241
Stephens, Alexander Hamilton, 103
Stephens, H. Morse, 227
Steuart, Sir James, 190
Stewart, Dugald, 4, 66, 231, 241
Stinzing, 241
Stoics, 21, 34, 35, 85, 116, 166, 186
Stöpel, 241
Strauss, David Friedrich, 38, 146

Stuarts, 170, 182
Stubbs, William, Bishop of Oxford, 154, 197, 227
Study of History, A, Professor A. J. Toynbee's, 40 n. 4
Suarez, Franciscus, 108, 169, 241
Success, test of, 136, 205
Swinburne, Algernon Charles, 73, 238
Swiss school, the, xii n. 1
Switzerland, 101 n. 2, 105, 182, 206, 211, 218
Sybel, Heinrich von, 132, 136, 155, 161, 162–163, 164
Sydenham, Doctor Thomas (d. 1689), 66, 67, 231
Syriac, 227

Tableau des Progrès (Condorcet), 145
Taborites, 121
Tacitus, 108
Taine, Hippolyte, 160, 162, 163, 164
Talleyrand, 182, 217, 224, 225
Tannenbaum, F., 219 n. 7, 220
Tawney, Professor R. H., 14 n. 3, 123 n. 2
Taxation, 167, 173, 175, 180, 192, 213, 216
Taylor, Professor A. E., 195 n. 2
Taylor, Sir Henry, 135
Télémaque, Fénelon's, 145
Temple, Sir William, 235
Tennyson, Alfred, Lord, 73, 238
Theodosian code, 84
Theology, 11, 169, 187, 207, 219
Théorie des Quatre Mouvements (Fourier), 145–146
Theory of Moral Sentiments, Adam Smith's, 188
Thierry, Amédée, 74, 87, 113, 117
Thiers, Louis Adolphe, 74, 154, 162, 163, 239
Third Estate, 87, 174, 175, 176, 215
Third Republic, 118, 183
Thirlwall, C., Bishop of St. David's, 135, 152
Thirty Years War, 170, 227
Thomasius, 145
Thoughts on the Present Discontents, Burke's, 74 n. 2
Thuanus, [i.e. De Thou], 22
Thucydides, 14, 15, 61, 106, 154, 186
Tibet, 147
Tiercelin, 241
Times, The, 131, n. 5
Tischendorf, 227
Tithe, 178
Tocqueville, Alexis de, 4, 24, 74, 101, 114, 117, 119, 161, 162, 186, 197, 200, 239, 242
Toland, John, 4, 67, 68, 232

Toledo, Councils of, 91
Toleration, 32, 40–47, 64 n. 4, 109, 138, 141, 144, 169, 175, 178, 189, 194, 196 and n. 1, 202, 243
Tolosanus, 241
Tolstoy, Count Leo, 196 n. 1
Toreno, Conde, de, Spanish statesman, 73, 238
Torture, 173
Toryism, 66 n. 1, 74, 75, 132, 171, 172, 184
Towns, 211, 213, 215
Toynbee, Professor A. J., 40 n. 4, 200, 223
Trade, 69, 168 n. 2, 171, 172, 212, 213, 214, 221
Trade associations, 19
Trade Unions, 121
Tradition, 53, 54, 55, 56, 61, 65, 66 n. 1, 102, 144, 165, 177, 195, 204 and n. 2, 243
Transvaal, 132
Treitschke, Heinrich, 13, 38, 132, 133, 134, 156, 210
Trendelenburg, 24, 154, 198
Trevelyan, Dr. G. M., Master of Trinity College, Cambridge, 131 and n. 4
Tribonian, 144
Trimmers, 64, 69, 229
Trinity College, Cambridge, 10
Troeltsch, 242
Truth, 53, 54, 55, 61, 187, 190, 201, 204 and n. 3, 226
Tubero, 222 n. 1
Tübingen, 53, 155
Tucker, Dean, 173
Tudors, 57, 168
Tuileries, 110
Turgot, 4, 12, 15, 27, 32, 41, 50, 61, 68, 75, 86, 88, 101, 135, 141, 145, 148, 174, 182, 190, and n. 10 199, 214, 221, 233, 240
Turkish invasion, 168
War, 132
Tuscany, 137
Twiss, Travers, 37 n. 4
Tyrannicide, 187
Tyrol, 128

Ultramontanes, 42, 141
Unbelief, 27, 39, 68, 145
Unemployment, 119
Unitarianism, 144
United States, 14, 126, 217
State Department, 131, *see also* America
Unity, 51, 130, 156, 166, 179, 206, 220
Universal suffrage, 99, 113, 117, 118, 160, 183, 243

INDEX

Universalism, 200
Universities, 124, 133, 155, 209
University College, v, 219
Usteri, Paulus, Swiss politician, 116 n. 1
Utilitarianism, 136, 141, 146, 162
Utility, 188
Utopia, More's, 117 n. 5

Valentin, German physiologist, 229
Valla, Lorenzo, 50, 144, 188
Valmy, battle of, 180
Value, 212
Vane, Sir Henry, the younger, 70, 234
Venice, 138, 212
Vergniaud, 160
Versailles, 101 n. 2, 175
Veto, 176, 177, 179
Vicaire Savoyard, 37
Vico, Giovanni Battista, 203 n. 1
Victoria, predecessor of Grotius, 241
Vienna, 225
Vienna, Congress of, 129, 181
Villiaumé, 160
Vincent of Lérins, Saint (d. c. 450), 54, 145
Vinet, Alexandre, xii, 1, 2, 24, 33, 38, 39, 43 n. 2, 146, 197, 203, 242
Vives, Luis, 241
Vollgraff, German liberal, 74, 239
Voltaire, 32, 37, 41, 68, 141, 145, 148, 174, 233
Voluntary Social Services (A. F. C. Bourdillon), 81 n. 5

Waddington, 71, 236
Wagner, Adolf, 17, 118, 123 n. 2, 125, 241
Wagram, battle of (July 1809), 225
Waitz, Georg, 157
Wakefield, Edward Gibbon, 70, 73, 74, 235, 238
Waldenses, 121
Walpole, Horace, 135
Walpole, Sir Robert, 73, 172, 214, 237
Walter, 116 n. 1
Wamba, 87
War, 5, 182, 196 n. 1, 201, 244
Warburton, William, bishop, 62
Washington, George, 4, 102, 138, 192, 243

Waterloo, 57
Watt, James, 59
Wealth, 19, 64, 79, 81, 113, 121, 122, 123, 125, 160, 168 and n. 2, 173, 174, 196, 209, 211, 212, 215, 216, 218, 221
Wealth of Nations, Adam Smith's, 17, 141, 145, 192, 241
Weber, Max, 123 n. 2
Webster, Daniel, 173
Welfare, 173, 194, 209
Wellesley, Arthur, First Duke of Wellington, 60
Westminster, 156
What the Independents would have, 40
Whately, Richard, Archbishop of Dublin, 74, 238
Wheaton, 241
Whichcote, Benjamin, Cambridge Platonist, 66, 231
Whiggism, xi, 25, 41, 62, 65–76, 85, 90, 98, 141, 187, 188, 192, 195
Whigs, 10, 62, 64–76, 98, 107, 115, 140, 145, 170, 171, 173, 180, 184, 191, 192, 194, 229–240
Wilberforce, William, 62
Will, 71–72, 88, 93, 105, 129, 150, 167, 168, 175, 176, 182, 196, 197, 244, *see also* General will, Rousseau
William III, King of England, 19, 214
William of Tyre, 222 n. 1
Williams, Roger, 169, 188, 196
Wilson, Woodrow, 129 n. 3
Witchcraft, 144
Wolf, Frederick Augustus, 61, 85
Woodhouse, Professor A. S. P., 196 n. 1, 199 n. 3
Woodruff, Douglas, xiii
Woodward, E. L., Professor, 29 n. 2, 43 n. 2, 45–46, 207 n. 1, 223
Wordsworth, William, 134
Workers, 176, 215
Wren, Matthew, the younger, 14
Wundt, Wilhelm, 39
Wyclif, John, 121, 226

Xenophon, 106, 186

Zeno, 21, 144, 186
Zollverein, 133
Zurich, 125